Sarah Chaker, Axel Petri-Preis (eds.)
Tuning up! The Innovative Potential of Musikvermittlung

Forum Musikvermittlung – Research and Practice | Volume 1

Editorial

The term »Musikvermittlung« was coined in German-speaking countries to describe a field of practice in music education which bridges the gap between music performance and the listener. The community of practice consists of musicians, music educators, ensembles, schools and concert halls, united by the wish to enable or deepen aesthetic experience with music. Today, the specific structures, formats and self-concepts of this community are increasingly subjected to scientific research. This book series is a platform for scientists and practitioners alike, bringing together a scholarly and practice-related discourse.

Johannes Voit and Constanze Wimmer (series editors)

Sarah Chaker (Dr. phil.) studied musicology and German language at the Carl von Ossietzky University of Oldenburg. She is currently an assistant professor at the Department of Music Sociology (IMS) at the mdw – University of Music and Performing Arts Vienna. Her research interests include street music, the transdisciplinary analysis of music, histories, theories and methods of music sociology, popular music (in particular metal music) and *Musikvermittlung*.

Axel Petri-Preis studied music education, German philology and musicology in Vienna. He has been active in the field of *Musikvermittlung* internationally for more than ten years, and his projects have received several awards. He is a senior scientist and Deputy Head at the Department of Music Education Research, Music Didactics and Elementary Music Education (IMP) at the mdw – University of Music and Performing Arts Vienna. His research currently focuses on the education and further training of (classical) musicians in relation to *Musikvermittlung* and on community engagement in classical music life.

Sarah Chaker, Axel Petri-Preis (eds.)
**Tuning up!
The Innovative Potential of Musikvermittlung**

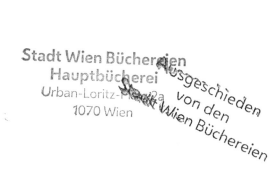

[transcript]

The authors acknowledge the financial support by the Open Access Fund of the mdw – University of Music and Performing Arts Vienna.

Bibliographic information published by the Deutsche Nationalbibliothek
The Deutsche Nationalbibliothek lists this publication in the Deutsche Nationalbibliografie; detailed bibliographic data are available in the Internet at http://dnb.d-nb.de

This work is licensed under the Creative Commons Attribution 4.0 (BY) license, which means that the text may be remixed, transformed and built upon and be copied and redistributed in any medium or format even commercially, provided credit is given to the author. For details go to http://creativecommons.org/licenses/by/4.0/
Creative Commons license terms for re-use do not apply to any content (such as graphs, figures, photos, excerpts, etc.) not original to the Open Access publication and further permission may be required from the rights holder. The obligation to research and clear permission lies solely with the party re-using the material.

First published in 2022 by transcript Verlag, Bielefeld
© Sarah Chaker, Axel Petri-Preis (eds.)

Cover layout: Maria Arndt, Bielefeld
Cover illustration: © Patrick T'Kindt/unsplash
Translation & proofread: Peter Waugh
Printed by Majuskel Medienproduktion GmbH, Wetzlar
Print-ISBN 978-3-8376-5681-7
PDF-ISBN 978-3-8394-5681-1
https://doi.org/10.14361/9783839456811

Printed on permanent acid-free text paper.

Contents

Preface 7

Welcome Notes 9

Musikvermittlung and Its Innovative Potential
Terminological, Historical and Sociological Remarks
Sarah Chaker & Axel Petri-Preis 11

Listening Twice to Bernhard Gander's "Peter Parker"
Axel Petri-Preis 39

The Big Bang of Musikvermittlung
On the Emergence of a New Social World
and Its Future Innovative Potential
Axel Petri-Preis 47

On the Translation of Music
Towards the Relation between Musikvermittlung and Innovation
Ronald Staples 71

Slam Poetry Meets Classical Music
Axel Petri-Preis 93

Under a Preservation Order?
The Innovative Potential of Musikvermittlung to Renew Concert Life
Constanze Wimmer 97

The Promotion of Pleasure in Individual Perception
Musikvermittlung as a Key Agenda in Concert Life
Matthias Naske 115

***Musikvermittlung* as Everyday Practice**
The Cello Quartet *Die Kolophonistinnen*
Sarah Chaker 121

Practical Intelligence and the Limitations of Practitioners
Multiple Forms of Knowledge, and Their Significance in Music
and *Musikvermittlung*
Tasos Zembylas 131

Engaging with New Audiences
Perspectives of Professional Musicians' Biographical Learning
and Its Innovative Potential for Higher Music Education
Rineke Smilde 151

Hear – Taste – See: UISGE BEATHA – Waters of Life
Towards the Innovative Potential of Synaesthetic Experiences
for *Musikvermittlung*
Sarah Chaker 169

Artful Innovation
Learning from Experiments with Audiences
in Symphonic Music Practice
Peter Peters, Ties van de Werff, Ruth Benschop & Imogen Eve 179

**Just join in? Audience Participation
in Classical Contemporary Music**
Empirical Insights into Theory and Practice
Jutta Toelle 199

Preface

Over the past four decades, *Musikvermittlung* has developed into a multifaceted field of practice that acts as a link between music production and reception. Musicians, educators, mediators, concert organisers, and many other actors form a steadily growing community of practice seek to open up new approaches to music for people of all ages. While *Musikvermittlung* has become an indispensable part of concert life and the cultural sector, it has so far been represented only sporadically at conservatories and universities in the German-speaking world. The increasing diversification and professionalisation of the field makes it obvious that there is an urgent need on the one hand for comprehensive and demand-oriented education and training structures, and on the other hand for scientific research into the field of *Musikvermittlung*, including social practices, institutional contexts, key success factors, power structures, and the forms and conditions of knowledge production. For this reason, the "Forum Musikvermittlung an Hochschulen und Universitäten" (https://www.forum-musikvermittlung.eu) was founded in 2016, bringing together researchers and teachers in the field of *Musikvermittlung* from Germany, Austria, Switzerland and South Tyrol. In the first five years, the focus was on initiating the networking of the actors and the discourse about the content and quality criteria of a university education which produces professionally qualified graduates. Currently, however, in the light of an increase of scientific publications and doctoral theses, the international network is increasingly focusing on tasks in the field of research.

With the first academic publication series on *Musikvermittlung*, which is inaugurated with the present volume, we would like to map and fuel the professional discourse of this young discipline in all its diversity, and to accompany the developments of the field of practice in a reflective way. We want to open up a space for reflecting on concert life, audiences, new concert and event formats, the role of different musical practices in a diverse society, and about new collaborations between cultural institutions and the various social actors and communities in urban and rural areas.

The German term *Musikvermittlung* is used throughout this volume. This is because, on the one hand, the term is simply difficult to translate, even if its overlaps with English terms such as "music education" or "community music" are obvious. On the other hand, it refers to the specific character of the field of practice it denotes, which can only be found in the German-speaking countries. However, this should not obscure the fact that *Musikvermittlung* has received many influential impulses from foreign countries (especially English-speaking ones) since the very beginning and that actors in the internationally oriented cultural sector are in constant exchange with colleagues and institutions all over the world. We are therefore particularly pleased to address an international readership with the first volume of the new publication series.

We wish the new series much success and you, dear readers, a stimulating read!

Constanze Wimmer and Johannes Voit
Series editors

Welcome Notes

It is a great pleasure to observe how the topic of *Musikvermittlung* is gaining ground at the mdw – University of Music and Performing Arts Vienna. From the area of preliminary studies to its emphasis in artistic and pedagogical studies, to special initiatives at the Department of Music Education Research, Music Didactics and Elementary Music Education (IMP), *Musikvermittlung* is being both practiced and researched here, the latter in cooperation with the Department of Music Sociology (IMS). Further major steps forward in the implementation of Musikvermittlung in courses at our university are imminent.

Many thanks and congratulations to Axel Petri-Preis (IMP) and Sarah Chaker (IMS) for the conception and realisation of the lecture and event series in 2019/2020 and for the conversion of this format into the present publication.

Barbara Gisler-Haase
Vice Rector for Academic Affairs and Young Artists' Promotion at the mdw – University of Music and Performing Arts Vienna

It remains a desideratum to further explore the young field of *Musikvermittlung* academically, in empirical research as well as from the starting point of the humanities – and both approaches are necessary. So the lecture series that took place in autumn and winter 2019/20 at the mdw – University of Music and Performing Arts Vienna contributed to this target in remarkable way: we faced lectures with a wide academic range, opening onto a broad horizon.

Yet the organisers and curators, Sarah Chaker and Axel Petri-Preis, also wanted to demonstrate what *Musikvermittlung* feels like, showing its possibilities, exploring what it could be, and so on these evenings fascinating musicians made appearances, inspiring settings could be experienced, involvement and resonance happened.

We, the audience, not only listened to interesting lectures, but were invited to co-act with the musicians, to listen, to watch, to feel and even to taste. The lecture hall was variously transformed into a concert hall and a performance venue, with the events switching between periods of listening and understanding on the one hand, and moments of being overwhelmed and moved on the other.

This publication includes the lectures which were given – as may be expected in a book like this – but it also tries to catch the aesthetic experience and the atmosphere of the evenings.

I therefore really appreciate that this attempt is being made and I am glad that the mdw – University of Music and Performing Arts Vienna has supported this project.

Peter Röbke
Head of the Department of Music Education Research, Music Didactics and Elementary Music Education at the mdw – University of Music and Performing Arts Vienna

Musikvermittlung and Its Innovative Potential
Terminological, Historical and Sociological Remarks

Sarah Chaker & Axel Petri-Preis

This anthology is dedicated to the innovative potential of *Musikvermittlung*, focusing on practices, concepts and formats that are ascribed a transformative power in relation to the ways in which music can be produced, experienced and perceived both individually and collectively.

The term, as we understand it here, refers to the manifold and divergent practices in an artistic-educational field in which actors with heterogeneous formal (academic) qualifications[1] and different professional backgrounds[2] are currently elaborating and implementing specialised artistic-educational concepts (both individual formats and series) for and with various social groups with regard to music (to be more precise: currently with a focus primarily on so-called Western art music respectively classical music), mostly on behalf of public institutions (for example festivals, concert halls, orchestras). Furthermore, in the course of an increasing institutionalisation and professionalisation of its practices, *Musikvermittlung* turns out to be a growing occupational field, as well as a field of research. Many hopes, if not expectations, are connected with *Musikvermittlung* in its various dimensions and novel practices, not least with regard to an increase in the quality of communal life in "super-diverse" (Vertovec 2012) societies. It cannot be predicted with certainty

---

1   Primarily, many actors in the field of *Musikvermittlung* participated in and completed artistic-pedagogical degree programs and/or instrumental studies, but may also have an academic background in musicology, cultural studies or dance studies. Specialised (master) courses on *Musikvermittlung* increasingly play an important role at (music) universities and conservatories (see educult/netzwerk junge ohren 2020).

2   In addition to the specialised practitioners of *Musikvermittlung*, (classically trained) musicians, music pedagogues and educators, as well as dramaturges, composers, conductors, cultural managers and musicologists also currently contribute to this field.

whether these practices will be able to unfold their full innovative potential[3], as this depends on various factors and how they will interplay. Our anthology therefore offers an inventory of current theoretical considerations, scientific observations and empirical documentations concerning *Musikvermittlung*. By broaching the issue of its innovative potential however, this anthology also provides a glimpse into possible futures.

Musikvermittlung – Attempt at an Exegesis

Even though some practices that are today subsumed under the term *Musikvermittlung* draw on somewhat longer traditions, like concerts for children[4], a massive agglomeration and diversification of activities can be cited over the past 20 to 25 years.[5] In a comparatively short time, a multitude of new and very different concepts for and practices of *Musikvermittlung* emerged, each of which was and is guided by different purposes and associated with different objectives, depending on the context. What Carmen Mörsch formulated for *Kunst- und Kulturvermittlung* (art and cultural mediation/education) in general also applies to the current practice of *Musikvermittlung* in particular, namely that this is an extremely "heterogeneous practice. Depending on one's objective, appreciation of art and education, it may take on very different positions and forms" (Mörsch n.d.: 36).[6] Correspondingly, the interpretation of the term *Musikvermittlung* is currently vague, fuzzy, iridescent and contested.

---

3   The term *potential* (coming from the Latin word *potentia*: "power", "strength", "might", "force", see Langenscheidt n.d.) refers in a somewhat scholarly sense to something "that might be possible (according to the circumstances) but is not actually given" (Duden n.d.).
4   See the contribution by Axel Petri-Preis in this anthology.
5   Generally speaking, classical concert life in the 19th century was, with regard to performance concepts, much more diverse than it is today. It was not until the turn of the 20th century that attention-controlling measures were introduced (blackout, applause rules and so forth), which were intended to put the musical work at the centre (Blaukopf 1972, Salmen 1988, Tröndle 2018). One could argue that *Musikvermittlung* reopens classical concert life towards more diverse performance practices.
6   All translations of original German quotations in this anthology by Jonathan Quinn and Peter Waugh.

Musikvermittlung in the realm of German music education – a short look back

The term *Musikvermittlung* is closely linked to German music education, in particular to the didactic approach Didactic Interpretation of Music which was established as a theory by Karl Heinrich Ehrenforth (1971) and made fruitful for teaching practice by Christoph Richter (1976). As the basic assumptions of this concept still prove to be influential on the current use of the term in the German-speaking countries, it is briefly described in the following section.[7]

The Didactic Interpretation of Music draws on the philosophical considerations of Hans-Georg Gadamer and especially on his seminal book on philosophical hermeneutics "Truth and Method" (1960), and unfolds a didactic foundation for the question "how to look at musical works" (Richter 1996). In the context of school music lessons, it thus became an influential pedagogical approach. A central thought of the conception is that there is "a continuous exchange between the individual's preconception and what is offered and demanded by the subject matter [a piece of music, author's note]" (Richter 1996: 34). A music teacher thus mediates between the student who is embedded in his lived experience (*Lebenswelt*) and the musical piece.

In 1998, the term *Musikvermittlung* was used as a name for the first degree program of its kind at the Detmold University of Music. The initiator Ernst Klaus Schneider, a music pedagogue and proponent of the Didactic Interpretation of Music, together with the conductor Joachim Harder and the music pedagogue Hermann Große-Jäger, deliberately detached the term *Musikvermittlung* from the context of music didactics and school teaching practice: "Our way of *Vermittlung* [mediation; emphasis added] was supposed to lead to an intensive experience of music for the listeners. [...] We wanted to enrich the listeners' experience of art, an offer that was oriented towards the art and its demands, and was not, in the narrower sense, pedagogical." (Schneider 2009: 77)[8] The Didactic Interpretation of Music however remained present as a central part of the teaching content of the course (Schneider 2009: 10,

---

7   For a more elaborate account of the history and use of the term *Musikvermittlung* see Petri-Preis 2019.

8   Wolfgang Rüdiger puts even more emphasis on the artistic dimension and calls *Musikvermittlung* an "artistic project with artistic-educational elements" (Rüdiger 2015: 9).

Schneider 2019: 15) and its ideas still have an impact, especially on the conception of children's concerts (Brenk 2008, Schneider 2015). Most importantly, with its use for the degree program, the term *Musikvermittlung* was quickly established as a widely accepted terminus technicus in the German-speaking countries.

Although the Didactic Interpretation of Music was very influential for *Musikvermittlung* both in terms of content and terminology, there were, of course, other significant influences within German music education. In particular, elementary music education (e.g. Stiller 2008) and the discourse around aesthetic experiences (e.g. Rolle 1999) are worth mentioning here.

Current attempts at a definition of *Musikvermittlung* in the German-speaking countries

Numerous attempts to define *Musikvermittlung* can be detected within the last twenty years. However, as a heterogeneous artistic-educational practice, *Musikvermittlung* can hardly be pinned down in a general definition. Accordingly, many authors point out that a widely accepted definition does not yet exist. Hendrikje Mautner-Obst (2018: 337) asserts: "There is still no agreement on a concrete, manageable and consistent definition of '*Musikvermittlung*' [emphasis added]." In the publication "Musical Life in Germany", edited by the German Music Information Center (miz), Johannes Voit states: "The use of the term is anything but unambiguous, as is evident in the difficulty all publications have faced in trying to define it." (Voit 2019: 110)

An analytical look at definitions of *Musikvermittlung* in different academic publications points to an inconsistent and fuzzy terminology that makes it a messy concept. It is variously described as a field of action in its own right (Voit 2019) or consisting of manifold fields of action (Müller-Brozovic 2017, Voit 2019), as a field of practice (Wimmer 2010a, Mautner-Obst 2018, Voit 2019), as an attitude (Weber 2018, Wimmer 2018a) or as a profession (Allwardt 2017, Weber 2018). Peter Mall und Ralf-Olivier Schwarz (2018: 25) regard *Musikvermittlung* from a system theoretical perspective, as a communicative effort that mediates between two systems and establishes a structural coupling[9], while Constanze Wimmer (2010b) describes *Musikvermittlung* as the translation and contextualisation of music. Finally, Mautner-Obst describes *Musikvermittlung* as a practice with certain objectives and special sites:

---

9 See also Ronald Staples in this anthology.

"*Musikvermittlung* [emphasis added] is an artistic, educational and communicative practice that aims to make music accessible to heterogeneous audiences in various formats, ranging from artistic-creative to cognitive-reflexive approaches, thereby enabling and deepening aesthetic experiences, as well as expanding and experimenting with creative means of expression. In this way, concerns of cultural policy or cultural management can also be supported." (Mautner-Obst 2018: 339)

Mautner-Obst points out that practices of *Musikvermittlung* are based on and able to meet quite different aims and demands at once. Amongst others, artistic-educational, socio-political and economic aims appear to be central. Artistic-educational aims may include the initiation of aesthetic experiences through musical practices and providing knowledge about pieces of music as well. Socio-political aims strive to strengthen self-confident cultural participation by making classical concerts accessible to everyone, as well as initiating social change and empowering people in community projects. Economic aims comprise acquiring new audiences and increasing occupancy rates. Whereas artistic-educational and socio-political aims serve the addressees of *Musikvermittlung* practices, economic aims primarily benefit the organisations.

The practices of *Musikvermittlung* become perceivable and observable when they manifest in a variety of presentation and participation formats, currently still predominantly in the realm of classical music life. Children's and family concerts, moderated or staged concerts, pre- or post-concert talks and workshops, participative community projects realised with different social groups in society, music events at unusual settings, as well as long-term partnerships with public institutions, such as schools, hospitals, prisons or refugee homes, are selected examples of new types of music formats and collaborations which break up conventional forms of music production, performance and appropriation and, in doing so, seek to enable a new kind of music experience for all of the people involved in the artistic process.[10]

Music education? Music mediation? *Musikvermittlung*!

In the context of an English-language publication, we had to face the challenge that there is no appropriate English translation of the German word

---

10   Wimmer (2010a) and Welch et al. (2012) offer an extensive overview of formats of *Musikvermittlung*.

Musikvermittlung. We refrain from using the term "music education" because it can also refer to music lessons in schools. Other terms, such as "participation", "outreach", "children's concerts", or "community engagement", merely designate subareas of the broader concept of *Musikvermittlung*.

As far as the literal translation, "music mediation", is concerned, further challenges arise: The term "mediation" is used heterogeneously in various semantic contexts. As Mörsch points out, "mediation is connected with the legal and social arena of conflict resolution, cultural mediation in particular is associated with translation and negotiation activities in the context of migration" (Mörsch n.d.: 19). In the realm of social sciences and the humanities, the word "mediation" is used in several different ways – in music sociology, for example, Antoine Hennion (2015) conceptualises music as an "accumulation of mediators" and Georgina Born (2005) conceives of music as a "constellation of mediations". So the term "mediation" is already strongly associated with other theoretical approaches, connotations, meanings and concepts. From this, it becomes clear that the literal translation of *Musikvermittlung*, music mediation, may lead to misunderstandings and irritations in a global scientific community rather than bring clarity, as it entails a whole new discourse space.[11] We therefore decided to maintain the original term *Musikvermittlung* in this publication, drawing on the long tradition of German loanwords in the realm of music, like lied, leitmotif or flatterzunge, to name just a few.

Nevertheless, it should be mentioned that even in German the term *Vermittlung* is ambiguous and its use in the context of *Musikvermittlung* and music education does not go undisputed (Petri-Preis 2019). As, for example, the members of the collective microsillons critically note, the term *Vermittlung* "contains etymologically the idea of a conflict solution (and so indicates that a conflict situation exists between the viewers [or listeners] and works, or between the non-viewers [non-listeners] and institutions)" (microsillons n.d.: 25). Alexander Henschel (2020) too refers to the fact that in the practice of *Kunstvermittlung* today there is mostly a reference to the harmonising, consensus-building significance of the term in the sense of the resolution of a conflict. In his publication about the meanings and history of the term *Vermittlung*, he goes back to the Middle High German meaning "to preventively step between" and develops from that a difference-theoretical understanding of *Kunstvermittlung*.

---

11   For an overview of the use of the concept in relation to music see Born/Barry (2018).

While the resolution of conflicts is frequently imposed upon the practice of *Musikvermittlung* as a central agenda from the outside, in particular by cultural policymakers, it seems at least questionable whether its primary purpose can in any way be "to repair or to close up the breaches between art and society" (Mörsch n.d.: 37). In the arts – and in the case of music to an especially marked extent – it is rather a matter of fields which are themselves structurally pervaded with hierarchies and inequalities, where power structures become effective and day-to-day struggles play out on a variety of levels.

So if the concept of *Vermittlung* implies that of conflict, and in particular also the "internal dispute about who has the respective right and possibility to own, see, show and discuss the arts" (Mörsch n.d.: 33), then this seems to us, from an analytical perspective, to tend to be a realistic and productive starting point, rather than a negative one. Cultural and social conflicts do exist – although this is obviously not something to be welcomed, it nevertheless has to be openly addressed, because only in this way is there a chance that these conflicts can be dealt with. At this point, it should once again be emphasised with Mörsch that in the practice of *Musikvermittlung*, just as in the field of *Kunst- und Kulturvermittlung*, it is not a matter of finding quick and easy solutions for cultural and social problems, but rather that with and through art, culture and music relatively open-ended social relations and interactions among people should be established:

> "accordingly, *vermitteln* [emphasis added] does not mean [...] to explain and to arbitrate. *Vermittlung* [emphasis added] realises the [...] implied potential of the prefix *Ver-* [emphasis added], in the sense of entanglement, of the loss of control and of missing the mark, in favour of the production of not (always) controllable networks of relationships and spaces for action." (Mörsch n.d.: 38, with recourse to Eva Sturm)

In this respect, Wimmer refers to a potential of *Musikvermittlung* "not to pursue art exclusively as an end in itself, but also as a means of enlightenment, social interaction, and empowerment of population groups that would otherwise have more difficult access to publicly funded cultural institutions" (Wimmer 2018b: 43).[12]

---

12 Nina Stoffers (2019) shows, however, that *Musikvermittlung* often oscillates between the poles of empowerment and othering, and Michael Wimmer states critically that there is "a considerable tendency to describe those to whom the offer is directed first of all as being deficient in a particular way [...]." (Wimmer 2012) Therefore, it is important

Musikvermittlung – Perspectives on a Track Record

Musikvermittlung as a professional field

The negotiation of the concept of *Musikvermittlung* takes place within the context of the increasing professionalisation, institutionalisation and theoretical consolidation of the practice of *Musikvermittlung* that has been observable since the beginning of the 2000s in German-speaking countries, if not all over Europe. *Musikvermittlung* today not only represents an elaborate artistic-educational field of practice, but as a professional field also forms an increasingly significant segment of the music labour market.

Fig. 1: Number of positions for Musikvermittlung at music institutions (orchestras, concert halls and festivals) in Austria (summated) in the period 1989-2019.

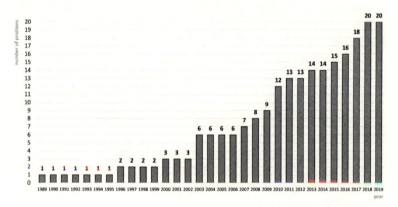

Source: own survey

Fig. 1 documents the number of positions for *Musikvermittlung* that have been created at music institutions in Austria (including festivals, orchestras and concert halls, but excluding the 'independent scene'), whereby this number has been constantly increasing, especially since the turn of the millennium. According to our study, two thirds of the 20 positions created are full-

---

for cooperation between different partners to take place on an equal footing, in which attributions of alterity and need are avoided.

time positions and 85% of them are filled by women[13]. Even though the number of fixed positions is admittedly still limited, it must be remembered that these were created in a geographically small country like Austria under conditions of impending budget cuts and savings in the public cultural sector – money was and is being invested in *Musikvermittlung*, yet elsewhere in the cultural sector massive cuts are being made. This seems quite remarkable, and it raises questions about the possible reasons for the increased attention that *Musikvermittlung* in particular, and *Kunst- und Kulturvermittlung* in general, has been receiving from established cultural institutions and cultural policymakers for some time.

Cultural policy – hopes and demands

From a more institutional (cultural management) perspective, *Musikvermittlung* is historically associated with the hope of building new audiences (or at least keeping the established ones), so as to counteract an audience decline. Peter Mall points out that back in the early 1970s German orchestras reacted to financial problems with a commitment to diversify their audience, to address all parts of society and so reach out to people who did not previously attend classical concerts (see Mall 2016). As Lukas Bugiel (2015) convincingly shows, a "crisis-discourse" around classical music and classical concert life eventually played a vital role in the legitimisation and justification of the practices of *Musikvermittlung* in the early 2000s. Reinhart von Gutzeit, for example, writes that *Musikvermittlung* emerged against the background of a "dramatically declining interest in classical (serious, sophisticated) music and its (public) performance" (Gutzeit 2015: 19). Schneider speaks of *Musikvermittlung* as "a response to the perceived or even real decline in concert attendance and interest in 'classical' music, a reaction to observed signs of erosion" (Schneider 2019: 11) and retrospectively characterises the central impetus behind the foundation of the first degree program for *Musikvermittlung* at the Detmold University of Music in 1998: "Is something that is important to us in musical life dying away? [...] If the orchestras and ensembles do not strive for a new audience today, they will not have one tomorrow" (Schneider 2009: 76). As this

---

13   Mörsch speaks in the context of *Kunstvermittlung* of a feminised practice (Mörsch n.d.: 36). This is also true for the field of *Musikvermittlung* (see educult/netzwerk junge ohren 2020).

quotation shows, economic considerations in the realm of audience development are linked to cultural considerations: on top of audience development, *Musikvermittlung* is assigned a further role, namely in the conservation of cultural heritage.

More than 20 years later, Heiner Gembris and Jonas Menze still identify one of the main challenges for classical music providers as being that a younger audience does not grow back (Gembris/Menze 2018: 319). Accordingly, orchestras and musicians have to "strive for the mediation and acceptance of classical music in their own interest" (Gembris/Menze 2018: 324), whereas "audience development also means redefining the role of the musician" (Gembris/Menze 2018: 325). Even if we are of the opinion that it is certainly beneficial for musical communication if musicians take an interest in their audience, we are nevertheless critical of the pressure to justify themselves which is increasingly being exerted upon them – and on publicly funded cultural institutions serving as organisers, particularly those with low attendance figures – and we consider this pressure to be rather counterproductive. If economic success becomes the prior factor, then the willingness and scope for experiments, for courageous, unpredictable projects, for spontaneous, improvised actions might diminish, both individually and institutionally. Furthermore, the compulsion to be economically successful, which is linked to the need to always keep an eye on visitor quotas, represents, in the words of Tasos Zembylas, a fundamental "reinterpretation of cultural policy", namely insofar as it is considered "an element of a more sweeping economic policy" (Zembylas 2017: 150). In actual fact, culture and cultural policy in the sense of a "'res publica' […] are a matter for the political community and not just for economic rationality" (Zembylas 2017: 150). Understood in this way, however, institutions – and this applies to the classical concert life in particular – should and must in future be much more self-critical than they have been up till now in addressing the following question: "Whose 'culture' is at present actually being taken into account or most promoted by the public purse? And what is the state's attitude to those marginalised cultures that do not belong to the mainstream and do not enjoy hegemonic preferential treatment?" (Zembylas 2017: 151) After all, a colourful, diverse society, in which ascriptive factors such as class, gender, ethnicity, religious affiliation and others are nevertheless highly affective, "argumentatively supports the demand for differentiation and pluralisation among the target group of public cultural funding" (Zembylas 2017: 151).

In *Musikvermittlung*, too, there has to date been a strong, largely unquestioned and apparently self-evident focus on classical music, implicitly promoting its hegemonic status (for a critical examination of this aspect see Hornberger 2020). A greater diversification with regard to the musical practices that are thematised and realised in and through *Musikvermittlung* in contemporary societies is well overdue.[14] At the same time, Michael Annoff urgently warns against merely simulating artistic diversity: "It is no use supposedly progressive cultural producers exploiting diversity for themselves on the level of representation if, at the same time, they cling to the oppressive institutions and structures whose exclusivity gave them their power in the first place." (Annoff 2021: 69) Instead, music-cultural institutions must (also) renew themselves structurally and therefore fundamentally from within: "Many theatres and museums are still managed like a feudal system today, with only a few institutions seriously looking for alternatives to that principle of directorship and management which often causes the failure of those who have (initially of necessity) professionalised themselves outside of white bourgeois institutions." (Annoff 2021: 68) So instead of outsourcing the problems to *Musikvermittlung* and passing them on, cultural institutions must enter much more intensely than before into a process of self-reflection, and question themselves, as a "component of the migration society, concerning their structurally conditioned exclusion mechanisms and their transformation potential" (Mörsch n.d.: 61) – this applies to music institutions and organisers, as well as to the institutions of (higher) music education. A similar demand is also made by Mark Terkessidis, who notes in this context: "In this sense, all efforts to allow participation should also serve the aim of self-examining the respective supporting structures – in connection with the question of whether our structures, planning and offers are fit for the diversity of society." (Terkessidis 2019: 84)

It is therefore a matter of some urgency that music universities and conservatories extend their view of artistic excellence beyond the mastery of musical instruments to include aspects such as pedagogical sensitivity and social responsibility. Courses both in artistic studies and in specific studies for *Musikvermittlung* are needed in order to enable graduates to address diverse audiences in a changing society affected by demographic change, digitisation, climate change and the aftermath of the Covid pandemic. Music institutions,

---

14   Already in 2012, Sophie Arenhövel was reflecting on the state of diversity-awareness of *Musikvermittlung* in the transitional German society.

such as orchestras and concert halls, on the other hand, will have to give their employees even more opportunities for further training, committing to the concept of lifelong learning to gain the social and pedagogical skills that are needed to enable truly inclusive cultural participation (Petri-Preis 2021).

Musikvermittlung in the Singularised Society

In light of the foregoing deliberations, it should be clear that *Musikvermittlung* is much more than *solely* audience development – although economic and cultural policy considerations do play a certain role, there are numerous other significant reasons that can help to explain why this field is at present becoming increasingly institutionalised and professionalised, and is attracting a great deal of attention. Social aspects in particular play a significant role in this context – the current prosperity of *Musikvermittlung* is related to the general state of contemporary postmodern societies.

Central concerns of *Musikvermittlung* include bringing people into contact with one another by means of music, and getting them involved in shared discussions and interaction with, through and around music, in short: to instigate social communication and entice them towards new kinds of music experience. This potential of *Musikvermittlung*, which is developed via specific artistic-educational practices and concepts, can become effective in a "society of singularities" (Reckwitz, 2020), with all its differentiations and individuations, in two ways:

Firstly, the artistic-educational practices of *Musikvermittlung* are in themselves practices of singularisation – what is culturally shared is produced via practices of singularisation – which is why its practices and methods appear appropriate and even convincing and functional in a "society of singularities" (Reckwitz 2020). By presenting previously unknown musics to their audiences in a contextualising manner, or by updating the supposedly well-known in a quasi-kaleidoscopic way through new performance practices and possibilities of participation, and so making it possible to experience it differently, those who work in *Musikvermittlung* are constantly developing new and unique qualities of experience that can be excellently reconciled with the individual demands and social expectations of late- and post-modernity.[15]

---

15   On the quality of the new, Reckwitz remarks: "In late modernism, a radical regime of the new predominates, which is at the same time momentary, i.e. it does not orient

Secondly, in singularised societies, with their countless "segmented media publics" (Reckwitz 2020: 440), the commonly shared can no longer be assumed to exist without any further ado, nor can it be "simply discovered; it must itself first be manufactured again – in an inevitably contentious manner" (Reckwitz 2020: 440), whereby Reckwitz assumes that "the endeavour of working on universality, on generally binding cultural norms and jointly shared goods [...] will become a permanent task" (Reckwitz 2020: 441). Even if we are not talking about a "parallel society" at this point[16], it must be noted that in the context of increasing globalisation, mobility and required flexibility, and not least in the context of neoliberal labour relations and pronounced migration movements, people's life plans are becoming increasingly diverse, less comparable and less predictable. As a result, the shared stores of knowledge and cultural practices are thinning out, or proving to be highly singularised. So what is it that holds a society together when there remains little that connects people? How can we, despite all our individuality and singularity, live well and peacefully together, mastering everyday life and productively shaping shared social spaces together?

In this context, art and culture are regarded by political functionaries as a possible cement (see e.g. Mandel 2019, Brosda 2020[17]) and are sometimes also instrumentalised as such. In the course of this, professional groups, who act as cultural translators, experience a revaluation and increasing respect, and by *"doing universality* [emphasis in the German original] [...] provide a counterweight to the omnipresent act of *doing singularity* [emphasis in the German original]" (Reckwitz 2020: 441), whereby "doing universality" may certainly involve practices of resistance. In this context, *Musikvermittlung* may be interpreted as a contribution to the "reconstitution of the general public sphere" (Reckwitz 2020: 440), with which, in the best case, it succeeds in bringing together people with diverse biographical backgrounds, equipped with different symbolic, cultural and economic capital and forms of habitus (Bourdieu 2009 [1972]), effecting their social contact and exchange with one another in one

---

itself to long-term innovation and revolution, but rather to the affectivity of the present moment." (Reckwitz 2020: 431).

16   On the concept of the "parallel society", see critically Kaschuba 2007.
17   For instance, Carsten Brosda, Senator for Culture and Media in Hamburg states: "In the end, culture can have an effect as an integrative force which creates social purpose and develops personality." (Brosda 2020: 129)

place through the medium of music. On a meta-level, this may well be where the greatest innovative potential of *Musikvermittlung* lies.

What we have just outlined theoretically will be illustrated in the next paragraph by a concrete and, in our opinion, innovative example from the field of *Musikvermittlung*, in which a heterogeneous audience is addressed in an exemplary way: the "klangberührt" concert series by the Wiener Konzerthaus[18]. As part of a special focus on the topic of inclusion – among other things, a necessary renovation to the building was undertaken for the purpose of providing accessibility, and an inclusive summer music week was launched – education manager Katja Frei also initiated a concert series in 2019 that was intended to make it possible for people with disabilities, in particular, to attend concerts.[19] As for the material arrangement, part of the seating was removed for this purpose, creating space for wheelchairs as well as cardboard boxes as mobile seats. Instead of playing on a raised stage, the musicians play in the hall, at eye level with the audience. The effect of their music is enhanced by a light dramaturgy. A moderator guides the audience through the concert, and together with the musicians she also performs a participatory music-making action with the audience. The musical program for the concert series is stylistically broad, and ranges from jazz to traditional music to contemporary classical music. In contrast to "disciplining as a cultivated and distinctive habitus" (Hornberger 2016) in the classical concert, traditional concert rituals are largely suspended. Physical participation in the music by dancing, rocking or swaying, as well as singing along or spontaneously expressing emotion, is explicitly possible. This informal character appeals not only to people with disabilities and their companions, but also to people who desire a greater closeness and immediacy – and so, "a much more symmetrical understanding of the relationship between producers and recipients of art" (Staples, in this anthology: 72) – arises in the concert. People of different ages meet in these concerts, subscription audiences as well as concert newcomers, people with and without disabilities. The opening of the hall half an hour before the concert begins also enables an exchange between the visitors.

From our point of view, a format like "klangberührt" is innovative in the sense that it fosters inclusion in the traditionally exclusive classical concert life and enables encounters between people who presumably would not have

---

18 See also the contribution of Matthias Naske in this anthology.
19 See also Petri-Preis (in press).

met otherwise, as well as enabling new perspectives on music. This already indicates that we are pursuing a broad concept of innovation that is not limited to economic or technical innovation, as we will show in the next section.

Musikvermittlung and Innovation

Innovation is a term and a claim that has been tied very closely to modern societies from their beginnings, as Michael Hutter et al. (2016: 2) state. In the origin of the word, the adjective "innovative" can be, as Jan-Felix Schrape elucidates, "derived from the Latin verb *innovare* [emphasis in the original], which may be translated as 'renew', but also as 'regenerate while sleeping'. *Innovatio* [emphasis in the original] accordingly describes a thorough internal renewal and not a superficial *renovation* [emphasis in the original]" (Schrape 2012: 3). "Change", "alteration" and "novelty" are further interpretations closely linked with the Latin origin *innovatio* (see Pons n.d.). Almost ubiquitous and overused in the everyday life of postmodern societies, the following central levels of meaning can be identified:

"Innovation is becoming increasingly reflexive, heterogeneously distributed, and ubiquitous. *Reflexive innovation* [emphasis in the original] implies more than the intentional transformation of routine actions; it also refers to the transformation of social practices based on continuously (re-)produced knowledge of innovation. Hence, innovation itself becomes the aim and purpose of social activities: as the meaning and motif of (what we call the 'semantics' of novelty), as a component of practical routines (the 'pragmatics' of creative performance), and, finally, as part of systematically (re-)produced social structures of generating novelty (grammar of innovative regimes). *Heterogeneously* [emphasis in the original] distributed innovation refers to the observed shift from the individual entrepreneur to a network of divergent actors. *Ubiquity* [emphasis in the original] indicates the current expansion of innovation beyond the traditional spheres of science and economy and its generalization into an imperative for social action." (Hutter et al. 2016: 2)

The ubiquity of innovation goes hand in hand with the ubiquity of creativity – as Reckwitz has shown, the more or less daily renewal and reinvention of oneself has become a "cultural imperative" (Reckwitz 2012) for individuals as well as for collectives, institutions and companies in societies stamped as postmodern and neoliberal.

As Werner Rammert points out, the term innovation is very often primarily, if not exclusively, associated with economic and scientific technological innovations. From a social and a scientific cultural point of view, this assumption must appear to be an unreliable abbreviation, as economic and technological innovations basically represent "two, admittedly concise, special cases of societal innovation" (Rammert 2010: 2). In everyday life, economic, technical, scientific, social and cultural innovations are often closely related to one another, sometimes even mutually dependent, so that "on closer inspection, a so-called 'technical' innovation turns out to be a 'social' innovation or a mixed bundle of innovations of various kinds" (Rammert 2010: 7).[20] In this respect, from a theoretical point of view, an expanded concept of innovation as proposed by Rammert appears expedient to us.

Furthermore, this broad perspective opens up the opportunity to think of innovation as a primarily collaborative heterogeneous, network-like practice, as proposed by Hutter et al. (2016, see above). With regard to the field of art, Howard S. Becker stated, back in 1982, that "[a]ll artistic work, like all human activity, involves the joint activity of a number, often a large number, of people" and that "[t]he work always shows signs of that cooperation" (Becker 1982: 1). Human cooperation is described by Becker as a precondition for the emergence of a new art world (Becker 1982: 310), and its continuous changes are also shaped by collaboration:

> "[C]hanges in art occur through changes in worlds. Innovations last when participants make them the basis of a new mode of cooperation, or incorporate a change into their ongoing cooperative activities. [...] Innovations begin as, and continue to incorporate, changes in an artistic vision or idea. But their success depends on the degree to which their proponent can mobilize the support of others. Ideas and visions are important, but their success and

---

20 As Max Weber showed in his fragment *Die rationalen und soziologischen Grundlagen der Musik* (*The Rational and Sociological Foundations of Music*) more than one hundred years ago, the gradual assertion and increasing dominance of the pianoforte in Europe in the 18th and 19th centuries turns out to be a complex interplay of very different factors: Technological inventions in combination with processes of societal, cultural and economic transformations, as well as musical-practical conditions, were interlocked in this process. See Weber 1972 [1921/22], 73–77.

permanence rest on organization, not on their intrinsic worth." (Becker 1982: 309–310)

An original and novel idea alone is not enough – it has to be recognised as such by others. In this way, human activity can "introduce significant differences into the world" (Schatzki 2019: 81), but it is the reaction of the social environment that ascribes the status of innovation to these changes: "This includes the reactions of observers, commentators, and researchers, that is, their judgments and juxtapositions of the differences in question with other phenomena." (Schatzki 2019: 81)

From the theoretical perspective of art as a collective human activity, Becker further points out that innovations in an art world might entail the necessity for the actors "to learn and do different things, inconveniencing them and threatening their interests" (Becker 1982: 304). Innovations break up routines of action and may be perceived as a challenge or even a crisis, because people have to learn new ways of "doing things together" (Becker 1986). Practitioners in the field of *Musikvermittlung* are also sometimes perceived as introducing a "moment of disruption" (Mörsch n.d.: 36) simply because they appear as persons "in the artistic field, [...] interrupting its routines through their presence and making it suddenly aware of itself" (Mörsch n.d.: 36). This points, not least, to the importance of lifelong learning, especially in a highly fluid late modern society (for lifelong learning in music see e.g. Smilde 2009).

These theoretical considerations raise questions of power and interpretive authority, as Rammert points out: "Why, when, and in what constellations are which actors and institutions able to define and enforce something as an innovation?" (Hutter et al. 2016: 9f.) We are fully aware that the presentation of selected practices of *Musikvermittlung* in the context of this anthology implies a setting on our part: as editors, authors, researchers, and educators, we speak from positions of power and contribute to the classification und fixation of selected practices of *Musikvermittlung* as *innovative*. To address this problem constructively, we have integrated into this anthology a variety of scholarly perspectives and interdisciplinary viewpoints, as well as practical examples, which we will briefly outline here.

The Structure of the Anthology

This publication is based on a transdisciplinary lecture series that was held in the winter semester of 2019/2020 at the mdw – University of Music and Performing Arts Vienna. From the beginning we planned the lecture series to consist of spoken papers as well as performances of *Musikvermittlung*. On the one hand, this was important to us because we wanted not only to talk about the respective practices, but also to present them. On the other hand, the performances and the partly subsequent conversations with the artists added yet another perspective on the topic. Although the live situation cannot be depicted 1:1 in an anthology, we tried to transfer the concrete and practical portrayals of *Musikvermittlung* in a written form, supplemented by audio examples (QR codes) and pictures, and also to include these in this anthology. An example of this follows directly after this essay: Petri-Preis illustrates the format "2xHören" ("Listening Twice") by means of the composition "Peter Parker" by Bernhard Gander, which is inspired by the movements of Spider-Man. Listening to the piece twice – the first time before, the second time after a conversation between pianist Joonas Ahonen, composer Bernhard Gander and Axel Petri-Preis as moderator, enables the audience to hear the piece with *new ears* the second time.

As stated at the beginning of this article, there has been a significant agglomeration and differentiation of activities in *Musikvermittlung* within the past 20 to 25 years. In the following essay, Axel Petri-Preis traces the roots of *Musikvermittlung* and argues that around the turn of the last millennium a social world of *Musikvermittlung* emerged. He analyses the conditions that initiated its emergence and evolution and sheds a light on its current situation vis-à-vis other social worlds. Ultimately, he argues, the central future innovative potential of *Musikvermittlung* lies in the promotion of inclusion and accessibility in concert life.

This is followed by Ronald Staples' approach to *Musikvermittlung* from the perspective of innovation sociology. He first outlines the concept of (doing) innovation in detail and then analyses the relationship between innovation, creativity and art. Building on this, he argues that *Musikvermittlung*, as a third thing between art and education, is firstly an innovation itself, secondly the result of translation services, and thirdly an instance of the subsystem of art that ensures communication beyond the system.

During the lecture series, Jonas Scheiner and Henrik Szanto (alias Kirmes Hanoi/FOMP), together with the woodwind ensemble qWINDtett, brought together slam poetry and classical music in their performance. Text and music commented on, reflected and complemented each other, providing an exciting and novel listening experience, as Axel Petri-Preis outlines in this anthology.

Drawing on Reckwitz, we stated that in a postmodern, singularised society, practitioners of *Musikvermittlung* strive for "doing universality". Accordingly, Constanze Wimmer argues that in the face of a multi-diverse society, contemporary concert life needs professional translators. Based on the metaphor of practitioners of *Musikvermittlung* as architects who renovate old houses and build new ones, she analyses the status quo of *Musikvermittlung* and eventually describes a contemporary concert hall as a vision for the renewal of concert life: one that offers participatory music-making, functions as a place of social exchange, and opens itself to a diverse audience with different concert formats.

From the perspective of cultural management, Matthias Naske describes *Musikvermittlung* as a key agenda in classical concert life. In his reflections he takes as a starting point Günther Anders' thoughts on musical situations, stating that the act of listening as attention directed at the musical event is a central aspect of *Musikvermittlung*. In this way, *Musikvermittlung*, based on excellent concert planning, is the key to stimulating interest in and openness to music as an art form.

The Austrian cello quartet Die Kolophonistinnen, with its young musicians Hannah Amann, Marlene Förstel, Elisabeth Herrmann and Theresa Laun, was founded in 2014 and is known for its creative performative strategies and special arrangements of works, which all aim to address and connect with the audience, as the lecture series also impressively showed. Based on an interview with Marlene Förstel, Sarah Chaker outlines the motivation and strategies of the ensemble.

As mentioned above, curiosity and a willingness to learn and to become constantly and repeatedly involved in something new seems to be a prerequisite for innovation, not only but also in the fields of the arts and music (Becker 1982, 1986, Smilde 2009, Mörsch n.d.). Subsequently, by drawing on concrete examples from the field of music, Tasos Zembylas analyses and differentiates multiple forms of knowledge and know-how, as he identifies them as motors of innovation and regards them in a quasi-holistic understanding as closely interrelated in concrete everyday practice. From his analysis, he also derives specific recommendations for the current practice of *Musikvermittlung*.

The contribution by Rineke Smilde connects to Zembylas' theoretical consideration as she highlights the biographical learning processes of professionally trained musicians who are able and willing to address new audiences. By referring to two ethnographically and exploratively informed research projects in which she was significantly involved – the first one carried out in a care home for people living with dementia, the second conducted in a hospital, focusing on patients and their nurses – Smilde convincingly demonstrates the innovative potential of biographical learning for all people involved in the process. A sustainable *Musikvermittlung* therefore has to consider how biographical learning processes can be implemented in an adequate way in higher music education in the future.

A special kind of synaesthetic experience could be seen, heard and tasted in "Works and Whiskies", as very different tastes of Scotch whisky flavours were transformed into notes and pieces of music for contrabass clarinet by composer Petra Stump-Linshalm. These were rendered audible by musician Heinz-Peter Linshalm and found their visual equivalent in paintings by Jutta Goldgruber. Sarah Chaker summarises the thoughts of the artists involved in this special kind of *Musikvermittlung*, which was retrospectively described by many of those present as particularly innovative and expedient, especially by many of our students, perhaps not only because of the stimulating ingredients mentioned.

More insights into current (artistic) research and mutual learning processes and practices in classical music is provided by the contribution of the team of authors Peter Peters, Ties van de Werff, Ruth Benschop and Imogen Eve. By the means of two experimental performance settings functioning as a lab, the orchestra members, as well as the staff involved and the audience members, are prompted to rethink their roles in the musical process – reflexive learning is encouraged.

Finally, Jutta Toelle focuses explicitly on the audience of contemporary classical music, its experiences and expectations, and the opportunities and limits of its involvement and participation in the musical process by drawing on empirical findings from a study she conducted at different participatory projects in the field of *Musikvermittlung*.

Thanks!

In realising this book publication and the lecture series on which it is based, we have received support from many sides, for which we would here like to express our sincere thanks: it was only the financial and institutional support provided by the rectorate of the mdw – the University of Music and Performing Arts Vienna – that made it possible to realise our event concept and the corresponding publication. For this, we are very grateful to the rector of the mdw, Ulrike Sych, as well as to the vice-rector Barbara Gisler-Haase, who also opened the lecture series in autumn 2019. We would also like to thank Therese Kaufmann and Vitali Bodnar from the mdw's Research Support Office for their help regarding the open access funding of this volume. Peter Röbke (back then head of the Department of Music Education Research, Music Didactics and Elementary Music Education at the mdw) and Tasos Zembylas (back then head of the Department of Music Sociology at the mdw) have accompanied both projects from the beginning in an extremely benevolent manner and supported them in a constructive and stimulating way – many thanks! We would also like to thank Rosa Reitsamer for her helpful feedback on our work. The interdisciplinary collaboration with our speakers and authors, as well as with the participating artists, was an honour and a great enrichment for us – many thanks for the wonderful cooperation. Barbara Balba Weber, Andreas Bernhofer, Irena Müller-Brozovic, Peter Mall, Hendrikje Mautner-Obst, Peter Röbke, Ernst-Klaus Schneider, Lisa Unterberg and Constanze Wimmer supported us as peer reviewers in a highly professional and constructive way – thank you for your commitment! In addition, Johannes Voit and Constanze Wimmer, as series editors, have reviewed the contributions to the volume and commented on them where necessary – many thanks for your feedback, and we are pleased to be able to open transcript's new book series "Forum Musikvermittlung – Perspektiven aus Forschung und Praxis" with our volume. The central creative impulse for a project on the innovative potential of *Musikvermittlung* came from Anna Rockenschaub and Antonia Grüner from Jeunesse, with Constanze Wimmer kindly putting us in touch – thank you for that! We would also like to thank Peter Waugh who, as proofreader and translator, meticulously commented on, corrected and discussed the present anthology with us. Last but not least we would like to thank our student assistants Laura Bezold, Matthias Gruber and Doria Thürr, who actively helped us with the lecture series and/or our book publication. Now we wish you an informative read.

Bibliography

Allwardt, Ingrid (2017): Musikvermittlung — Ein Überblick über Ziele, Angebotsformate, Strukturen und statistische Erhebungen, [online] https://www.kubi-online.de/artikel/musikvermittlung-ueberblick-ueber-ziele-angebotsformate-strukturen-statistische-erhebungen [22.3.2021].

Annoff, Michael (2021): Sich die Krone aufsetzen. Wer darf Diversität in deutschen Kulturinstitutionen managen?, in: *Kulturpolitische Mitteilungen* No. 172, 1/2021, 67–69.

Arenhövel, Sophie (2012): Zur Komplexität von Differenz – Notwendige Haltungen und Reflexionen für eine diversitätsbewusste Musikvermittlung, in: Binas-Preisendörfer, Susanne/Unseld, Melanie (eds.): *Transkulturalität und Musikvermittlung. Möglichkeiten und Herausforderungen in Forschung, Kulturpolitik und musikpädagogischer Praxis*, book series Musik und Gesellschaft, Vol. 33, Frankfurt am Main: Peter Lang, 263–284.

Becker, Howard S. (1982): *Art Worlds*, Berkeley, Los Angeles, London: University of California Press.

Becker, Howard S. (1986): *Doing Things Together*, Evanston: Northwestern University Press.

Blaukopf, Kurt (1972): Symphonie, Konzertwesen, Publikum, in: Rauchhaupt, Ursula von (ed.): *Die Welt der Symphonie*. Sonderauszug, Wien: mdw-Bibliothek, 9–16.

Born, Georgina (2005): Musical Mediation: Ontology, Technology and Creativity, in: *Twentieth Century Music* Vol. 2, No. 1, 7–36.

Born, Georgina/Barry, Andrew (2018): Music, Mediation Theories and Actor-Network Theory, in: *Contemporary Music Review*, Vol. 37, No. 5-6, 443–487.

Bourdieu, Pierre (2009 [1972]): *Entwurf einer Theorie der Praxis auf der ethnologischen Grundlage der kabylischen Gesellschaft*, [2nd edition], Frankfurt am Main: Suhrkamp.

Brenk, Markus (2008): Konzertpädagogik/Musikvermittlung im Rahmen einer Musikhochschule am Beispiel Detmold: Porträt sowie didaktische und professionstheoretische Analyse einer musikpädagogischen Konzeption, in: Pfeffer, Martin/ Rolle, Christian/Vogt, Jürgen (eds.), *Musikpädagogik auf dem Wege zur Vermittlungswissenschaft?*, Hamburg: Lit Verlag, 34–56.

Brosda, Carsten (2020): *Die Kunst der Demokratie. Die Bedeutung der Kultur für eine offene Gesellschaft*, Hamburg: Hoffmann und Campe.

Bugiel, Lukas (2015): Wenn man von der Krise spricht. Diskursanalytische Untersuchung zur 'Krise des Konzerts' in Musik- und musikpädagogischen Zeitschriften, in: Rora, Constanze/Cvetko, Alexander (eds.), *Konzertpädagogik*, Aachen: Shaker, 61–81.

Duden (n.d.): *potenzial, potential*, [online] https://www.duden.de/rechtschreibung/potenzial [8.7.2021].

educult/netzwerk junge ohren (eds.) (2020): *Arbeitsbedingungen für Musikvermittler*innen im deutschsprachigen Raum. Hochmotiviert, exzellent ausgebildet, prekär bezahlt*, Berlin: netzwerk junge ohren.

Ehrenforth, Karl Heinrich (1971): *Verstehen und Auslegen: die hermeneutischen Grundlagen einer Lehre von der didaktischen Interpretation der Musik*, Frankfurt am Main, Berlin, Munich: Diesterweg.

Gadamer, Hans-Georg (1989): *Truth and Method*, London: Sheed and Ward.

Gembris, Heiner/Menze, Jonas (2018): Zwischen Publikumsschwund und Publikumsentwicklung. Perspektiven für Musikerberuf, Musikpädagogik und Kulturpolitik, in: Tröndle, Martin (ed.), *Das Konzert^{II}. Beiträge zum Forschungsfeld der Concert Studies*, Bielefeld: transcript, 305–331.

Gutzeit, Reinhart von (2015): Musikvermittlung — was ist das nun wirklich? In: Rüdiger, Wolfgang (ed.), *Musikvermittlung — wozu? Umrisse und Perspektiven eines jungen Arbeitsfeldes*, Mainz: Schott, 19–36.

Hennion, Antoine (2015): *The Passion for Music: A Sociology of Mediation*, London: Taylor & Francis Ltd.

Henschel, Alexander (2020): *Was heisst hier Vermittlung? Kunstvermittlung und ihr umstrittener Begriff*. Vienna: Zaglossus.

Hornberger, Barbara (2016): *Informelle Orte, informelles Lernen: Herausforderung für Kulturelle Bildung*, [online] https://www.kubi-online.de/index.php/artikel/informelle-orte-informelles-lernen-herausforderung-kulturelle-bildung [1.7.2021].

Hornberger, Barbara (2020): Was wir uns ein-bilden. Musikpädagogik aus der Perspektive der Cultural Studies, in: Berg, Ivo/Lindmaier, Hannah/Röbke, Peter (eds.): *Vorzeichenwechsel. Gesellschaftspolitische Dimensionen von Musikpädagogik heute*, Münster: Waxmann, 47–68.

Hutter, Michael/Knoblauch, Herbert/Rammert, Werner/Windeler, Arnold (2016): Innovationsgesellschaft heute: *Die reflexive Herstellung des Neuen. Technical University Technology Studies Working Papers, TU Berlin*, [online] https://www.researchgate.net/publication/303375531_Innovationsgesellschaft_heute [8.7.2021].

Kaschuba, Wolfgang (2007): Ethnische Parallelgesellschaften? Zur kulturellen Konstruktion des Fremden in der europäischen Migration, in: *Zeitschrift für Volkskunde*, 1 / 2007, 65–85. [online] http://www.wolfgang-kaschuba.de/texte/parallel_zfv.pdf [8.7.2021].

Langenscheidt (n.d.): *Potentia*, [online] https://de.langenscheidt.com/latein-deutsch/potentia [8.7.2021].

Mall, Peter (2016): *Schule und Orchester. Aspekte des Zusammenspiels von schulischer und außerschulischer Musikvermittlung in kooperativer Projektarbeit*, Augsburg: Wissner.

Mall, Peter/Schwarz, Ralf-Olivier (2018): Musikvermittlung aus soziologischer Perspektive, in: Voit, Johannes (ed.), *Schule und Konzertbetrieb als "Blackbox". Überlegungen zu möglichen Schnittstellen zwischen Musikvermittlung und Musikpädagogik*, Hamburg. Hildegard-Junker-Verlag, 18–30.

Mandel, Birgit (2019): Teilhabeorientierte Kulturvermittlung. Neue Herausforderungen für Kulturinstitutionen und Kulturpolitik, in: Nationaler Kulturdialog (ed.), *Kulturelle Teilhabe. Ein Handbuch*, Zurich: Seismo Verlag, 69–78.

Mautner-Obst, Hendrikje (2018): Musikvermittlung, in: Gruhn, Wilfried/Röbke, Peter (eds.), *Musiklernen. Bedingungen, Handlungsfelder, Positionen*, Innsbruck, Esslingen: Helbling, 335–357.

microsillons (n.d.): Vermittlung. (Kontra)punkte, in: *Zeit für Vermittlung. Eine online Publikation zur Kulturvermittlung, herausgegeben vom Institute for Art Education der Zürcher Hochschule der Künste (ZHdK), im Auftrag von Pro Helvetia*, [online] https://www.kultur-vermittlung.ch/zeit-fuer-vermittlung/download/pdf-d/ZfV_0_gesamte_Publikation.pdf [8.7.2021], 25–26.

Mörsch, Carmen (n.d.): *Zeit für Vermittlung. Eine online Publikation zur Kulturvermittlung, herausgegeben vom Institute for Art Education der Zürcher Hochschule der Künste (ZHdK), im Auftrag von Pro Helvetia*, [online] https://www.kultur-vermittlung.ch/zeit-fuer-vermittlung/download/pdf-d/ZfV_0_gesamte_Publikation.pdf [8.7.2021].

Müller-Brozovic, Irena (2017): Musikvermittlung, [online] https://www.kubi-online.de/artikel/musikvermittlung [22.3.2021].

Petri-Preis, Axel (2019): Musikvermittlung. Ein musikpädagogischer Streitbegriff, in: *Diskussion Musikpädagogik*, Vol. 84, 5–9.

Petri-Preis, Axel (2021): *Musikvermittlung lernen. Eine Analyse von Lernwegen klassischer Musiker_innen*, Dissertation: Department of Music Education Research, Music Didactics and Elementary Music Education, mdw – University of Music and Performing Arts Vienna.

Petri-Preis (in press): Musikvermittlung und Community Music als Motoren von Inklusion im klassischen Konzertleben, in: Hennenberg, Beate/Röbke, Peter, *Inklusion am Wiener Institut für musikpädagogische Forschung, Musikdidaktik und Elementares Musizieren — am Beispiel der Band All Stars inclusive*, Münster: Waxmann.

Pons Online-Wörterbuch (n.d.): *innovatio*, [online] https://de.pons.com/%C3%BCbersetzung/latein-deutsch/innovatio [8.7.2021].

Rammert, Werner (2010): *Die Innovationen der Gesellschaft*. Technical University Technology Studies Working Papers, TU Berlin, [online] https://www.researchgate.net/publication/226058346_Die_Innovationen_der_Gesellschaft [9.7.2021].

Reckwitz, Andreas (2012): *Die Erfindung der Kreativität: Zum Prozess gesellschaftlicher Ästhetisierung*. Berlin: Suhrkamp.

Reckwitz, Andreas (2020): *Die Gesellschaft der Singularitäten. Zum Strukturwandel der Moderne*, [3rd edition], Berlin: Suhrkamp.

Richter, Christoph (1976): *Theorie und Praxis der didaktischen Interpretation von Musik*, Frankfurt am Main/Berlin/München: Diesterweg.

Richter, Christoph (1996): The Didactic Interpretation of Music, in: *Philosophy of Music Education Review*, Vol. 4, No. 1, 33–49.

Rolle, Christian (1999): *Musikalisch-ästhetische Bildung. Über die Bedeutung ästhetischer Erfahrung für musikalische Bildungsprozesse*, Kassel: Bosse.

Rüdiger, Wolfgang (2015): *Musikvermittlung – wozu. Umrisse und Perspektiven eines jungen Arbeitsfeldes*. Mainz: Schott.

Salmen, Walter (1988): *Das Konzert. Eine Kulturgeschichte*, München: C.H. Beck.

Schatzki, Theodore R. (2019): *Social Change in a Material World*, New York: Routledge.

Schneider, Ernst Klaus (2009): Wie aus einem kleinen Pilotprojekt ein erfolgreicher Masterstudiengang (Weiterbildung) wurde, in: Richter, Christoph (ed.), *Musikvermittlung - Konzertpädagogik in Detmold*, Hamburg: Hildegard Juncker Verlag, 75–87.

Schneider, Ernst Klaus (2015): Kann man Musikvermittlung lernen? In: Rüdiger, Wolfgang (ed.), *Musikvermittlung – wozu? Umrisse und Perspektiven eines jungen Arbeitsfeldes*, Mainz: Schott, 37–58.

Schneider, Ernst Klaus (2019): Entwicklung eines 1998 entstandenen Studiengangs. "Musikvermittlung in Detmold", in: *Diskussion Musikpädagogik*, Vol. 84, 10–18.

Schrape, Jan-Felix (2012): *Was ist Innovationssoziologie?* [online] https://gedank enstrich.org/wp-content/uploads/2012/04/Was-ist-Innovationssoziologi e.pdf [8.7.2021].

Smilde, Rineke (2009): *Musicians as lifelong learners. Discovery through biography*, Delft: Eburon.

Stiller, Barbara (2008): *Erlebnisraum Konzert. Prozesse der Musikvermittlung in Konzerten für Kinder*, Regensburg: ConBrio.

Stoffers, Nina (2019): *Kulturelle Teilhabe durch Musik? Transkulturelle Kinder- und Jugendbildung im Spannungsfeld von Empowerment und Othering*, Bielefeld: transcript.

Terkessidis, Mark (2019): Kulturelle Teil-Gabe. Das Prinzip der Kollaboration, in: Nationaler Kulturdialog (ed.), *Kulturelle Teilhabe – Ein Handbuch*, Zürich: Seismo Verlag, 79–85.

Tröndle, Martin (2018): Eine Konzerttheorie, in: Tröndle, Martin (ed.), *Das Konzert^{II}. Beiträge zum Forschungsfeld der Concert Studies*, Bielefeld: transcript, 25–52.

Vertovec, Steven (2012): *Superdiversität*, [online] https://heimatkunde.boell.de /de/2012/11/18/superdiversitaet [8.7.2021].

Voit, Johannes (2019): Music Communication, in: Schulmeistrat Stephan/ Schwerdtfeger Christiane/German Music Council, German Music Information Centre [miz] (eds.), *Musical Life in Germany*, Bonn: German Music Council, 108–129.

Weber, Barbara Balba (2018): *Entfesselte Klassik. Grenzen öffnen mit künstlerischer Musikvermittlung*, Bern: Stämpfli Verlag.

Weber, Max (1972/[1921/22]): *Die rationalen und soziologischen Grundlagen der Musik*. Tübingen: Mohr/Siebeck.

Welch, Graham F./Saunders, Jo/Himonides, Evangelos (2012): *European Concert Hall Organisation (ECHO): An initial benchmarking study of Education, Learning and Participation*, London: International Music Education Research Centre (iMerc).

Wimmer, Constanze (2010a): *Exchange. Die Kunst, Musik zu vermitteln. Qualitäten in der Musikvermittlung und Konzertpädagogik*, [online] http://www.ku nstdervermittlung.at/ [22.3.2021].

Wimmer, Constanze (2010b): *Musikvermittlung im Kontext. Impulse-Strategien-Berufsfelder*, Regensburg: Con Brio.

Wimmer, Constanze (2018a): Einen Sehnsuchtsort der Wahrnehmung öffnen. Musikvermittlung im Konzertbetrieb, in: Tröndle, Martin (ed.), *Das Konzert[II]. Beiträge zum Forschungsfeld der Concert Studies*, Bielefeld: transcript, 197–216.

Wimmer, Constanze (2018b): Musik als gesellschaftliche Interaktion. Musikvermittler auf dem Weg zu Artistic Citizenship, in: *positionen. Texte zur aktuellen Musik*, Vol. 115, 41–43.

Wimmer, Michael (2012): Kulturelle Bildung und Ungleichheit, [online] https://educult.at/wimmers-weekly/kulturelle-bildung-und-ungleichheit [13.9.2021].

Zembylas, Tasos (2017): Kulturpolitik in Österreich, in: Klein, Armin (ed.): *Kompendium Kulturmanagement. Handbuch für Studium und Praxis*, [4th edition], München: Franz Vahlen Verlag, 141–156.

Biographical notes

Sarah Chaker studied musicology and German language at the Carl von Ossietzky University of Oldenburg. She is currently an assistant professor at the Department of Music Sociology (IMS) at the mdw – University of Music and Performing Arts Vienna. Her research interests include street music, the transdisciplinary analysis of music, histories, theories and methods of music sociology, popular music (in particular metal music) and *Musikvermittlung*.

Axel Petri-Preis studied music education, German philology and musicology in Vienna. He has been active in the field of *Musikvermittlung* internationally for more than ten years, and his projects have received several awards. He is a senior scientist and Deputy Head at the Department of Music Education Research, Music Didactics and Elementary Music Education (IMP) at the mdw – University of Music and Performing Arts Vienna. His research currently focuses on the education and further training of (classical) musicians in relation to *Musikvermittlung* and on community engagement in classical music life.

Listening Twice to Bernhard Gander's "Peter Parker"

Axel Petri-Preis

Artists
Joonas Ahonen, piano & Bernhard Gander, composer

Concept and moderation
Axel Petri-Preis

Programme
Bernhard Gander: "Peter Parker" (2004)

The concept of the "2xHören" [listening twice] format is as simple as it is brilliant: the audience listens to a piece of music twice, at the beginning and at the end of a concert. In between, a moderator provides the audience with insights, for example by talking to the artists, zooming in on parts of the piece, conducting listening experiments, or giving information about its sociocultural context.

"2xhören" was developed by the Körber Stiftung Hamburg.[1] It started in 2006 with Markus Fein as moderator and soon found its way into the *Musikvermittlung* repertoire of concert halls (e.g. Konzerthaus Berlin).[2] The idea of listening to an artwork twice isn't entirely new. The pianist Hans von Bülow used to perform Ludwig van Beethoven's monumental "Sonate for Hammerklavier" twice and thus enabled the work, which was extraordinary for the ears of the time, to find a place in the concert repertoire. Willem Mengelberg played

---

1   For video recordings see https://www.koerber-stiftung.de/veranstaltungsuebersicht/re ihen/2-x-hoeren-1.
2   For more information about the history and the educational approach, see Musil (2013).

Gustav Mahler's "Symphony No. 4" twice in a 1903 concert, first conducting it himself and then with Mahler on the podium. Mahler wrote to his wife that this was a great idea to make the audience comfortable with his piece. Lastly, the concept of playing a piece repeatedly in order to allow for more informed listening also played an important role in Arnold Schönberg's "Verein für musikalische Privataufführungen".

What can be seen from these historical examples is that the intention behind listening to a piece twice in the course of a concert was to support the audience in getting accustomed to a new piece of music and in listening to it differently the second time. This is exactly the idea behind the "2xHören" format, which seeks to lead the audience to deeper and more informed listening and facilitate aesthetic experiences.

In the course of our lecture series, we invited the pianist Joonas Ahonen and the composer Bernhard Gander for a "2xHören" of Gander's piece "Peter Parker". In order to get an impression of the format, we recommend that you listen to the piece by scanning the QR-Code provided on this page, then read the interview with the composer and eventually listen to the piece a second time.

Interview with Bernhard Gander

Axel Petri-Preis (APP): Bernhard, your composition is called "Peter Parker". That's Spider-Man's civic alter-ego and a thoroughly unusual source of inspiration for a contemporary piano piece. How did this reference come about?

Bernhard Gander (BG): The first ideas for the piano piece came to me when I saw the film in the cinema. The unbelievably good 3D-shots of the flying scenes really stuck with me. It was very clear to me that I wanted to process these flying scenes, these dynamic 3D-scenes, into music. At the time, I thought that maybe the piano wasn't the best instrument for that. It would probably be better to represent this spatiality with a spatially distributed string quartet. But it was the restriction to the piano that eventually made the composition process interesting to me.

APP: You say you might have preferred a string quartet. One of your string quartets is inspired by the superhero Hulk. What predestines superheroes to serve as a source of inspiration for your music?

BG: In retrospect, I'm very glad that I wrote "Peter Parker" for piano, because Spider-Man himself is virtuosic and filigree, and that's better suited for the piano than for string instruments. Because with string instruments – when I think of the Hulk – I can blow up the physicality more. I have four string instruments, and I also associate the sonority more with that gross, pompous Hulk. So I'm glad about the choice of instrument. As for superheroes, musicians have always been superheroes to me. That's probably why they're such a good connecting point (laughs).

APP: "Peter Parker" is highly virtuosic and places the highest technical demands on the pianists. What is striking, however, is that you stick to a conventional way of playing the instrument, which you don't necessarily do in other pieces and with other instruments. What is behind this decision?

BG: With the piano, I'm only interested in the use of the keys. So the plucking in the piano or the percussion sounds on the piano don't interest me from a purely sonic point of view.

APP: In many of your piece titles and short introductory texts you refer to sources of inspiration outside of music. Do these references serve more for the process of composing or are they meant as a listening aid for the audience?

BG: It's both. For example, I could work musically in a purely abstract way. I could say I'm doing a theme with variations. "Peter Parker" would be that, too. I could also explain the piece that way. But because I was inspired by this story, I also make an inner script and work on it musically. Firstly, because it refreshes my musical workday and makes it more interesting, and I also think that listeners can discover quite a lot of correspondences when they listen, for example, when Spider-Man flies or crawls around on the ground. So when the audience hears a virtuoso passage, it's not just mere virtuosity on the instrument, there's a struggle going on. So that could also be an auditory aid.

APP: How important is it to you that the musicians who perform your pieces know about your thoughts on the piece?

BG: I'm almost more interested if they don't know anything about my background and approach the material purely musically, but I always leave that up to the musicians. If they ask me what I was thinking, I tell them. But I don't send them the instruction manual with the sheet music (laughs).

APP: You worked a lot with sketches at the beginning of the composition process for "Peter Parker". Can you please talk about how you went about that?

BG: I worked with graph paper in this piece, using mostly dots to represent individual notes and strokes to symbolize clusters. This way I get a good overview: do the individual elements occur very densely or rather loosely, do they make a distinctive rhythm? I can see on the sketch how it will sound. I can also improvise freely on it (sings).

APP: When you talk about improvising, do you also try things out on the piano while composing?

BG: No, mostly only on paper. I have a rough idea of the sound and make quick sketches. It's precisely in this quick writing that I get new results that I might not get with rigorous musing.

APP: Is the overall dramaturgy of the piece fixed from the beginning, or does it develop during improvisation while composing?

BG: I usually have the big dramaturgical arc in my head as an energy. So I know roughly how long the piece is going to be and I think about whether it's going to be divided into many parts or whether it's going to be one big rearing shape, for example. I determine something like that in my head fairly quickly and then start working it out in more detail.

APP: Let's come back to Spider-Man. How does this character flow into the music in concrete terms?

Fig. 1: Sketch (extract) for Peter Parker

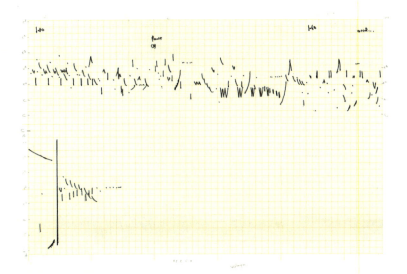

Source: private

BG: There are different scenes or adventures that Spider-Man has. In some scenes he just casts his web. At the very beginning, you hear a little bite where he gets infected by the spider. There are also fight scenes where he gets knocked to the ground, or he jumps in the air. Then, of course, there are these three-dimensional movements in space. The whole piece is like a comic book with different adventures.

APP: Comic book is a good keyword. You also used concrete images from Spider-Man comics as a template. Did you try to translate those images into music?

BG: Yes, they're actually 1:1 translations, because in comics, after all, bodies are depicted particularly well and clearly. When a body is tense, for example, you can see how the muscles stand out under the clothes, how the body is built up in a plastic and muscular way. I drew that for myself and then also tried to depict muscle progressions in short formal sections.

APP: Do you have a favorite part of the piece?

BG: I think my favorite parts are the ones where he flutters through the New York skyscrapers really fast.

APP: If you were to give a listening tip to the listeners, what could they focus on in particular?

BG: The first time, you could really think of the character of Spider-Man based on the title. And the second time, just listen to what happens sonically. Like a Beethoven sonata.

Dibliography

Gander, Bernhard (2003): *Peter Parker*, Leipzig, London, New York: Edition Peters.

Musil, Monika (2013): *Formate des Zwei- und Mehrfachhörens. Analytische Betrachtung des Musikvermittlungsformats "2 x hören" der Körber-Stiftung*, unpublished Master's Thesis (Anton Bruckner Privatuniversität Oberösterreich).

QR-code: Joonas Ahonen performing Bernhard Gander's "Peter Parker"; Source: YouTube [online: https://www.youtube.com/watch?v=0SxD6iNrxwU].

Biographical notes

Pianist **Joonas Ahonen's** musical interests take him from performing late 18th century music on the fortepiano to giving premiere performances of the music of our times. He is a member of Klangforum Wien, one of the leading ensembles for contemporary music, and a member of the Rödberg fortepianotrio. Over the years, Ahonen has performed as a soloist with the Helsinki Philharmonic Orchestra, the Finnish Radio Symphony Orchestra, the BBC Symphony Orchestra and Ictus. His recordings on BIS label of Ligeti's Piano Concerto and Ives' Piano Sonata No. 2, "Concord" have received critical acclaim in the music press. https://www.joonasahonen.com

Born in Lienz in 1969, **Bernhard Gander** studied piano and conducting at the Tyrolean Provincial Conservatoire and composition with Beat Furrer in Graz. He also studied at the Studio UPIC in Paris and at the Swiss Centre for Computer Music in Zurich. In 2004 he received the Musikförderungspreis of the City of Vienna, in 2006 the Erste Bank Composition Prize, in 2005 a government grant, and in 2012 the Ernst-Krenek Prize. He has also received commissions among others from Klangforum Wien, Ensemble Modern, RSO, Musikprotokoll, Wiener Konzerthaus, Donaueschinger Musiktage, Wiener Festwochen, Biennale Munich, Wittener Tage für neue Kammermusik. https://www.bernhardgander.at

Fig. 2: Joonas Ahonen, Bernhard Gander and Axel Petri-Preis in conversation at the lecture series, October 2019

Source: private

The Big Bang of *Musikvermittlung*
On the Emergence of a New Social World and Its Future Innovative Potential

Axel Petri-Preis

The years around the turn of the last millenium launched the remarkable career of *Musikvermittlung*[1] in the German-speaking countries.[2] Ever since then, concert halls, orchestras and ensembles have been creating new positions and even departments, and their range of *Musikvermittlung* formats has been constantly increasing (Keuchel/Weil 2010). The annual concert statistics of the Deutsche Orchestervereinigung (DOV)[3] and the Deutsches Musikinformationszentrum (miz) shows that the numbers of "music-pedagogical events"[4] tripled between 2003/04 and 2017/18 (from 2,141 events to 6,325 events), whereas there has been a steady decline in classical symphonic concerts (from a peak of 6,158 concerts in the 2011/12 season to 5,557 concerts in 2017/18). In the 2017/18 season *Musikvermittlung* performances even outreached the numbers of classical symphony concerts for the first time (Deutsches Musikinformationszentrum 2019).

---

1   For a definition of *Musikvermittlung* see the introduction to this anthology.
2   Practices of *Musikvermittlung* (variously termed "education", "education and community", "learning and engagement" or "learning and participation" in the English-speaking countries) gained importance in all those parts of the world with a tradition of performing classical music. I will however restrict myself to Germany, Austria and Switzerland in this article.
3   The Deutsche Orchestervereinigung (DOV) is the German union for orchestra musicians.
4   The statistics cover publicly funded orchestras and radio symphony orchestras in Germany. *Musikvermittlung* offers are labelled "music-pedagogical events" and comprise children's and youth concerts, school concerts and workshops in schools. It is reasonable to assume that the number would be even higher if formats for adults and outreach activities were also to be included in this calculation.

Practices of *Musikvermittlung* aren't entirely new inventions. They draw on concerts for children, collaborative projects of music institutions and educational institutions and also community music practices that have long traditions, especially in the Anglo-American world. However, in this chapter, I will show that around the year 2000 a new "social world of *Musikvermittlung*"[5] constituted itself and will analyse the conditions under which this innovation[6] took place. To give a comprehensive picture, after having outlined my theoretical framework and methodical approach, I will first shed a light on the current structure of the social world and subsequently elaborate on its emergence and development. Eventually, I will conclude with some final remarks about the future innovative potential that I think lies in *Musikvermittlung*, especially in regard to classical concert life.

Theoretical Framework

Musikvermittlung has been approached from the theoretical background of cultural studies (Wimmer 2010), Pierre Bourdieu's field theory (Mall/Schwarz 2018, Ardila-Mantilla/Busch/Göllner 2018) and Niklas Luhmann's system theory (Mall 2016, Schmitz 2017, Staples in this anthology). My analysis is informed by pragmatist/symbolic interactionist and practice-theoretical thinking. Essentially, I am drawing on the social-theoretical assumptions of Adele E. Clarke's situational analysis and Theodore Schatzki's site ontology.

As a "theory-methods package", situational analysis is a postmodern and poststructural version of grounded theory methodology that encompasses "epistemological *and* ontological assumptions along with concrete practices through which social scientists go about their work" (Clarke et al. 2018: 24, emphasis in the original). Clarke extends the pragmatist and symbolic interactionist theoretical foundation of grounded theory methodology, which she calls "always already around the postmodern, poststructural and interpretive turns in many ways" (Clarke et al. 2018: 25), by building centrally on Anselm Strauss' social worlds/arenas theory and including elements of Foucauldian discourse theory and actor-network theory, as well as linking it to

---

5   I will use the abbreviation SW for social worlds in the following.
6   In reference to Schatzki, I understand innovation as actions that "introduce significant differences into the world" (Schatzki 2019: 81).

practice theory.[7] Clarke contends that social worlds are the "principal affiliative mechanisms through which people organize social life" (Clarke 1991: 131) and defines them as "groups with shared commitments to certain activities, sharing resources of many kinds to achieve their goals, and building shared ideologies about how to go about their business" (Clarke 2008: 115). In his seminal essay "A Social World Perspective" (1978), Strauss conceptualises the main features of social worlds: there is at least one primary activity that is performed by members of the world at specific sites. Many social worlds evolve complex technologies to carry out their activities. Formal organisations[8] usually emerge during the legitimation process of a social world and can be situated either in a single social world or at the borders of different social worlds. Visibility and perceptibility can differ significantly and, unlike formal organisations, the borders of social worlds are more or less permeable.

The primary activity of a social world can be understood as practices[9] in Schatzki's sense, who defines them as "organized, spatio-temporal nexuses of doings and sayings" (Schatzki 2014: 18). Together with material arrangements ("humans, artifacts, organisms, and phenomena of nature", Schatzki 2019: 35), they link to bundles. In his article "Art Bundles", Schatzki compares his depiction of art, which is informed by practice theory, to Howard Becker's (1982) theory of "art worlds" claiming that the latter conception, which is deeply rooted in the symbolic interactionist tradition, comes closest to his own ideas (Schatzki 2014: 20). A social world can thus be seen as a "constellation of practices" – in Schatzki's sense[10]: "[B]undles [of practices] link into larger constellations, in this case, one – let's call it the 'rock music world' – that embraces concerts and auditoriums, record deals and companies, radio broadcasts and stations, meetings and firms, equipment manufacturers

---

7 Clarke et al. (2018) reference Schatzki's work several times in their book, although they do not elaborate on intersections between pragmatism/symbolic interactionism and practice theory in detail. Jörg Strübing (2017) however sees a reciprocal complementary relation between pragmatism and practice theories and suggests a combination of practice theory and situational analysis.
8 Clarke et al. (2018: 172) have a broad understanding of organisations encompassing both professional organisations and NGOs.
9 Both Clarke et al. (2018: 74) and Schatzki (2014: 21) point out the conceptual proximity of the symbolic interactionist terms "collective action" or "joint action" and "practices".
10 Etienne Wenger (1998: 183) also asserts that Strauss' theory of social worlds is closely related to his own approach, albeit with a different analytical focus, and that many social worlds are constellations of practices.

and their products, etc." (Schatzki 2014: 20) According to Strauss ([1993] 2017: 215f.), social change transpires through the intersection, segmentation and legitimation of social worlds. Segmentation typically occurs around innovations and specialisations within social worlds. New subworlds often emerge around newly differentiated activities and may lead to the establishment of new social worlds. Schatzki contends that "social changes consist in significant configurations of differences in bundles" (Schatzki 2019: 214), resulting from human activity and material events or processes. New worlds that emerge around innovations have to legitimise and newly define themselves through the use of resources, shared commitments and specific activities (Strauss [1993] 2017: 215f.). According to Strauss, the intersection of social worlds is the most important process. It leads to joint actions between members of different social (sub)worlds and can subsequently result in the emergence of arenas, in which negotiations about the further principles of action take place (Strauss [1993] 2017: 227). Smaller arenas dissolve after a certain period of time because their problem has been solved, whereas larger arenas can exist permanently.

The frame of reference presented serves as a theoretical lens or "prior picture" (Blumer 1969: 24) for the analysis, the methodical approach to which I will outline in the next section.

Methodical Approach

For this article I am drawing on data from my dissertation study of musicians' learning trajectories in relation to practices of *Musikvermittlung* (Petri-Preis 2021). Between June 2018 and December 2019, I conducted 22 semi-structured interviews with six male and six female musicians, aged between 23 and 59, who engage in practices of *Musikvermittlung*. Their degree of involvement spans the whole range, from merely taking part in children's concerts to developing and leading the *Musikvermittlung* offers of an orchestra. Using Clarke's situational analysis, an important part of the analysis was to construct the "big picture" (Clarke et al. 2018: 104) of the situation of inquiry, in order to situate the musicians' learning processes. To do so, I used academic literature about *Musikvermittlung* and related it to the interview data, as well as to my own expert knowledge.[11] It is this big picture that I will focus on in this chapter.

Today's Social World of *Musikvermittlung*

Against the background of two examples of formats which the musicians described in their interviews, I will first analyse the "central work" (Clarke 2018: 157) as the primary activity of the social world of *Musikvermittlung* (SW *Musikvermittlung*), and will then focus on its formal organisations. Subsequently, I will briefly elaborate on intersecting social worlds and highlight two significant arenas of negotiation.

Primary activity

Dora[12] is a musician in her mid-30s with a portfolio career encompassing orchestra playing as well as chamber music. Already during her instrumental and pedagogic studies she founded an artist's collective. Her aim was to experiment with new, interdisciplinary modes of display for classical concerts. She came into contact with practices of *Musikvermittlung* in the early 2000s through kindergarten projects when she was an academy student in a renowned orchestra. One year later, after having won an orchestra audition, she started to implement formats of *Musikvermittlung* in her new working place and eventually became the head of *Musikvermittlung* for some years. In the interview she describes one of the first formats that she developed, where orchestra musicians play in chamber formations and curate the programs themselves. Beyond the usual doings and sayings of a classical concert, they tell, for example, life stories that connect to certain musical pieces, show pictures on a canvas, act out little scenes and conduct a quiz to raffle tickets for a subscription concert. As for the location and its material arrangement, they perform in a sociocultural center which – holding just 100 seats – has a much smaller capacity than a classical concert hall, and a close proximity between audience and musicians. The admission to the concert starts at 8 p.m.,

---

11   About the role of expert knowledge in qualitative research see Corbin/Strauss (2015: 78f.).
12   The names of the interviewees have been anonymised.

giving the audience the possibility to have drinks at the bar before the 60-minute concert half an hour later. After the concert, a DJ set and the bar offer possibilities for socialising. Moreover, the musicians do not perform in their concert clothes, but usually just wear private clothing. The material arrangement described thus results in what Dora calls a "living room atmosphere" (UPT4_1: 6, own translation)[13]. The format is supposed to address new audiences and win them over for the regular subscription concerts, which is why Dora calls it an "appetizer".

Anita, a freelance musician and instrumental teacher in her late 40s, started her first collaborative projects involving children and artists in the realm of music school concerts. After a colleague told her that what she was doing could be termed *Musikvermittlung*, she started to become interested and decided to enroll in a postgraduate course. Ever since, the practices of *Musikvermittlung* have become an important part of her portfolio career. In one of her projects, an orchestra and a school class worked together over the course of several weeks to create a piece of music theater. It was based on the musical work the orchestra was going to play in a concert that the children would visit after the project. Together with the teachers and fellow musicians, Anita conducted workshops with the pupils, where they developed a story, invented a stage design, and improvised and composed music. Eventually, the whole piece was performed by musicians and pupils together.

The projects described can be understood as bundles of practices and material arrangements. They encompass artistic practices like playing an instrument, singing or creating a lighting and stage concept, as well as educational practices like explaining, rehearsing and practicing a piece of music with pupils, or teaching them how to play an instrument. The distinction between artistic and educational practices is not always clear-cut; for example joint music-making involving musicians and pupils, or a concert moderation, can be described as artistic-educational practices. The site where the practices are realised, as well as the people involved, are part of the material arrangement. It encompasses socio-cultural centers, schools or hospitals[14], and people who usually do not attend classical concerts. As can be seen from this description,

---

13   In the code, each participant and each interview is assigned a number. The number after the colon refers to the corresponding paragraph in the transcript. UPT4_1: 6, for example, is the first interview with the fourth research participant, and the quote can be found in paragraph 6 of the transcript.

14   See Rineke Smilde in this anthology.

bundles of *Musikvermittlung* consist of practices and material arrangements that differ considerably from bundles of classical concerts.

Formal organisations

Concert halls, opera houses and orchestras are located in the intersections of the SW classical concert life and the SW *Musikvermittlung*, since practices of both worlds are realised in them.[15] Especially in the course of the last two decades, those organisations have changed considerably, from institutions that exclusively offer and perform classical music concerts to places of cultural education (Mertens [2012] 2013, see also Keuchel/Weil 2010: 17) offering a wide range of *Musikvermittlung* formats and creating new infrastructure, as well as new positions and even departments. This is also reflected in the architecture of new concert halls. When the Elbphilharmonie in Hamburg (opened in 2017) was built, the infrastructure for *Musikvermittlung* was part of the planning process, so that there are rooms (Kaistudios) that are specifically dedicated to *Musikvermittlung* workshops. The Sage Gateshead, opened in 2004 and situated in Newcastle, in the UK, was designed as both a concert hall and a place for *Musikvermittlung* from the beginning. Nevertheless, in both buildings the hierarchies existing in the practices of classical concerts and *Musikvermittlung*[16] partly become visible through the spatial arrangement. In contrast to the halls for symphonic concerts and chamber music, which are located on the upper levels, the rooms for the workshop formats of *Musikvermittlung* can be found downstairs.

Apart from concert halls, opera houses and orchestras, schools and other public organisations, such as prisons (Ziegenmayer 2020) or hospitals, are at least temporarily located in the intersections of the SW *Musikvermittlung* and their respective worlds, when their actors cooperate in formats like workshops or long-term partnerships. In the collaborative projects of schools and orchestras, for example, different practices of music teaching and *Musikvermittlung*

---

15   Strauss (1978: 125) contends that organisations can be viewed as arenas "wherein members of various subworlds or social worlds stake differential claims, seek differential ends, engage in contests, and make or break alliances in order to do the things they wish to do."
16   For the analysis of hierarchies in practices in the hospital see Wenger-Trayner/Wenger-Trayner (2015: 16) and Clarke (2018: 154).

have to be negotiated and also adapted to the respective material arrangements, resulting in questions like "What are the roles of musicians, music teachers and other actors in the process?" or "How can a final performance be staged within the infrastructure of a school building?"[17]

Music universities and conservatories, located in the intersection of the SW higher music education, SW classical concert life and SW *Musikvermittlung*, have reacted to the increasing importance of *Musikvermittlung* by offering new degree courses, postgraduate studies and further training, as well as implementing special courses in existing artistic curricula. The Detmold University of Music in Germany (1998) and the Anton Bruckner Private University in Austria (2009) were the first institutions in higher music education in the German-speaking countries to offer postgraduate studies for *Musikvermittlung*. Since then, many more study programs have emerged, such as, for example, a bachelor's degree program at the University of Cologne, a master's degree program at the Leopold Mozart Center in Augsburg, and a postgraduate study at the Bern University of the Arts – just to name a few. Alongside the implementation of degree programs, the universities also founded new chairs for *Musikvermittlung*.

Over the course of the last few years, in addition to the permanently or temporarily intersectional organisations described above, organisations have emerged that can be assigned specifically to the world of *Musikvermittlung*. The Netzwerk Junge Ohren [network young ears] (2007) in Germany, the Plattform Musikvermittlung Österreich (2012) and Musikvermittlung+ (2017) in Switzerland were founded to serve as networking organisations for practitioners of *Musikvermittlung*. The "Forum Musikvermittlung an Hochschulen und Universitäten" (2016) connects researchers and teachers of *Musikvermittlung* in higher music education. Those organisations, some of which are still loosely organised and in the process of professionalisation, are of central importance in furthering the social world's agenda (Strauss 1978: 122, Clarke et al. 2018: 71) by offering networking events, workshops, conferences, doing lobbying work and, in the case of Netzwerk Junge Ohren, also coordinating their own

---

17   Mall (2016) offers an in-depth analysis of cooperations between orchestras and schools.

projects, such as the "Junge Ohren Preis" [Young Ears Award][18], or contract projects like "Klangradar"[19] or "The Power of the Arts"[20].

Intersecting social worlds and arenas

Due to the history of the SW *Musikvermittlung*, as I will show a little later, there is a strong and permanent interconnectedness with the SW classical concert life. Through joint projects and performances, temporary overlappings arise with the SWs music education in schools, instrumental pedagogy and social work. Those intersections often result in arenas as places of negotiation. From the perspectives of the interviewed musicians, I will give examples for arenas between the SWs *Musikvermittlung* and music education in schools, as well as between *Musikvermittlung* and classical concert life.

Bernhard is an orchestra musician in his 30s who regularly engages in workshop formats of *Musikvermittlung* in his orchestra. He usually conducts two-hour workshops together with a second musician in school classes, playing some pieces, presenting their instruments, getting into conversation with the students and sometimes working on a collaborative musical improvisation. With regard to the schools' teachers, he states that there is no real cooperation in the sense of collaborative preparation or team teaching, rather he expects the teachers to be responsible for the discipline during the workshop (UPT2_1: 45–51). The interview data shows that musicians engaged in collaborative formats of *Musikvermittlung* construct clear differences between themselves as artists on the one hand and music teachers on the other.[21] Ilia, an orchestra musician in his 40s, and Carsten, an orchestra musician and

---

18 The "Junge Ohren Preis" is the central competition for projects of *Musikvermittlung* in the German-speaking countries and was established in 2006. Actors and projects are nominated and awarded prizes annually in different and varying categories, thus boosting their public visibility. Other competitions dedicated to the performances and projects of *Musikvermittlung* are "Find it" (2000 and 2004), founded by Jeunesse Austria, the "YAM Awards" (since 2008), hosted by the Jeunesse Musicales Internationale and the "YEAH! Young EARopean Award" (2010-2015), again founded by the "netzwerk junge ohren".
19 "Klangradar" brings together composers, teachers and pupils in experimental composition workshops. For more information see https://www.klangradar.de [7.1.2020].
20 For more information see https://www.thepowerofthearts.de/ [7.1.2020].
21 See types of musicians in a collaborative project between orchestra and school in Mall (2016).

university lecturer for *Musikvermittlung* in his late 50s, state that musicians authentically embody and live music, whereas music teachers merely transmit knowledge about music (UPT3_1: 44, UPT9_1: 18). Consistent with this, Christian Rolle et al. (2018: 58) contend with regard to research about a collaborative composition project that "[t]he role of artistic expert is more likely to be attributed to composers than to educators. Teachers are often described as nonartistic supporters, acting more often as organizers." Carsten also describes skepticism that he encountered during a school project. One of the teachers feared that he as an artist would merely use the students and the project to stand out. Following Lars Brinck (2018: 193), my descriptions can be seen as examples for conflicts in teacher-musician collaborations "especially with regards to the roles and mutual expectations".

As for the intersection between the SW *Musikvermittlung* and the SW classical concert life, it is interesting to look at power relations between different practices, and especially the devaluation of a practice. Wenger-Trayner/Wenger-Trayner (2015: 15) state that the landscape of practices[22] is political and includes power dynamics between different practices which can be made visible in the following examples. Klara, an orchestra musician in her mid 40s, describes symbolic devaluation of practices of *Musikvermittlung* in her orchestra. She states that formats of *Musikvermittlung* are not considered as very important: "[I]t's just *Musikvermittlung*, it is somehow part of what we do, but it is not great art" (UPT11_1: 25, own translation). Among other things, this has an effect on the rehearsal morale of the orchestra musicians: "The people make a difference, that's quite classical, the hierarchy in the company is also noticeable in the concentration of the rehearsals" (UPT11_1: 115f., own translation). This quotation clearly reflects the argument of Wenger-Trayner/Wenger-Trayner (2015) that in a landscape of practice, hierarchies between individual practices prevail. In Klara's orchestra, more symbolic value is placed on traditional subscription concerts than on formats of *Musikvermittlung*. Klara also describes that it is difficult to engage good conductors for concerts of *Musikvermittlung*. It can be assumed that this is, on the one hand, due to lower fees paid for these formats compared to regular concerts (economic devaluation)[23], but on the other hand conductors

---

22 Wenger's concept of a landscape of practices is very close to Schatzki's constellation of practices and Strauss' idea of social worlds.

23 Several of my interview partners refer to this fact.

themselves often do not consider an engagement in these formats, favoring the symbolically more highly valued regular symphonic concerts. The hierarchies and power relations between the practices of classical concert performance and the practices of *Musikvermittlung* are also evident in the access to personnel, as well as spatial and temporal resources. Carsten, for example, tells of "struggles with the logistical framework" (UPT3_1: 14, own translation) in a participatory project he conducted with schoolchildren, patients in a drug ward and university students, in the context of an opera production. It was not clear "whether one gets the lighting equipment in such a house [the opera house] and how much time one gets, where one is allowed to do a dress rehearsal, so it was all insanely elaborate" (UPT3_1: 14, own translation).

A Look Back: Roots of *Musikvermittlung*

Strauss stresses the importance of analysing the history of a social world, "that is, what are its origins, where is it now, what changes has it undergone, and where does it seem to be moving?" (Strauss 1978: 127). The roots of *Musikvermittlung* lie in practices with a long tradition, predating the turn of the last millennium when the term was coined. To this day, they form part of the core of *Musikvermittlung* and illustrate its different influences.

Children's concerts

Concerts for children[24] are still a core practice of *Musikvermittlung* and date back as far as the 19th century (Gruhn 1986, Eberwein 1998, Wimmer 2011, Schilling-Sandvoß 2015, Mall 2016). Orchestras in the US play a pioneering role in this respect. One of the first documented children's concerts took place in 1858 in Cincinnati, organised by the Philharmonic Society. In New York, the first educational concerts started in the 1880s with the New York Symphony Orchestra. The "Young People's Concerts" with the New York Philharmonic started in 1914 (Rosenberg 2000: 119) and became famous and influential when Leonard Bernstein began presenting the concert series nationwide on CBS in 1958. From 1928 to 1942, Walter Damrosch was already hosting the nationally broadcast "Music Appreciation Hour" on NBC. In Cleveland, the foundation

---

24 For an extensive overview over the history of children's concerts see Mall (2016).

of the orchestra was closely linked with educational aims, so that the first children's concerts took place three years after the orchestra was founded in 1918. In 1931 Lillian Baldwin was hired as consultant in music education and developed the "Cleveland plan", a series of educational concerts with preparation and follow-up. Under the impression made by a children's concert in New York in 1919, Sir Robert Mayer started the first British Children's Concerts at Central Hall in Westminster in 1923, under the baton of Sir Adrian Boult. In the Soviet Union, Natalia Sats founded a theater for children in 1921 and later commissioned a work that soon became a standard piece at children's concerts, Sergei Prokofiev's "Peter and the Wolf" (1936). In Germany, the first children's concerts date back to the end of the 19th century and stand in close relation to ideas of progressive education. Richard Barth presented his ideas for children's concerts at the arts education conference of 1905 ("Kunsterziehungstag"). He argued that children should be exposed to musical artworks in order to lift their spirits. In contrast to the singing education that was prevalent in German schools around this time, Barth intended to introduce children to classical music in the realm of live performances. In contrast to the US, however, children's concerts in the German-speaking countries remained singular events. Only in the 1970s, against the background of German orchestras facing economic problems, were more efforts once again made in this direction (Mall 2016). However, there remained a strong connection between music education in schools and children's concerts in the 1970s and 1980s, whereas in the 1990s orchestras started to establish independent offers (Eberwein 1998, Stiller 1999).

Participative projects

The second root can be seen in participative composition projects in the realm of contemporary art music. In 1985, Gillian Moore, Education Organiser for the London Sinfonietta, organised the first so called "Response Projects" where children react to an existing piece of contemporary music that serves as a reference for their own composition (Voit 2018). They are supported by composers and instrumentalists and present their piece in a public final performance. This concept was brought to Germany by the Ensemble Modern in 1988 and subsequently inspired the "Klangnetze" project in Austria

(Schneider/Bösze/Stangl 2000) that started in 1992/93, as well as projects like "Querklang"[25] and "Klangradar".

Community Music

Another root of *Musikvermittlung* comprises Community Music practices (see Petri-Preis in press). Community Music, defined by Lee Higgins (2012) as an active intervention aimed at social change, originated in the late 1960s and 1970s, as part of the Community Arts Movement in the UK. As an activist and countercultural movement, its members turned against the established cultural institutions ("highbrow culture") and put the focus on topics like inclusion and cultural participation. In the 1980s, however, a rapprochement with institutions of the so-called high culture took place when community musicians took up posts as music animateurs in orchestras (Higgins 2012: 47). One of those animateurs was the flutist Richard McNicol, who later led the German response projects with Ensemble Modern and helped Sir Simon Rattle establish a *Musikvermittlung* department with the Berlin Philharmonic.

The Big Bang of *Musikvermittlung*[26]

The conditions in the years around the turn of the millennium were just right for the big bang of *Musikvermittlung* that initiated the emergence and evolution of a new social world, where several practices and bundles of practices were linked up to the SW *Musikvermittlung*. Both the social worlds/arenas theory and site ontology highlight collaboration as imperative for social change. Schatzki (2019: 134) states that "changes arise from nexuses of action chains and material/other events and processes" and for Becker a new world is likely to emerge "when it brings together people who never cooperated before" (Becker 1986: 324). This is what can be observed around the year 2000,

---

25 For more information see https://www.udk-berlin.de/universitaet/fakultaet-musik/institute/institut-fuer-musikpaedagogik/studium/projekte-und-ensembles/querklang/#c682 [7.1.2021].
26 For a chronological overview of developments in *Musikvermittlung* from 2000 to 2014, see Barbara Stiller (2014).

which is why I call this period the "big bang of *Musikvermittlung*"[27]. In this section I will analyse some aspects of the conditions that proved conducive to the emergence and evolution of the social world of *Musikvermittlung*.

The crisis discourse

As Heiner Gembris and Jonas Menze (2018) show, there has been a significant decrease of 10.1% in attendance numbers at classical concerts in Germany since the 2005/06 season. They state that this might be related to the age structure of concert-attendees, who have an average age of 55 to 60, and assert that by the year 2035 the audience for classical music could shrink dramatically by 36%. Against the background of this long term development, which was already apparent before 2000 (see Hamann 2008), there evolved a crisis discourse in music pedagogical journals, as well as magazines like "das Orchester" and "Neue Musikzeitung",[28] that subsequently served as a justification narrative for the need for *Musikvermittlung* (Bugiel 2015). On the basis of 66 articles from music pedagogical journals and books between 2001 and 2015, Lukas Bugiel states that the discourse is "determined by a teleological course that began in the 18th or 19th century [...] and whose end point as a catastrophe, or the downfall of the current concert ritual and practice, still lies in the future" (Bugiel 2015: 72, own translation). He concludes that speaking about a crisis of the concert proved to be effective in two respects: "on the one hand, because the crisis of the concert, which began in 2001, can relatively quickly establish itself as a pattern of interpretation. On the other hand, the discourse implicitly legitimises all the measures which were introduced and decisions that were taken by the authors in their role as experts" (Bugiel 2015: 75f., own translation). As Schatzki shows, "texts [and] sayings [...] can give people ideas, shape their motivations, direct them to particular events and phenomena, lead them to respond and contribute to what actions they subsequently perform, individually, connectedly or collectively" (Schatzki 2017: 135). This is what can be observed in regard to the crisis discourse that con-

---

27 Obviously, the metaphor of the big bang is not meant to give the impression that the SW *Musikvermittlung* came out of nowhere. Rather, it points out that it emerged in this period of time.
28 For more information on the importance of those two magazines for *Musikvermittlung*, see the section Media and Research in this article.

structed a necessity for the practices of *Musikvermittlung* in order to counteract dwindling audiences.

Higher music education

In 1998, the degree program "Musikvermittlung – Konzertpädagogik" was launched at the Detmold University of Music by Ernst Klaus Schneider, together with Joachim Harder and Hermann Große-Jäger. It was a reaction both to the rising number of children's concerts in the 1990s, in relation to which it aimed at professionalising musicians for this kind of innovative practice, and to the perceived crisis of the classical concert (Schneider 2019: 12). Against the background of ageing audiences and decreasing attendance numbers, Schneider was convinced that musicians will increasingly have to address new audiences. This event proved to be significant in several ways: firstly, *Musikvermittlung* was established as a *terminus technicus*[29], secondly, the degree program served as a role model for other universities that developed similar programs in the following years, and finally, many graduates from Detmold subsequently received jobs in renowned orchestras and concert halls, thereby significantly influencing the practice of *Musikvermittlung*.

The initiative "Konzerte für Kinder"

In 2000, the initiative "Konzerte für Kinder" [concerts for children], funded by the German foundation "Stiftung Deutsche Jugendmarke", was launched by Jeunesse Musicale Germany and proved to be influential in many ways. Two international conferences – "Neue Wege für Junge Ohren" [new ways for young ears] in 2001 and "Konzerte für Kinder – Zukunftsaufgabe für Orchester" [concerts for children – a future task for orchestras] in 2002 – provided a space for exchange between actors from the German-speaking countries and the Anglo-American world, with its long tradition of children's concerts and community music practices. The second conference led to the publication of a handbook called "Spielräume Musikvermittlung" (Stiller/Wimmer/Schneider 2002) that was aimed at practitioners of *Musikvermittlung*. Another result was a special section at the "Neue Musikzeitung", starting in 2001, which was first

---

29 The term "Konzertpädagogik", which was coined by Anke Eberwein (1998), soon lost its significance and is hardly used anymore. For a more detailed account of the history and usage of the term *Musikvermittlung*, see Petri-Preis (2019).

called "Konzerte für Kinder" and eventually renamed *Musikvermittlung* in 2003. Not least, the first ideas for a network organisation that eventually resulted in the first "Junge Ohren Preis" in 2006 and the foundation of the Netzwerk Junge Ohren in 2007 were discussed.

Deutsche Orchestervereinigung

The German Orchestra Union was an early partner of Jeunesse Musicale Germany in the initiative "Konzerte für Kinder" and served as a significant multiplicator of its member organisations. It was a founding partner of the Netzwerk Junge Ohren, where its managing director Gerald Mertens has been chairman of the board since the start. He is also chief editor of the magazine "das Orchester", which has been featuring articles about *Musikvermittlung* regularly since 2004 and has served as the official newsletter of the Netzwerk Junge Ohren since 2009.

First departments of *Musikvermittlung*

The first departments of *Musikvermittlung* in German and Austrian orchestras were initiated by the conductors Sir Simon Rattle and Dennis Russell Davies. With their orientation towards social goals, their work reflects the influence of Community Music. Davies founded the Move on department at the Bruckner Orchestra Linz in Upper Austria, and Rattle launched Zukunft@BPhil in 2002, in collaboration with McNicol, who could draw on extensive expertise from his activities as animateur with the London Symphony Orchestra. Not only did these new departments serve as models for other institutions, but their projects also received considerable media coverage. The film-documentary "Rhythm is it", a large-scale community dance project by the Berlin Philharmonic, involving the British community dancer Royston Maldoom, became a big commercial success and received multiple awards.

Media and research

The "Neue Musikzeitung", as well as the magazines "üben & musizieren" and "das Orchester", have been publishing articles about *Musikvermittlung* on a regular basis since the early 2000s. The "Diskussion Musikpädagogik", a music pedagogical research journal, published a focus edition on *Musikvermitt-*

lung in 2005[30]. Furthermore, research on *Musikvermittlung* started with first dissertations by Schwanse (2003), Stiller (2008) and Wimmer (2010). Schatzki (2019: 82) states that "[a]ctivities can generate differences, but it is how the world reacts to these differences that bestows significance on or accords them status as innovative or inventive." Media as well as research placed significance on the practices of *Musikvermittlung*, thus making them visible and attributing innovative character to them. Moreover, both journalistic and academic texts play a vital role in the "hanging together of bundles" (Schatzki 2017: 140), and serve as a "connecting-and-threading-infrastructure" (Schatzki 2017: 133) for the social world of *Musikvermittlung*.

An Outlook: The Future Innovative Potential of *Musikvermittlung*

In the last two sections I have argued that practices of children's concerts, community music and participative projects have led to the emergence of the social world of *Musikvermittlung* and analysed the conditions that proved conducive to this. In this final section I will claim that the future innovative potential of *Musikvermittlung* lies in its transformational potential to foster inclusion and accessability[31] in a classical concert life which can still be considered as an exclusive place of distinction and bourgeois self-assurance (Borwick 2012).

In the 2019/20 season, the Wiener Konzerthaus launched a concert series called "klangberührt" [touched by sound] that aims at addressing people who, due to different mechanisms of exclusion, especially those relating to mental or physical disability, are not able to attend classical concerts. The doings and sayings, as well as the material arrangements, in this concert series differ considerably from regular classical concerts: there is no stage, only half of the hall is equipped with seats, leaving room for flexible cardboard stools and wheelchairs, the concert duration is limited to 60 minutes, there is a moderator guiding the audience through the program, lighting creates a special atmosphere and the musicians include participative and interactive musical elements to involve the audience. Classical concert rituals largely do not apply in this concert, so the audience is, for example, allowed to express itself

---

30   Further focus editions followed in 2012 and 2019, special issues were published in 2009 and 2018.
31   For a more elaborate account of this argument see Petri-Preis (in press).

spontaneously without having to fear being disciplined by others. This format shows how practices of *Musikvermittlung* display "a much more symmetrical understanding of the relationship between the producers and recipients" (see Staples, in this anthology: 72) by eliminating the hierarchies between audience and performers. Musicians engaged in practices of *Musikvermittlung* as in "klangberührt" play an important role in the potential transformation of and innovation within classical performance practices. By doing *Musikvermittlung* they engage in learning processes comprising the acquisition of specific knowledge and skills, as well as the development of their identity and social membership (Lave/Wenger 1991). Thomas Alkemeyer and Nikolaus Buschman (2017: 12) argue that, through learning, people "become enabled via the interplay with other participants to not automatically reproducing the social order, but also to reflectively modifying and critically transcending it." In other words: musicians might change their performance practices through the experiences they have made in practices of *Musikvermittlung*. They might moderate their concerts, collaborate with actors from other social worlds, think about alternative formats and venues, or modify their repertoire subsequently. Possibly this will lead to transformations and innovations in the social worlds of school education, university education, social work and of course the classical concert life.

Bibliography

Alkemeyer, Thomas/Buschmann, Nikolaus (2017): Learning in and across Practices. Enablement as Subjectivation, in: Hui, Allison/Schatzki, Theodore/Shove, Elisabeth (eds.), *The Nexus of Practices. Connections, Constellations, Practitioners*, London/New York: Routledge, 9–23.

Ardila-Mantilla, Natalia/Busch, Thomas/Göllner, Michael (2018): Musiklernen als sozialer Prozess. Drei theoretische Perspektiven, in: Gruhn Wilfried/Röbke, Peter (eds.): *Musik lernen. Bedingungen, Handlungsfelder, Positionen*, Innsbruck, Esslingen, Bern-Belp: Helbling, 178–203.

Becker, Howard S. (1982): *Art Worlds*, Berkely/Los Angeles/London: University of California Press.

Becker, Howard S. (1986): *Doing Things Together: Selected Papers*, Evanston: Northwestern University Press.

Blumer, Herbert (1969): Symbolic Interactionism. Perspective and Method. Englewood Cliffs, NJ: Prentice-Hall.

Borwick, Doug (2012): *Building Communities not Audiences. The Future of the Arts in the United States*, Winston-Salem: ArtsEngaged.

Brinck, Lars (2018): "I'm Just the Bass Player in Their Band": Dissolving Artistic and Educational Dichotomies in Music Education, in: Christophersen Catharina/Kenny, Alibhe (eds.), *Musician-Teacher Collaborations. Altering the Chord*, London/New York: Routledge, 193–203.

Bugiel, Lukas (2015): Wenn man von der Krise spricht. Diskursanalytische Untersuchung zur Krise des Konzerts' in Musik- und musikpädagogischen Zeitschriften, in: Cvetko, Alexander/Rora, Constanze (eds.), *Konzertpädagogik*, Aachen: Shaker, 61–81.

Clarke, Adele E. (1991): Social world/arenas theory as organizational theory, in: Maines, David (ed.), *Social Organization and Social Process. Essays in Honor of Anselm Strauss*, New York: Aldine de Gruyter.

Clarke, Adele E/Star, Susan Leigh (2008): *The Social Worlds Framework: A Theory/Method Package*, [online] https://www.researchgate.net/publicatio n/261948477_The_Social_Worlds_Framework_A_TheoryMethods_Package [12.01.2021]

Clarke, Adele E./Friese, Carrie/Washburn, Rachel S. (2018): *Situational Analysis: Grounded Theory after the Interpretive Turn* [2nd edition], Los Angeles: Sage.

Deutsches Musikinformationszentrum (2019): *Konzertstatistik*, [online] http:// www.miz.org/downloads/statistik/78/78_Veranstaltungen_oeffentlich_fi nanzierter_Orchester.pdf [12.01.2021]

Eberwein, Anke (1998): *Konzertpädagogik. Konzeptionen von Konzerten für Kinder und Jugendliche*, Hildesheim: Hildesheimer Universitätsschriften.

Gembris, Heiner/Menze, Jonas (2018): Zwischen Publikumsschwund und Publikumsentwicklung: Perspektiven für Musikerberuf, Musikpädagogik und Kulturpolitik, in: Tröndle, Martin (ed.), *Das Konzert^{II}. Beiträge zum Forschungsfeld der Concert Studies*, Bielefeld: transcript, 305–331.

Gruhn, Wilfried (1986): Die Vermittlung von Musik in Kinder- und Jugendkonzerten, in: *Österreichische Musikzeitschrift*, Vol. 41, 346–369.

Hamann (2008): Musikkultur – Einfluss der Bevölkerungsentwicklung auf Publikum und Konzertwesen, in: Gembris Heiner (ed.): *Musik im Alter. Soziokulturelle Rahmenbedingungen und individuelle Möglichkeiten*, Frankfurt am Main: Peter Lang, 159–211.

Higgins, Lee (2012): *Community Music. In Theory and Practice*. New York: Oxford University Press.

Keuchel, Susanne/Weil, Benjamin (2010): LERNORTE oder KULTURTEMPEL. Infrastrukturerhebung: Bildungsangebote in klassischen Kultureinrichtungen, Cologne: ARCult Media.

Lave, Jean/Wenger Etienne (1991): *Situated learning. Legitimate peripheral participation*, New York: Cambridge University Press.

Mall, Peter (2016): *Schule und Orchester. Aspekte des Zusammenspiels von schulischer und außerschulischer Musikvermittlung in kooperativer Projektarbeit*, Augsburg: Wißner.

Mall, Peter/Schwarz, Ralf-Olivier (2018): Musikvermittlung aus soziologischer Perspektive, in: Voit, Johannes (ed.): *Zusammenspiel? Musikprojekte an der Schnittstelle von Kultur- und Bildungseinrichtungen*, Hamburg: Hildegard-Junker-Verlag, 18–29.

Mertens, Gerald ([2012] 2013): *Konzerthäuser und Orchester als Orte Kultureller Bildung*, [online] https://www.kubi-online.de/artikel/konzerthaeuser-orchester-orte-kultureller-bildung [12.01.2021]

Petri-Preis (2019): Musikvermittlung. Ein musikpädagogischer Streitbegriff, in: *Diskussion Musikpädagogik*, Vol. 84, 5–10.

Petri-Preis, Axel (2021): *Musikvermittlung lernen. Eine Analyse von Lernwegen klassischer Musiker_innen*, Dissertation: Department of Music Education Research, Music Didactics and Elementary Music Education, mdw – University of Music and Performing Arts Vienna.

Petri-Preis (in press): Musikvermittlung und Community Music als Motoren von Inklusion im klassischen Konzertleben, in: Röbke, Peter/Hennenberg, Beate (eds.): *Inklusion am Wiener Institut für musikpädagogische Forschung, Musikdidaktik und Elementares Musizieren – am Beispiel der Band All Stars inclusive*, Münster: Waxmann.

Rolle, Christian/Weidner, Verena/Weber, Julia/Schlothfeldt, Matthias (2018): Role Expectations and Role Conflicts within Collaborative Composing Projects Musician-Teacher Collaborations, in: Christophersen Catharina/Kenny, Alibhe (eds.), *Musician–Teacher Collaborations. Altering the Chord*. London/New York: Routledge, 50–61.

Rosenberg, Donald (2000): *The Cleveland Orchestra Story: "Second to None"*. Cleveland: Gray & Company Publishers.

Schatzki, Theodore (2014): Art Bundles, in: Zembylas, Tasos (ed.), *Artistic Practices. Social Interactions and Cultural Dynamics*, London/New York: Routledge, 17–31.

Schatzki, Theodore (2017): Sayings, Texts and Discursive Formations, in: Hui, Allison/Schatzki, Theodore/Shove, Elisabeth (eds.): *The Nexus of Practices*.

Connections, constellations, practitioners, London/New York: Routledge, 126-140.

Schatzki, Theodore (2019): *Social Change in a Material World*, London/New York: Routledge.

Schilling-Sandvoß, Katharina (2015): Konzertpädagogik aus historischer Perspektive – Ein Rückblick in Hunderterschritten, in: Cvetko, Alexander/Rora, Constanze, *Konzertpädagogik*, Aachen: Shaker, 24–34.

Schmitz, Peter (2017): Das Kinderkonzert, ein außerschulischer Lernort, in: *Diskussion Musikpädagogik Vol. 76*, 31–37.

Schneider, Hans/Bösze, Cordula/Stangl, Burkhard/Aichinger, Oskar/Brandstätter, Ursula (eds.) (2000): *Klangnetze: Ein Versuch, die Wirklichkeit mit den Ohren zu erfinden*, Friedberg: Pfau.

Schneider, Ernst Klaus (2019): Entwicklung eines 1998 entstandenen Studiengangs. "Musikvermittlung" in Detmold, in: *Diskussion Musikpädagogik Vol. 84*, 10–18.

Schwanse, Ulrike (2003): Familienkonzerte in Kooperation mit Grundschulen – ein Konzept und seine Wirkungen. [online] http://ubdata.uni-paderborn.de/ediss/04/2003/schwanse/ [12.01.2021]

Stiller, Barbara/Wimmer, Constanze/Schneider, Ernst Klaus (eds.) (2002): *Spielräume Musikvermittlung: Konzerte für Kinder entwickeln, gestalten, erleben*, Regensburg: ConBrio.

Stiller, Barbara (2008): *Erlebnisraum Konzert: Prozesse der Musikvermittlung in Konzerten für Kinder*, Regensburg: ConBrio.

Stiller, Barbara (1999): Die Kinderkonzerte deutscher Orchester. Überraschende Ergebnisse einer Umfrage, in: *das Orchester Vol. 9*, 22–25.

Stiller, Barbara (2014): Musikvermittlung: Am Anfang war das Modewort. Versuch einer kritischen Chronik, in: Rüdiger Wolfgang (ed.): *Musikvermittlung – wozu?*, Mainz: Schott, 81–98.

Strauss, Anselm (1978): A Social World Perspective, in: Denzin, Norman (ed.), *Studies in Symbolic Interaction, Vol. 1*, Greenwich, CT: Jai Press, 119–128.

Strauss, Anselm ([1993] 2017): *Continual Permutations of Action*, New York: Routledge.

Strübing, Jörg (2017): Where is the Meat/d? Pragmatismus und Praxistheorien als reziprokes Ergänzungsverhältnis, in: Dietz, Hella/Nungesser, Frithjof/Pettenkofer, Andreas (eds.): *Pragmatismus und Theorien sozialer Praktiken*, 41-76.

Voit, Johannes (2018): *30 Jahre Response. Historischer Rückblick und Typologie aktueller Erscheinungsformen*, [online] https://www.kompaed.de/artikel/praxisbeispiele/johannes-voit-30-jahre-response/ [26.08.2020]

Wenger, Etienne (1998): *Communities of Practice. Learning, Meaning, and Identity*, Cambridge, UK/New York, NY: Cambridge University Press.

Wenger-Trayner, Etienne/Wenger-Trayner Beverly (2015): Learning in a Landscape of Practice. A Framework, in: Wenger-Trayner, Etienne/Fenton-O'Creevy, Mark/Hutchinson, Steven, Kubiak, Chris/Wenger-Trayner, Beverly (eds.): *Learning in Landscapes of Practice. Boundaries, Identity, and Knowledgeability in Practice-Based Learning*, London/New York: Routledge, 13–29.

Wimmer, Constanze (2010): *Musikvermittlung im Kontext: Impulse - Strategien - Berufsfelder*, Regensburg: ConBrio

Wimmer, Constanze (2011): Konzerte für Kinder gestern & heute. Perspektiven der historischen und aktuellen Praxis in der Musikvermittlung, in: Schneider, Ernst Klaus/Wimmer, Constanze (eds.), *Hörräume öffnen. Spielräume gestalten. Konzerte für Kinder*, Regensburg: ConBrio, 9–19.

Wimmer, Constanze (2018): Einen Sehnsuchtsort der Wahrnehmung öffnen. Musikvermittlung im Konzertbetrieb, in: Tröndle, Martin (ed.), *Das Konzert[II]. Beiträge zum Forschungsfeld der Concert Studies*, Bielefeld: transcript, 197–216.

Ziegenmayer, Annette (2020): Musik im Strafvollzug – Bedeutung, Vielfalt und Potenziale, [online] https://www.kubi-online.de/artikel/musik-strafvollzug-bedeutung-vielfalt-potenziale [12.01.2021].

Interviews (own data)

UPT2_1, Bernhard, first interview, March 21st 2019.
UPT3_1, Carsten, first interview, April 3rd 2019.
UPT4_1, Dora, first interview, May 21st 2019.
UPT9_1, Ilia, first interview, November 11th 2019.
UPT11_1, Klara, first interview, December 2nd 2019.

Biographical note

Axel Petri-Preis studied music education, German philology and musicology in Vienna. He has been active in the field of *Musikvermittlung* internationally for more than ten years, and his projects have received several awards. He is a senior scientist and Deputy Head at the Department of Music Education Research, Music Didactics and Elementary Music Education (IMP) at the mdw – University of Music and Performing Arts Vienna. His research currently focuses on the education and further training of (classical) musicians in relation to *Musikvermittlung* and on community engagement in classical music life.

On the Translation of Music
Towards the Relation between *Musikvermittlung* and Innovation

Ronald Staples

Over the last hundred years, innovation semantics has had a remarkable career. Not only has the term "innovation" now become part of everyday language, but it has also managed to become synonymous with progress, creativity, inventiveness, and economic growth. Innovation thus covers a very large semantic space. For art, this means a loss of interpretative sovereignty, since innovation has at least partially usurped fields of interpretation that were once processed by art. At the turn of the 20th century, creativity semantics shifted from deviant, exceptional and ingenious to new, desirable and innovative, combined with useful (Reckwitz 2012). Subsequently, the semantics of creativity and innovation merged in a way, as result of what Andreas Reckwitz calls the dispositive of creativity (Reckwitz 2016). Accordingly, at least the so-called creative industries demand that art be innovative in order to keep the creative motors running in the service of societal progress (Berg 2009, Florida 2004). This is usually linked to the expectation of commercial success. A look at the differentiated field of art shows that this is achieved to varying degrees. While in the visual arts a radicalised market[1] promises exorbitant profits for a few (Velthuis/Baia Curioni 2015), the picture is not so clear-cut in the other arts.

In the last two decades, art institutions (and organisations) have increasingly set up departments that are concerned with the mediation of their creations. These departments focus on communication between art producers

---

[1] To put it more precisely, one could say it is a 'winner takes all' market. Most artists find it very difficult to gain a foothold in the art market and accordingly convert their cultural capital into economic capital. Only a handful of players dominate the global market, regulating access and prices.

and their audiences. Their efforts first became visible in (art) museums, as instances of cultural memory, and then increasingly in performing arts and music organisations (Garoian 2001). Initially often positioned somewhat bashfully in the pedagogical corner, the diversity of current mediation practices show a much more symmetrical understanding of the relationship between the producers and recipients of art than at the beginnings of *Musikvermittlung*.

In the following, I will reflect – from a system-theoretical point of view – on the relationship between contemporary society's expectations of the innovativeness of its cultural institutions, the appearance and function of art, and the practices of *Musikvermittlung* and its organisations. That *Musikvermittlung* seems to play a prominent role has less to do with the central theme of this volume than with the specifics of music as an art form. Its "non-representational nature" (Adorno 1981) makes it both abstract and ephemeral. If technical reproducibility (Benjamin [1935] 2015) has led to an exponential increase in the availability of music, not to mention the emergence of purely technical music, the consumption of music is also accompanied by an intensive individualisation. With its spread and availability, music seems to have lost its aesthetically unique qualities. Rather, it turns into a means of distinction, an expression of identity and social belonging (DeNora 2000). Classical music organisations that produce highly professional music have come under pressure to determine who the addressees of their performances are and what social function they have[2]. Institutions such as orchestras, music theatres, concert halls, and classical music festivals are thus increasingly pressured economically. It seems that, of necessity, they have to communicate their products in new and other ways, rather than simply performing an art piece. Innovation seems to be a key term in this context. For this reason, I will firstly take a look at the societal function of innovation and how its relationship with art is shaped. From this perspective, I assume that innovation is a certain communicative act that differs from the communicative act called art. In a second step, I reconstruct – with the aid of illustrative examples – the extent to which *Musikvermittlung* can be understood as a certain translational practice[3].

---

2   This is certainly also true of other cultural institutions, such as spoken theatre, dance, or museums of contemporary visual arts. This pressure was created through the differentiation of art. At the latest since the differentiation of E and U music, the former has had to justify itself for being financed primarily by the community. For a discussion of pop and high culture, see Wilson (1991).

3   Joachim Renn coined for this specific phenomenon the term "Übersetzungsleistung" (Renn, 2006). In an analogue translation, one could say "translational effort", but this

The Time of Innovation

If one generally asks the question about significant innovations, one often gets a list of artifacts that receive the attribute "innovative". An example of this is the Edison light bulb. On closer inspection, however, it quickly becomes unclear what exactly the innovative content of the light bulb metaphor is: does it lie in the electrification of households, in the possibility of transporting electrical charge over a certain distance, or is it actually in the standardisation of the light source itself, so that all light bulbs are given the same socket? Does innovation now show itself in the one artifact, or in this bundle of problems that must be solved all around the light bulbs for them to shine? This leads directly to the question of what innovation actually is. In other words: How can innovations be recognised as such? There are different perspectives on how to find an answer.

From an economic point of view, innovation would be something that would prevail in a market (Kelley 2001). Taking a sociological approach to the question means dissolving it from the context of the invention, but also asking what social conditions make innovations possible, or even prevent them. Consequently, it is interesting how innovation processes are triggered and take place at the different levels of society. In everyday life, new artifacts are usually attributed to innovation, or a technology, and a system, or a social practice, is expected to trigger a changed form of practice, or to provoke a need in consumers that was previously unknown to them. Expectations do not arise spontaneously, but are the expression of social processes connected with how the world is epistemologically framed and the assumptions about how it can be manipulated (Alexander 1987).

In the analysis of innovation, two relationships are crucial: on the one hand, the relationship of old/new, and on the other that of past/present/future (Luhmann 1976). In this sense, innovations are novel treatments of an unknown future (Schütz [1945] 2003). Yet how is something to be dealt with socially when it is not yet clear what it will be? So before we can start looking for innovation in, or with, the practices of *Musikvermittlung*, we have to talk about the modern understanding of past, present, and future. In the course of modernity (beginning, for example, with the era of the Enlightenment) modern societies have come to acknowledge that the future is not determined by

---

does not denote the situated process, and therefore "translational performance" will be used.

God or any other transcendental entity – that it is not fate – but that it can be molded. In retrospect, this makes the past problematisable, because it did not have to be the way it was (Luhmann 1999). This also means that action or the making of decisions becomes contingent, and this means a radical change at the societal level regarding society's control options (Holzinger 2007: 52ff.). Finally, the idea associated with the present becomes more and more punctiform, because the future – and thus the demands on society to shape it – becomes a permanent task. In a certain sense, the modern, functionally differentiated society is working on its *telos*, which it has to reaffirm again and again now that the religious world view has receded into the background, thus opening the field for something new (Luhmann 2008: 39) and changing it according to the respective possibilities for processing complexity. Demographic change, economic growth, sustainable management of material resources and climate change are global social problems whose complexity produces possibilities of variation that seem to be impossible to handle with the current (semantic) means of complexity processing. The innovation society is a variation of social order within the framework of a functionally differentiated society, which cannot solve the problem of complexity, but which can be rationalised by semantically anticipating what has not yet been found and thus integrated into current programs for complexity processing (Rammert et al. 2016).

In this respect, the production of innovations represents a recursive form of this processing (Ortmann 1999: 250). Ultimately, innovations do not solve current problems, but are possible solutions for future problems. This could also explain why the modern sense of time has changed considerably in terms of speed and intensity – as in the acceleration discourse (Rosa 2013). Helga Nowotny very pointedly remarks that "this is the dynamic of innovation and multiplicity of the new: the next round of the game has already begun while we still believe we are in the present one" (Nowotny 1999: 111).

In abstract terms, this means that so-called functional systems, organisations, and society as a whole try to anticipate themselves and reduce complexity. This complexity arises from the uncertain, what has not yet been decided (Baecker 2011). If many possibilities are equally contingent, then procedures are needed to make the resulting complexity smaller and to make a certain future seem more likely. This is why it is so tempting to give the innovative award to things that promise a favorable, less contingent future. In Niklas Luhmann's sense, society is thus structurally geared towards novelty "and indeed towards more novelties than can realistically occur. In this sense, it has created redundancies to bear its dynamics. This corresponds to the radicalisation of its contingency experience" (Luhmann 2008: 40).

Innovations are therefore not only something that can be found in the difference between old and new, but also an expression of our relationship to past, present, and future (Luhmann 1999). As already indicated, modern and late modern societies see their future as open and thus shapeable. But this immediately raises the question of how the future should/can be shaped in such a way that it also becomes a determinable future, even if the future necessarily remains open. The mode of deciding for one or the other practice changes dramatically[4]. For *Musikvermittlung*, this means: how do you contextualise an idea into a "Vermittlungskonzept"/mediation offer in such a way that the uncertainty of acceptance (i.e. of communicative connectivity) can be rationalised? This is preceded by the fact that music (or art in general) is associated with uncertainty about possible acceptance by the audience and other producers. At this point, "acceptance" does not yet mean a judgment of taste, but merely the possibility of consumption; is it possible to go to a concert, to take out subscriptions, to purchase audio recordings? From this perspective, acceptance is also not a passive acceptance of something, but rather a communicative event that makes further events possible.

The rationality of decision-making acquires a different basis through these changed time references; it is no longer a matter of decisions being "right" (Luhmann 1997: 171), but of transforming contingency (Luhmann 1987: 402, 1992c: 206). The rationality of decisions can then take the form of innovation. The advantage of this is that something can be called a variation and that further decisions (or social practice) can then follow on from that variation. This sounds banal at first sight, but it makes a difference whether variations are called (rejectable) deviations or (desirable) innovations. Although art has the advantage that creativity is generally attributed to it, it is not yet clear that the respective artistic creativity is also acceptable in society. However, "innovative ability", or the imperative to produce innovations, denotes an unmarked space, because we do not know which form of knowledge will actually have led to innovation or a variation of practice (Reckwitz 2016). We can make estimates that rationalise this uncertainty by

---

4   Ulrich Beck coined the term "risk society" in the context of his theory of reflexive modernity. In my opinion, he describes very well how precarious decision-making has become in modern societies and that it is, therefore, becoming increasingly presuppositional (Beck 1986).

probabilistic methods and thus try to establish predictability for the design of the open future, but we cannot obtain certainty. Nevertheless, innovation with a view to the past is the key driver of social and technological development. Various attempts have been made to reconstruct social development as a history of innovation (Barnett 1953, Gilfillan 1963). This is certainly one of the decisive reasons for the central role of innovation in the context of industrial revolutions. At the latest with Joseph Schumpeter's analyses of economic development, innovation is attributed a key position for both social and economic prosperity. However, in his view, the "entrepreneur" needs the "creative destroyer" in order to put real innovation into action (Schumpeter 1961: 95ff.). This connotation has long shaped the image of innovation: on the one hand, it is attributed to autonomous subjects – individuals – and on the other hand, it seems to be linked to the downfall – destruction – of the old. In the language of today's innovation managers, one speaks of evolutionary or even disruptive innovation (Augsdörfer et al. 2013). Spelling out these Schumpeterian semantics has led to a culture of innovation that has seen it as precarious and difficult to achieve – also potentially dangerous – and something that needs to be carefully planned and contained. In the economy, the result is then R&D departments[5] and a gradual upgrading of the male engineer as a specific, inventive social figure (see Paulitz 2012). In art, too, radical creativity always seems acceptable only if it is linked to form. In short, a harmonious piece of music is more likely to be recognised as a work of art than one that contradicts the harmonic convention[6].

Nevertheless, William Ogburn (1964), in his seminal "Analysis on Culture and Social Change", shows that important inventions or innovations are not just the product of an ingenious mind, but always an amalgam of different overlapping practices and ideas. The light bulb as an artifact is just the material substrate of various innovative practices. Modern innovation research, therefore, asks less about who innovates and more about how framework conditions must be designed so that possible innovations find the most fertile milieu possible. Currently, the most far-reaching concept in this direction is that of "open innovation". It has not only enriched the economic debate (Chesbrough 2003, Hippel 2005), but has also gained great importance in the practi-

---

5   **R**esearch and **D**evelopment is the usual term for units in companies that are mainly concerned with product development.

6   See, for example, Hans-Friedrich Bormann (2005) on the relationship between aesthetics and performance in the work of John Cage.

cal design of innovation processes (Augsdörfer et al. 2013, Dornaus et al. 2015). The basic idea is impressively simple, but from a business (entrepreneurial) perspective, it is revolutionary. The Open Innovation paradigm assumes that the temporary use of different, even external, sources of knowledge leads to better solutions to innovation problems than iclosed departments (systems) of "closed innovation" (Chesbrough 2003). This is risky for companies, but also for research, because it is more difficult to attribute authorship, or to keep results secret. However, in a world of networked value chains, the strategy of understanding knowledge as exclusive property to be exploited is hardly enforceable[7]. Moreover, even if Open Innovation currently exists parallel to closed innovation, networked approaches seem to be more suitable for dealing with the complex challenges of late modern societies than concepts based on isolation (Gray/Vander Wal 2014). This suggests that innovation is a social practice that at some point in the future will have made a difference and will then no longer be new, but routine (Howaldt/Jacobsen 2010).

After this outline of the concept of innovation and a brief classification of its development and mode of operation, the following section discusses the relationship between innovation, creativity and art. Although innovation semantics implicitly carry the sign of the creative, it is still up in the air to what extent it can be applied in a field that is considered creative in itself – art. Constant change (which also means self-referential change) is the ancestral domain of art, so why should innovation be introduced additionally?

Art, *Musikvermittlung* and Innovation

If we now turn to the relationship between music, *Musikvermittlung*, and innovation, we change the terrain or switch to another social subsystem. Up to now, the debate about innovation semantics has moved between the systems of science and economy. In a very brief semantical genealogy of innovation, I state that innovation from a systemic standpoint marks an ex-post decision and it is typical for modern societies. Decisions are denoted as a certain type of communication in the Luhmannian Systems Theory. More basically, social

---

7   Manuel Castells has widely reconstructed how firms are embedded in networks. There are cultural differences, but one can recognise that, especially in an economy depending on global value chains, a single firm is always part of at least one larger network (Castells 2010).

systems themselves only exist as communication. Luhmann thus directs the view away from actors and their intentions and makes communicative connectivity the interface for social entities. From this perspective, a specific work of art is not interesting in terms of its materiality, but only – as will be shown – with regard to whether it can be connected to by communication (Luhmann 1981, 1987). However, creativity and the function of *Musikvermittlung* seem to be more relevant in the system of art[8] than in economy or science[9]. Therefore, it seems of interest to take a closer look at how innovation, *Musikvermittlung* and the social system of art are connected.

If we observe music as events in the field (or system) of art, then we must ask ourselves a question: is music or art innovative – and should it be? In other words, is this one of its functions? From this perspective, an event denotes the specific occurrence of art. This includes the performance of a symphony on a certain evening, as well as a picture presented in an exhibition. If pieces of art and the performance of them are both observed as communication offers, then Luhmann (1995: 481) asserts: "Works of art differ from other things by a self-referential relationship: they claim to be art in themselves; and this is possible because it is about communication and not about mere things." Communicative events that arise – and are communicated in the system of art[10] – thus have something of intrinsic value through their "self-referential relationship", which distinguishes them from other artifacts or communication offers, as well as from innovations. To put it bluntly, this would mean that an art work – a piece of music and its performance – can be either art or innovative, but not both. This is analytical reasoning that takes the threefold construction of communication very seriously: information-message-comprehension (Luhmann 1997:190). So communication is usually structured in such a way as to minimise the risk of misunderstanding, which is inherent in communication. To this end, media are employed. This minimising of risk can be called reducing the chance of variation. However, as discussed above, innovation is

---

8   For a discussion on radical constructivism and music see Daniel Müllensiefen (1999).
9   Creativity is of course a constitutive element of science and more recently it seems to be required also for economic growth. However, science is carefully concerned to enclose creativity systematically, while economy transforms it into techniques. Reckwitz (2012) intriguingly discusses how modern economy aestheticises itself and Bruno Latour (2002) shows in great detail how science is produced.
10 This may sound redundant at first sight. Yet events like a concert are themselves communicative and the institution hosting the event has to communicate about it. This kind of communication addresses possible audiences and the art system.

about variation and creativity, too. So what is the difference between art (a piece of art) and (an) innovation? How can they be distinguished?

If we want to reflect a bit deeper on the relation of *Musikvermittlung* and innovation it seems necessary to explain further the mutual exclusion of art and innovation. A look at Siegfried Schmidt's reflections on the relationship between creativity and communication may perhaps shed light on this point: in his analysis, a creative performance is something that interrupts the flow of communication – which is highly precarious for social systems – but at the same time offers new possibilities for communication to continue (Schmidt 1988: 48). In this respect, creative performances can be very different manifestations of social systems. What is important is that they are communicative acts, i.e. genuinely social events and not the products of ingenious subjects[11]. Schmidt differentiates these possibilities basally according to "Gestaltswitch" and complexity. With regards to "Gestaltswitch" he states:

> "Creative performances that essentially change the model of reality of a social group in any field (such as scientific or technical inventions) soon belong to the self-evident nature of communication and their innovativeness must be consciously held by narration if the social group considers them worthy of being passed on." (Schmidt 1988: 9)

Here the tragedy of innovations is also evident. For if they do indeed change reality, they disappear with the occurrence of that very change, and what was special and new just then becomes normalised and mainstream (Luhmann 1999). This trap of temporality then requires the establishment of innovation systems in a post-demand economy, which constantly oscillates between stable framework conditions and productive irritation (Blättel-Mink/Ebner 2009). The situation is different with creative efforts whose complexity is so high that each time they are dealt with again, they contain the possibility of a new and different follow-up communication. This can be the performance of a musical work, the viewing of a sculpture, or the feeling of an installation.

---

11   The debate about creativity cannot be continued at this point. Reference has already been made to Reckwitz' genealogy of creativity. At another well-known point, creativity is embedded in a broad cultural-anthropological horizon around imagination (Popitz 1997). Hans Joas (1996), on the other hand, with recourse to pragmatism, substantiates creativity as a prerequisite for social action as such. References to creativity increasingly testify to a normalisation, i.e. the desire for extraordinary action is increasingly giving way to the view that the ability to act in a surprisingly abductive manner is just normal action.

According to Schmidt, this kind of communicative interruption characterises art and coincides with Luhmann's assumption of the self-referentiality of art, or in Schmidt's words: "A creative work of art represents ambiguity and multistability in the long run" (Schmidt 1988: 49). Dodecaphony, mainly invented by Arnold Schönberg, is usually described as art and as a musical innovation. It is certainly a musical invention, but to what extent did it have an effect on music outside the system of art? One could state that it is more a kind of an internal differentiation and not so much an innovation that changed harmonics as a whole.

This digression into the radical constructivist theory of communication is necessary, above all so that we can reformulate the question of the relationship between music (art) and *Musikvermittlung* (innovation?). Art is therefore not to be regarded as downstream of society, since in functionally differentiated societies, art is an autonomous system and hence not only concerned with its environment, society, the world, and nature, but – as an autonomous system – it is also concerned with itself. This it has in common with other functional systems.

L'art pour l'art is thus not a genre narcissism, but an important differentiation step for social systems. Once this step has been taken – art in the 20th century has definitely left its representational relationship to its environment behind – art becomes "in need of commentary", as Luhmann remarks with reference to Arnold Gehlen (1965). The exact relationship between art and its reflective instances cannot be answered at this point. However, it should be noted that a functional system of art shows the same contradictions as other systems on this level. Above all, this also addresses[12] the popular problem of the question about whether something is considered as art (or not). This is not a discourse stemming from the environment of art but a self-thematisation that can contain its own negation. Emblematic of this can be the ready-mades dating from the beginning of the 20th century, or Joseph Beuys' garbage installations. The musical works of Beuys, which were significantly influenced by the Fluxus movement and the works of Cage, draw attention to the exceptional position of music within the art system (Geisenberger 1999). Music enables the most radical variations of this differentiation: "It consists of the concentration on the sound that is current at the moment and in the destruction of every possibility of remembering and expecting, as is guaranteed by

---

12   Which is also repeatedly addressed by art itself. Here we need only recall Yasmina Reza's piece "Art" (Reza/Helmlé 2008).

melodies. Only the present should count, and every new present should come as a surprise." (Luhmann 1995: 477)

Casting a glance at the contemporary world of musical styles shows that they have become highly differentiated and that even former basic distinctions, such as serious and popular music, have largely lost their power of allocation. The enjoyment of music has thus become more preconditioned, and for art organisations the urgent question arises of how access to musical events can be made easier. A directive educational approach seems to be less and less acceptable, as Constanze Wimmer remarks, because it would not enable visitors to experience art individually (see Wimmer 2018: 197). Yet how can this deepening hiatus be bridged when the differentiation of musical art forms has progressed so far that a simply performative aesthetic enjoyment of music seems less likely. From an innovation theory perspective, translation performances must be provided for this. There is more to be said about the concept of translation and how it relates to *Musikvermittlung*, yet it seems necessary, first of all, to take an illustrative look at the practices of *Musikvermittlung*, in order to sharpen our subsequent theoretical analysis.

Observation of *Musikvermittlung* Practices

Summing up, an informed guess is that *Musikvermittlung* is trying to make the products of musical art and performances for heterogeneous audiences more accessible. However, it is necessary to take a closer look at the current practices of *Musikvermittlung*, in order to draw conclusions as to what extent "translation performances"[13] are functions of *Musikvermittlung*. In what follows, the concert section of the Nuremberg State Theatre and the Berlin Philharmonic will provide two examples. Nevertheless, they cannot be regarded as exemplary; the selection is too arbitrary for that, and the comparative moments are not systematic enough. In justification of their selection, it should be said that the Berlin Philharmonic has, since its high-profile actions such as "Rhythm is it", served as a kind of role model in terms of modern *Musikvermitt-*

---

13   "Performance" is an ambiguous term here. In contradiction to the above mentioned musical performances, the meaning here addresses the process of translation and the outcome of this process at the same time.

lung for a world-class orchestra[14]. The concert section at the Nuremberg State Theatre was chosen because of its typical character of staging multipart theatre in German-speaking countries. In other words, the orchestra is not only an independent ensemble, but also part of a larger organisation and thus has other tasks than an independent concert orchestra. Obviously, the following examples do not show the concrete practices of *Musikvermittlung* within these organisations. Data of this kind would require extensive fieldwork, observing how practitioners are talking and acting with their audiences. Nevertheless these examples are helpful in illustrating the argument.[15][16]

---

14   For deeper insights into the economic relevance of developing audiences, see Klaus Georg Koch (2014).

15   Translation of the contents of Fig. 1: "There is music in everyone. The Education Program of the Berlin Philharmonic Orchestra. For me, the most important thing that music can achieve is to bring people together." (Sir Simon Rattle, Chief Conductor of the Berlin Philharmonic Orchestra from 2002 to 2018 and initiator of the Education Program) The Berlin Philharmonic's Education Program has been in existence since 2002 and - initiated by Sir Simon Rattle - has become part of the orchestra's DNA after 16 years. Giving everyone the opportunity to experience music, and especially bringing it closer to those who would normally have no access to our music, is the responsibility, task and challenge of the Berlin Philharmonic's Education Program, which has been made possible by Deutsche Bank since its inception. As part of the Education Program, we - together with the musicians of the orchestra - want to make the music experience as multifaceted as possible. We seek to meet the most diverse people in order to listen to and explore music together, to make and invent music, to think about music and learn more about it. A special emphasis is placed on making music together, because this is where the unifying power of music is most effective. This is where something that is very familiar to the musicians of the orchestra succeeds."

16   Translation of the contents of Fig. 2: "THE ART OF VERMITTLUNG. With Freestyle and Xplore the theater youth club and the program for educators at the Staatstheater Nürnberg started twenty years ago. Thousands of students have discovered the theater more intensively as a result. Hundreds of young people were able to stand on stage, negotiate and artistically shape their themes. With the start of the new teams in opera, concert and drama, we have once again increased our activities in the last season. Now clubs, the Tempo 100 Senior Theater, the children's and youth choir and other groups come to our house almost daily. Up to 300 creative people perform on our stages in their free time, secretly transforming the square between Südstadt and Altstadt into a vibrant cultural forum. Together with the sections, we invite the city society to discussions, further education and rehearsal visits. We inspire each other in workshops, workshop presentations and the big shows, because one thing connects us: the desire for theater."

Fig. 1: Self-description and concept of the music education program of the Berlin Philharmonic

> Das Education-Programm soll uns daran erinnern, dass Musik kein Luxus ist, sondern ein Grundbedürfnis.
>
> *Sir Simon Rattle*

Die Berliner Philharmoniker und Sir Simon Rattle waren auf dem Gebiet der Education-Arbeit Pioniere. Von Anfang an wollten sie vermitteln, dass Musik ganzheitlich ist, denn sie spricht gleichermaßen Seele, Körper und Geist an. Und, was besonders durch die Education-Arbeit sichtbar wird: Musik ist Motor für Weiterentwicklung und Wandel. Sie fördert Aktivität, Mitgestaltung und Kreativität, Begegnung und Austausch, die Überwindung von Hemmschwellen und Berührungsängsten. In den vergangenen zehn Jahren haben über 3.000 Menschen im Alter von 3 bis 73 Jahren aktiv an Education-Projekten der Berliner Philharmoniker teilgenommen, und die Ergebnisse wurden vor über 200.000 Zuschauern präsentiert. Die verschiedenen Aspekte der Education-Arbeit sind in den folgenden Fragen und Antworten zusammengefasst.

> Am schönsten sind die Momente, wenn sich die Schüler gegenseitig motivieren oder helfen, und wenn man sie während der Proben beobachtet und auf ihren Gesichtern ein Lächeln sieht. Alles Dinge, die im normalen Schulalltag eher selten sind.
>
> *Lehrerin, Tanzprojekt 2010*

- Wie begann alles?
- Für wen gibt es das Education-Programm – und wozu?
- Was ist Education – und was nicht?
- Wie ist das Education-Programm aufgebaut?
- Welche Herausforderungen stellen sich den Musikern des Orchesters?
- »Rhythm is it!« – Und die Folgen?
- Wie sieht es bei anderen Kulturinstitutionen aus?
- Education – unverzichtbar für die Musiker der Zukunft?
- Education oder Pädagogik?
- Und wie geht es weiter?

> Die Education-Arbeit ist genauso wichtig wie Bruckner-Symphonien zu spielen.
>
> *Christian Stadelmann, Mitglied der Berliner Philharmoniker, 2003*
>
> Ich empfinde beim Tanzen das Gefühl, dass ich die Welt entdecke. Ich bin da, wo ich sein soll.
>
> *Gina, Grundschülerin, Tanzprojekt 2010*

Source: https://www.berliner-philharmoniker.de/education/, screenshot, taken 2019/06/11

If we take a closer look at these examples, they illustrate the fact that the practice of this kind of *Musikvermittlung* seems to move on the edge between art and education in general. The educational offers, however, must be differentiated: on the one hand, they educate aesthetically, as the different (vertical) choices in capital letters in the second example, such as 'making', 'exploring', 'watching' theatre indicate. On the other hand, what is not said explicitly is that a future paying audience shall be educated (for an overview of audience development see Siebenhaar/Braun 2009). Besides, aesthetic communication

Fig. 2: Mission statement of the education program at the Staatstheater Nürnberg

| STAATSTHEATER NÜRNBERG | | SPIELPLAN | DIGITALER FUNDUS | ≡ |

MUSIK ENTDECKEN

Welche Magie von Musik ausgehen kann, zeigt sich besonders dann, wenn Kinder und Jugendliche sich zum ersten Mal von ihr verzaubern und berühren lassen. Um diese kostbaren Momente allen ermöglichen zu können, bauen wir auf zahlreiche starke Bündnispartner, wie den Nürnberger Kulturrucksack, die Nürnberger Musikschule, die Stadtbibliothek, das Germanische Nationalmuseum oder die zahllosen engagierten Pädagog*innen in der Stadt. Jede Konzerteinführung für Schüler*innen, jede Konzertmoderation und jede Konzeptentwicklung ist geprägt von dem Wunsch, dass danach durch die Musik etwas in uns allen nachklingen möge.

Kontakt PLUS:

SCHAUSPIEL / BALLETT
Leiterin PLUS
Anja Sparberg
Tel.: +49-(0)911-66069-3037
E-Mail

PERFORMANCE / CHOREOGRAFIE
Ingo Schweiger
Tel.: +49-(0)911-66069-3038
E-Mail

- KINDEROPER
- KINDERKONZERT
- JUGENDKONZERT
- KINDER IM GLUCK
- IN DER MEISTERWERKSTATT
- TON-ANGEBER
- ORCHESTERPAT*INNEN
- APP2MUSIC_DE
- DAS OPERNSTUDIO ZU BESUCH
- SIT-IN-PROBEN
- ICH LADE GERN MIR GÄSTE EIN …

MUSIKTHEATER / KONZERT
Philipp Roosz
Tel.: +49 (0)911 66069-8666
E-Mail

STAATSTHEATER NÜRNBERG
PLUS / Theaterpädagogik
Richard-Wagner-Platz 2-10
90443 Nürnberg
E-Mail

Folgen Sie uns auch im Social Web:
> Facebook
> Twitter
> Instagram
> YouTube

Source: https://www.staatstheater-nuernberg.de/content/plus, screenshot, taken 2019/06/11

work also makes the claim that it is offering something meaningful for the creation of a good life. This can be read as a key offer, because meaningful action is indispensable for social beings. If one takes a look at lines like "Giving everyone the opportunity to experience music, and especially bringing it closer to those who would normally have no access to our music," or "Together with the sections, we invite the city society to discussions, further education and rehearsal visits" it seems quite obvious that the organisations do understand their relationship with their potential audiences as being an educational one. Moreover, the self-description of the organisations promises social participation via art[17]. Hence, both descriptions of *Musikvermittlung* are implicitly operating with the assumption that participating in the (classical) arts is an

---

17   As has been mentioned before, the examples presented do not show *real* practices of *Musikvermittlung*. But they do show how the organisations depicted present themselves as organisations that produce art and communicate on it. There is a vast body of literature on the gap between what organisations show to the public and how they act,

important element for social participation. What then, in turn, makes sense is a normative, cultural-political question. The analysis of the concrete depiction of *Musikvermittlung* must be put aside at this point. In this context, the semantics on the surface are sufficient. It is interesting to note that "*Musikvermittlung* [emphasis by the author] creates a space in which we can exchange musical and aesthetic experiences" (Wimmer 2018: 207). However, this space must be able to link aesthetic experiences with economic and educational motives without the space being usurped by a single motive. In addition to the theme of aesthetic experience, or the pragmatic theme of reflecting on what it means to have an "experience" (Dewey 2005), it becomes clear that *Musikvermittlung* has an observational function. Wimmer emphasises the exchange, and tries to find a spatial metaphor for *Musikvermittlung* that observes both the production of music and the making of musical experiences. In a banalised way, this could be summarised as a task to make music consumable, i.e. to reduce its complexity to such an extent that its consumption is possible without any obstacles. Concerning the necessary economic marketing of music events, this may be left as it is, but it does not do justice to the complexity-processing potential of *Musikvermittlung*. For if we think of the problem of the self-negation of art in the art system, then the function of *Musikvermittlung* is rather to open up a protected space of experience that enables both the music and the audience to have an irritating experience. This in turn functions as an offer of communication. "Together" as a term for community can be found in both the examples presented above, and this may point to that protected space mentioned above, where a musical experience can be had without the constraint of already knowing the score.

What now remains irritating is that art, and thus also music, has an intrinsic value, so why does this have to be conveyed? Is the communicative interruption in Schmidt's sense otherwise too intense? The answers one can give at this point should all be equally bad. For it cannot be sufficiently argued either that people are simply not interested enough, or that they are too uneducated to appreciate art. From a historical perspective, it could be stated at least that society is in the middle of a media revolution whose end and transforming effect cannot yet be foreseen (Floridi 2014). Similar to the spread of printing, digitalisation will have a profound impact on the way we acquire and reproduce knowledge, as well as on our understanding of and taste in

---

but at least their self-descriptions show how they wish to be perceived (see Kieserling 2004).

art. From a differentiation-theoretical point of view, however, another offer of justification can be made, which is not suitable as an explanation, but perhaps offers a starting point for further thinking and problematising.

As already mentioned in the section on the temporality of innovation, sociological differentiation theories assume that societies form special fields for certain functions, which then only devote themselves to the provision of these functions. Modern social formations are considered to be those which have become very strongly differentiated (Luhmann 1997). According to Luhmann's theory of differentiation, we are no longer dealing with society as a whole, but with a significant number of functional systems (Luhmann 1997). The most important ones are politics, religion, science, economy, education, and art. All these functional systems try to fulfill their internal functions and also to differentiate themselves further. Within the system this is usually unproblematic, but how do the individual systems contact each other, or how does information get from politics to school or from science to business? If autopoietic functional systems like art develop the possibility of self-negation due to their internal differentiation, and this in turn becomes the object of observation of art, then "there is a danger that the communicative relationship between artist and viewer will break down" (Luhmann 1995: 478). In Schmidt's sense, there is then the danger that the communicative interruption by the work of art can no longer be eliminated. This problem is typical for functionally differentiated systems; they are incommensurable with one another.

In a final step, I will now try to show, with recourse to Renn's translation theory, that this system difference cannot be overcome, but can be translated with/via *Musikvermittlung*.

On the Translation of Music

The theory of translation relations enables a change of perspective by interpreting the shaping (Weick 1979) of social order not as the opposition of structure and practice, but as the mutual integration of the opposition of structure in practice and practice in structure, which allows a description of social order (and its empirical phenomena) that takes into account the dynamics and complexity of the same (Renn 2006: 206). Thus, the treatment of an uncertain future by means of innovation semantics is not treated as an object of economics, as is usually the case in the "Open Innovation Paradigm" (see above), but as a general problem of modern social order. This means that no structural coupling between functional systems is possible, since each social area operates in a sense-specific way and sense from other social areas can only process its own formats of meaning. This leads to the incommensurability just mentioned. Nevertheless, if we look around us, it is still possible for surgeons and civil servants, mechatronics engineers, and concert pianists to coordinate and communicate with each other. It succeeds through translations. However, this does not mean a form of linear transfer, in which the vocabulary of the other sense area is organised according to analogy principles, but rather that if sense can only be processed as a systemic sense, then the translation service consists in drawing the external offer of meaning equally spirally inwards and in attaching[18] one's own semantics or practice to it. From this it follows that if a variation is created, innovation can result also. In his theory of translational relations, Renn coined the term "Translate" for the specific results of these translation processes (Renn 2006: 445 f.). The question now is: what is the Translate in art (music) in which the translation performances of the art system become visible? The crystallisation point for this seems to be organisations. These organisations coordinate their operations usually within one functional system. A philharmonic orchestra operates mainly within the system of art. For this reason, they produce self-descriptions – which include a specific view on innovation – always in reference to art. In the end, the translational performance comprises attempts by the philharmonic orchestra to make sense out of the term for itself and to stay in touch with the organisational environment at the same time (Weick et al. 2005). The members of organisations in their respective milieus perform translations analogously, and the same happens at the level of functional systems, of abstract language games such as semantics (Renn 2006: 362–366). Innovation in this sense is then neither an economic growth utopia nor a product of individual self-surprise (invention), but an organisational strategy for dealing with contingency and uncertainty.

---

18   "Translation must take place between generalised formats of the meaning of action or communication ('types') and specific events ('tokens'), whose current meaning simultaneously exceeds (in the sense of situational specificity) and falls short of (because it does not exhaust) the general horizon of meaning (the 'semantics') typical and identifying for a context." (Renn 2011: 321)

According to this reading, *Musikvermittlung* is on the one hand an innovation, because it is neither art nor education, but something which is a third[19] thing, which establishes its own form of practices. On the other hand, it is the result of translation services, in other words, it is a translation of the re-specification of meaning in the art system. This is what we need in a late modern, highly differentiated society in order to be able to maintain this plurality and to be able to endure it. Finally, *Musikvermittlung* seems to have an observational function for music, so that music can observe itself under certain conditions and ensure that the ambiguity of art – as I mentioned earlier – does not lead to a breakdown in communication, to speechlessness, but continues to enable communicative connections. *Musikvermittlung* is thus an instance within the subsystem of art (music) which can observe and reflect the self-negation possibility of art. This enables music and its organisations to develop offers of communication that are to be heard beyond the system. This then also includes educational goals or economic functions of *Musikvermittlung*, as has been shown in the two examples above. The explicit offer of meaningfulness is also part of this. These are then specific translations in the context of the respective art organisation and its embedding in the art system. Scientific observations of *Musikvermittlung* should therefore not ask about its function. It is more important to find out where, and under what conditions, practices of *Musikvermittlung* arise and which musical events are subsequently made possible.

Bibliography

Adorno, Theodor W. (1981): *Einleitung in die Musiksoziologie*, Frankfurt am Main: Suhrkamp Taschenbuch Verlag.
Alexander, Jeffrey C. (1987): *Twenty Lectures: Sociological Theory since World War II*, New York: Columbia University Press.
Augsdörfer, Peter/Möslein, Kathrin/Richter, Andreas (2013): Radical, Discontinuous and Disruptive Innovation – What's the Difference? in: Augsdörfer, Peter/Bessant, John/Stamm, Bettina von (eds.), *Discontinuous innovation*, London: Imperial College Press, 9–39.

---

19 See Ilja Srubar 2009 on the emergence of a *third* as the result of translating between two different sense- making systems.

Baecker, Dirk (2011): Organisation als temporale Form, in: *Organisation und Störung: Aufsätze*, Berlin: Suhrkamp, 310–334.

Barnett, Homer Garner (1953): *Innovation: The Basis of Cultural Change*, McGraw-Hill Paperbacks. Problems of Civilization, New York: McGraw-Hill.

Beck, Ulrich (1986): *Risikogesellschaft*, Frankfurt am Main: Suhrkamp.

Benjamin, Walter ([1935] 2015): *Das Kunstwerk im Zeitalter seiner technischen Reproduzierbarkeit und weitere Dokumente*, Frankfurt am Main: Suhrkamp.

Berg, Karen van den (2009): Kreativität. Drei Absagen der Kunst an ihren erweiterten Begriff, in Jansen, Stephan/Schröter, Eckhard/Stehr, Nico (eds), *Rationalität der Kreativität?*, Wiesbaden: VS Verlag für Sozialwissenschaften, 207–224.

Blättel-Mink, Birgit/Ebner, Alexander (eds.) (2009): *Innovationssysteme*. VS Verlag für Sozialwissenschaften.

Bormann, Hans-Friedrich (2005): *Verschwiegene Stille: John Cages performative Ästhetik*, München: Wilhelm Fink.

Castells, Manuel (2010): *The Rise of the Network Society*, Chichester u.a.: Wiley-Blackwell.

Chesbrough, Henry W. (2003): *Open Innovation. The New Imperative for Creating and Profiting from Technology*, Boston: Harvard Business School Publishing Corporation.

DeNora, Tia (2000): *Music in Everyday Life*, Cambridge: Cambridge University Press.

Dewey, John (2005): *Art as Experience*, New York: Perigee.

Dornaus, Christina/Staples, Ronald/Wendelken, Anke/Wolf, Daniel (2015): *Innovationspotenziale - Entdecken! Wertschätzen! Nutzen!*, [online] https://opus 4.kobv.de/opus4-fau/frontdoor/index/index/docId/6442 [30.12.2020].

Florida, Richard (2004): *The Rise of the Creative Class*. New York, NY: Basic Books.

Floridi, Luciano (2014): *The 4th Revolution: How the Infosphere is Reshaping Human Reality*, New York; Oxford: Oxford University Press.

Garoian, Charles R. (2001): Performing the Museum, in: *Studies in Art Education*, Routledge, Vol. 42, No. 3, 234–248.

Gehlen, Arnold (1965): *Zeit-Bilder: zur Soziologie und Ästhetik der modernen Malerei*, Frankfurt am Main: Athänum-Verlag.

Geisenberger, Jürgen (1999): *Joseph Beuys und die Musik*, Marburg: Tectum.

Gilfillan, S. Colum (1963): *The Sociology of Invention*, Cambridge: MIT Press.

Gray, Dave/Vander Wal, Thomas (2014): *The Connected Company*, Sebastopol, California: Oreilly & Associates.

Hippel, Eric von (2005): *Democratizing Innovation*, Cambridge et al.: MIT Press.
Holzinger, Markus (2007): *Kontingenz in der Gegenwartsgesellschaft: Dimensionen eines Leitbegriffs moderner Sozialtheorie*, Bielefeld: transcript.
Howaldt, Jürgen/Jacobsen, Heike (eds.) (2010): *Soziale Innovation*, Wiesbaden: VS Verlag für Sozialwissenschaften.
Joas, Hans (1996): *Die Kreativität des Handelns*, Frankfurt am Main: Suhrkamp.
Kelley, Tom (2001): *The Art of Innovation*, New York, NY: Doubleday.
Kieserling, André (2004): *Selbstbeschreibung und Fremdbeschreibung: Beiträge zur Soziologie soziologischen Wissens*. Frankfurt am Main: Suhrkamp.
Koch, Klaus Georg (2014): *Innovation in Kulturorganisationen: Die Entfaltung unternehmerischen Handelns und die Kunst des Überlebens*, Bielefeld: transcript.
Latour, Bruno (2002): *Die Hoffnung der Pandora. Untersuchungen zur Wirklichkeit der Wissenschaft*, Frankfurt am Main: Suhrkamp.
Luhmann, Niklas (1976): The Future Cannot Begin: Temporal Structures in Modern Society, in: *Social Research*, Vol. 43, No.1, 130–152.
Luhmann, Niklas (1981): Ist Kunst codierbar?, in: *Soziologische Aufklärung 3. Soziales System, Gesellschaft, Organisation*, Opladen: VS Verlag für Sozialwissenschaften (Soziologische Aufklärung, 3), 245–266.
Luhmann, Niklas (1987): *Soziale Systeme: Grundriss einer allgemeinen Theorie*, Frankfurt am Main: Suhrkamp.
Luhmann, Niklas (1992): Ökologie des Nichtwissens. In: *Beobachtungen der Moderne*, Opladen: Westdeutscher Verlag, 149–220.
Luhmann, Niklas (1995): *Die Kunst der Gesellschaft*, Frankfurt am Main: Suhrkamp.
Luhmann, Niklas (1997): *Die Gesellschaft der Gesellschaft*, Frankfurt am Main: Suhrkamp.
Luhmann, Niklas (1999): Die Behandlung von Irritationen: Abweichung oder Neuheit?, in: *Gesellschaftsstruktur und Semantik: Studien zur Wissenssoziologie der modernen Gesellschaft*, 4, Frankfurt am Main: Suhrkamp, 55–100.
Luhmann, Niklas (2008): *Ideenevolution: Beiträge zur Wissenssoziologie*, Frankfurt am Main: Suhrkamp.
Müllensiefen, Daniel (1999): Radikaler Konstruktivismus und Musikwissenschaft: Ideen und Perspektiven, in: *Musicae Scientiae*, SAGE Publications Ltd, Vol. 3, No. 1, 95–116.
Nowotny, Helga (1999): *Es ist so. Es könnte auch anders sein: über das veränderte Verhältnis von Wissenschaft und Gesellschaft*, Frankfurt am Main: Suhrkamp.
Ogburn, William F./Duncan, Otis D. (1964): *On Culture and Social Change*, Chicago: The University of Chicago Press.

Ortmann, Günther (1999): Innovation als Paradoxieentfaltung – eine Schlußbemerkung, in: Sauer, Dieter/Lang, Christa (eds.), *Paradoxien der Innovation: Perspektiven sozialwissenschaftlicher Innovationsforschung*, Frankfurt am Main/New York: Campus, 249–262.
Paulitz, Tanja (2012): *Mann und Maschine*. ScienceStudies. Bielefeld: transcript.
Popitz, Heinrich (1997): *Wege der Kreativität*, Tübingen: Mohr Siebeck.
Rammert, Werner/Windeler, Arnold/Knoblauch, Hubert and Hutter, Michael (eds.) (2016): *Innovationsgesellschaft Heute: Perspektiven, Felder Und Fälle*, Wiesbaden: Springer VS.
Reckwitz, Andreas (2012): *Die Erfindung der Kreativität: Zum Prozess gesellschaftlicher Ästhetisierung*. Berlin: Suhrkamp.
Reckwitz, Andreas (2016): Jenseits Der Innovationsgesellschaft das Kreativitätsdispositiv und die Transformation der sozialen Regime des Neuen, in: *Kreativität und Soziale Praxis, Studien zur Sozial- und Gesellschaftstheorie*, Berlin/Boston: De Gruyter, 249–270.
Renn, Joachim (2006): *Übersetzungsverhältnisse: Perspektiven einer pragmatistischen Gesellschaftstheorie*, Weilerswist: Velbrück Wissenschaft.
Renn, Joachim (2011): Koordination durch Übersetzung. Das Problem gesellschaftlicher Steuerung aus der Sicht einer pragmatistischen Differenzierungstheorie, in: Albert, Gert, Sigmund, Steffen (ed.), *Soziologische Theorie kontrovers*, Wiesbaden: VS Verlag für Sozialwissenschaften, 311–327.
Reza, Yasmina/Helmlé, Eugen (2008): *Kunst*, Lengwil am Bodensee: Libelle.
Rosa, Hartmut (2013): *Beschleunigung und Entfremdung*, Berlin: Suhrkamp.
Schmidt, Siegfried J. (1988): Kreativität aus der Beobachterperspektive, in: Gumbrecht, Hans-Ulrich (ed.), *Kreativität – Ein verbrauchter Begriff?*, Munich: Fink.
Schumpeter, Joseph (1961): *Konjunkturzyklen. Eine Theoretische, Historische und statistische Analyse des kapitalistischen Prozesses. Band 1*, Göttingen: Vandenhoek&Ruprecht.
Schütz, Alfred ([1945] 2003): Teiresias oder unser Wissen von zukünftigen Ereignissen, in: Endreß, Martin/Srubar, Ilja (eds.): *Alfred Schütz Werkausgabe V.I - Theorie der Lebenswelt 1 Die pragmatische Schichtung der Lebenswelt*, Konstanz: UVK Verlagsgesellschaft, 249–284.
Siebenhaar, Klaus/Braun, Günter (eds.) (2009): *Audience Development: oder die Kunst, neues Publikum zu gewinnen*. Berlin: B & S Siebenhaar Verlag.
Srubar, Ilja (2009): Strukturen des Übersetzens und interkultureller Vergleich, in: Srubar, Ilja (ed.), *Kultur und Semantik*. Wiesbaden: VS Verlag für Sozialwissenschaften, 155–178.

Velthuis, Olav/Baia Curioni, Stefano (eds.) (2015): *Cosmopolitan Canvases: the Globalization of Markets for Contemporary Art*, Oxford/New York: Oxford University Press.

Weick, Karl E. (1979): *The Social Psychology of Organizing*, Reading, u.a.: Addison-Wesley.

Weick, Karl E./Sutcliffe, Katherine M./Obstfeld, David (2005): *Organizing and the Process of Sensemaking*, in *Organization Science*, Vol. 16, No. 4, 409–421.

Wilson, Peter (1997): Pop- und «Hoch»Kultur: Elf unsortierte Gedankensplitter zu einem nicht mehr ganz neuen Thema, in: *Neue Zeitschrift Für Musik* (1991-) 158 (2): 10–12.

Wimmer, Constanze (2018): Einen Sehnsuchtsort der Wahrnehmung öffnen. Musikvermittlung im Konzertbetrieb, in: Tröndle, Martin (ed.): *Das Konzert[11]*, Bielefeld: transcript, 197–214.

Biographical note

Ronald Staples teaches and conducts research at Friedrich Alexander Universität Erlangen-Nürnberg. He did his doctorate on the relationship between innovation and organisation and continues to ask how creativity and organisation are connected. This includes the question of the extent to which the bureaucratic organisation has passed its zenith as the dominant type of organisation. He is currently working on the changes in employment relationships and organisations due to the digital transformation.

Slam Poetry Meets Classical Music

Axel Petri-Preis

Artists
Henrik Szanto, slam poetry
Jonas Scheiner, slam poetry

qWINDtett
Silvio Trachsel, oboe
Veronika Vitazkova, flute
Wolfgang Lücking, horn
Nikolaus Höckner, bassoon
Benjamin Schachinger, clarinet

Programme
Alexander von Zemlinsky: "Humoreske" (1941)
   - *Intro by Jonas and Henrik*
Malcolm Arnold: Beginning of the 3rd movement from "Three Chanties" (1943)
   - *Finnish Idioms*
Darius Milhaud: Madrigal nocturne from "La Cheminée du Roi René" (1939) &
Eugène Bozza: "Scherzo" (1944)
   - *Wenn fliegen träumen lernen*
Terence Greaves: "Mozart's Turkey Rock Mambo" (1993)
   - *Bathrobe*

In their performance "Windrichtungen" (Wind Directions), the ensemble qWINDtett, a classical wind quintet, and the two slam poets Henrik Szanto and Jonas Scheiner bring together their respective art forms in a virtuoso manner. They have built a program where music and text stand in a reciprocal relationship, each commenting on, reflecting and complementing the other.

When the slam poets and the musicians met each other for the first time, through the mediation of the Wiener Konzerthaus, the first thing they did was present each other with pieces of music and texts. Up to that stage, there had been only a few points of contact with each other's art form. In retrospect, this was a leap into cold water, but everyone involved very quickly became enthusiastic about the cooperation. So they sought for possibilities of how to bring music and slam poetry together. The rehearsals developed into a work in progress, combinations were found and discarded, new paths were taken. At the beginning, it was by no means clear what the final result would be. While at first it was very important to the musicians to present complete works, they subsequently began to use only excerpts or individual movements. In the final program, the music and the texts are performed one after the other or simultaneously, complete or in extracts, and thereby comment on, intensify or counteract each other.

Fig. 1: *Henrik Szanto & Jonas Scheiner performing at the lecture series, November 2019*

Source: private

The artists highlight two outcomes of their joint project: firstly, they found it valuable that their horizons were broadened by this collaboration, and that multiple learning processes were initiated on all sides. The improvisational way of rehearsing and developing the program, for example, proved to be irri-

Fig. 2: The qWINDtett performing at the lecture series, November 2019

Source: private

tating for the musicians at first, but opened up new perspectives and a desire for unconventional concert formats. Secondly, their collaboration provided the possibility of bringing together different audiences that would otherwise not have met. In this way, both art forms, classical music and slam poetry, may have served as door openers for each other. Not least, the combination of text and music opens up a new level of perception, so that something third emerges, which text and music could not have achieved on their own.

Biographical notes

Jonas Scheiner and **Henrik Szanto** are writers, slam poets and organisers of cultural events in Vienna and Austria. They perform together under the name Kirmes Hanoi, and as such have become one of the most influential poetry slam teams in the German-speaking world, having won several regional, national, and international awards and championships. For the "Windrichtungen" project, Scheiner and Szanto curated the literature segment, for which they contributed their own pieces and will act as hosts during live performances.

The qWINDtett, founded in Vienna, is a classical woodwind quintet in its formation. Its members – **Desislava Dobreva** (flute), **Sebastian Sima** (oboe), **Benjamin Schachinger** (clarinet), **Nikolaus Höckner** (bassoon) and **Thomas Steinwender** (horn) – come from Vienna, Lower Austria, Upper Austria, Salzburg and Bulgaria. They met in 2013 at the Angela Prokopp Summer Academy of the Vienna Philharmonic in Salzburg, since when their collaboration has continued. During their chamber music studies at the mdw – University of Music and Performing Arts Vienna, the musicians' interplay was further refined. The ensemble has presented its by now large repertoire at the Vienna State Opera, the Musikverein Wien and also at the Wiener Konzerthaus. Together with the poetry slam collective FOMP, they performed as part of Music for You at the Wiener Konzerthaus and at Radio Kulturhaus Wien.

Under a Preservation Order?
The Innovative Potential of *Musikvermittlung* to Renew Concert Life

Constanze Wimmer

"Just as one is told about the advantages of a frying-pan cleaner at a trade-fair stall, today art is explained by professional "interpreters" before one can enjoy it. It can apparently no longer speak for itself and about itself – that, too, is a statement about its condition",

wrote the four authors of the pamphlet "Der Kulturinfarkt" [The Culture Heart Attack] in 2012, when – long before the COVID-19 crisis – they polemically painted a picture of what they saw as a cultural sector too heavily financed by public funding and on the verge of collapse (Haselbach et al. 2012a: 111).

The collapse has indeed occurred, but in the light of the Corona pandemic in a different way than expected. Practitioners of *Musikvermittlung* or "professional interpreters" (see above) have to struggle with the same problems as other actors in the (classical) music business, whether musicians, promoters or agents – resilience, creativity and savings are needed to deal with the current crisis in the concert business. After the initial shock at the beginning of the pandemic, the cultural sector was divided into two factions: one that hoped that everything would soon return to the way it was before the crisis and the other that hoped that this dramatic emergency braking might lead to a categorical rethinking.

"Politics has always given subsidised culture an increasingly costlier place, driven by the belief in growth and the bubbling taxes of the boom years. The idea that public culture is systemically relevant, that every production site is indispensable, is just an attempt to delay the presentation of the bill." (Haselbach et al. 2012b)

Much has been said and written about the systemic relevance and indispensability of culture in German-language (social) media in recent months, but the realisation remains that the systemic relevance is mainly invoked by or apparent to those who are part of the art system. Outside the arts and culture scene, priorities are assessed differently in the face of exponentially rising unemployment, national debt for years to come, insolvencies and a profound sense of COVID-19 insecurity gripping all parts of society. On the other hand, there is a music business that is picking up speed under strict conditions, and in order to continue to exist needs interpreters between the inside of the concert hall and the outside social conditions even more than before: "This pandemic has shaken the ground under our organizations, and those without deep community foundations are in danger of collapse. The audience is just shaken: people are suffering financially, emotionally and psychologically." (McIntyre 2020)

Today, practitioners of *Musikvermittlung*, in particular, are confronted with diverse challenges of interpretation: if they were already the actors within the concert business who were most aware that their own cultural standpoint can only be a starting point for projects with people in a differentiated society, it will become even more important in the future to mediate between different cultures, to negotiate cultural differences without violence and to find new interfaces to make concert halls, orchestras and ensembles relevant places of conversation and encounter (see Richter-Ibánez 2018). If it was already difficult to address "everyone" in the 1970s, when Hilmar Hoffmann coined the catchphrase of "culture for all", then today the situation seems even more confusing due to the current profound changes brought about by global migration. The anthropologist Steven Vertovec uses the term "super-diversity" for societies shaped by the changes in international migration patterns. He does not mean *more* or *larger*, but *more complex*, in terms of the present composition of the population in European states. While the traditional migration movement after World War II followed a simple pattern and large, homogeneous groups of people immigrated into Europe, such as rural Turks from Anatolia or workers from Southern Europe, the number of countries of origin has now increased exponentially. Regions from all over the world are now represented in the population of European states: refugees from wars and crises, reunited families, educational migrants, commuters and the permanent migration of global "high-performers" are changing our society (see Vertovec 2007).

Of course, art can speak for itself in this super-diverse society, but only to and with those who have learned and therefore understand its different codes. It is therefore very urgent to have mediators who have mastered several artistic and cultural languages and are willing to learn them, who are open and curious about what a diverse audience feels, thinks and associates. This is not what the authors of *Kulturinfarkt* meant, but their polemic only really makes sense today.

In this article, I first describe the current state of *Musikvermittlung* in the cultural sector on the basis of primary modes of action such as moderation, interaction and staging, and on this basis ask what potential for innovation might lie in these modes of action for the classical concert and the staging of classical music in view of the expected consequences of the Corona pandemic.

Format versus Content

"When I say I am a Kunstvermittlerin [emphasis added] I have to explain myself. I have to describe, and possibly justify, what I mean by it. It's not an easy business, *Kunstvermittlung* [emphasis added], let alone the term," complain Carmen Mörsch and Eva Sturm, two pivotal figures in *Kunstvermittlung* (Henschel 2020: 5). The actors in Musikvermittlung are not much better off. Just like *Kunstvermittlung* (art mediation/education), *Musikvermittlung* also covers various fields of activity that are sometimes difficult to combine – from cultural education to audience development, from community art to audience engagement, from curating to visitor orientation, the paths are sometimes longer than expected. Once again, a finding from *Kunstvermittlung* that also applies to the field of music: "The term is used as a marker for art-related educational work in a wide variety of institutional settings as well as for forms of curating, art criticism, gallery sales or cultural management" (Henschel 2020: 19).

To explain and illustrate their professional practice to the uninitiated, the actors often list the formats through which *Musikvermittlung* is practised. They then speak, for example, of

- staged and moderated concerts for children,
- staged and contextualised concert formats,
- moderated concerts,
- introductory workshops and talks before or after concerts, or of
- outreach and community projects.

The listener quickly gets a superficial "aha" feeling: "Yes, I know that, I've heard of that before – so that's what you call *Musikvermittlung*". But if the conversation ends here, the core of *Musikvermittlung* is already missed. Because that would be like explaining love by listing forms of possible partnership, e.g.: love is found in

- registered partnerships,
- same-sex marriage,
- marriage in the church,
- long-distance relationships, or
- life-stage partnerships.

We would not accept these as a descriptions of love. Admittedly, I could say with the Austrian poet Erich Fried (1921–1988) "It is what it is, says *Musikvermittlung*",[1] but then the article would be finished, and perhaps you would find that a shame.

When a Swiss colleague asked me for a metaphor of *Musikvermittlung* for her book, I sent her the following text:

"When architects are commissioned to renovate an old house [emphasis added], they consider what new lines of sight could be opened up, which walls should be moved or knocked down, and how the wooden floor could be given a fresh shine without destroying its texture.
When architects build a new house [emphasis added], they plan it together with the inhabitants and create places of communication, reflection and retreat.
Practitioners of Musikvermittlung are architects in concert life – they renovate and build new aesthetic spaces, definitely wheelchair accessible, but definitely not prefabricated." (Wimmer in Weber 2018: 103)

Practitioners of *Musikvermittlung* often find themselves serving institutions in need of renovation, such as concert halls or orchestras. Like the many *Gründerzeit* era[2] buildings in Vienna, they could be left largely as they are, the stucco is quietly crumbling, but the substance is incredibly stable. However,

---

[1] In reference to the poem "Was es ist" by Erich Fried, [online] https://www.deutschelyrik.de/was-es-ist-1039.html [10.4.2021].

[2] Gründerzeit era: the Central European version of late 19th/early 20th century historicism.

you could also start renovating from the inside, because the needs of some of the residents have changed and by residents in this context I mean everyone involved in concert life: artists, artistic directors and the audience! Sometimes it is even time to build a new house altogether, because 19th-century architecture does not suit the new concert formats, nor the democratic societies of the 21st century.

"Opening New Perspectives", or Putting Music into Context

Musikvermittlung looks for ways to continually create new relationships between music and its audience – one possible approach is to expose the cultural-historical or socio-cultural context of a composition in an original way during and before a concert, or to put the composition itself in a current or unusual context and so give it a surprising meaning. The social, historical or formal general conditions of a work influence its performance practice and can change and deepen the audience's perception if this context is itself made the subject in an exciting way. The perspective basically defines an imaginary line that connects different things and points, and in this way makes new aspects possible. As such, it forms the conceptual line between context(s) and work that stimulates the audience's listening and supports them in their transient perception of music.

Why do practitioners of *Musikvermittlung* use this method? I would like to quote Markus Poschner, the principal conductor of the Bruckner Orchestra Linz, who answered the question of whether classical music is in crisis in an interview:

> "It would be news to me if Bruckner, Schubert and Mozart had a crisis. But what we have to think about every day is the way we communicate art. [...] How do I bring Schubert or Schönberg together with a school class, for example? **How do I arrange a meeting?** [emphasis added] This is not only an Upper Austrian problem, but a worldwide one. It is certainly no longer enough always to go on stage at the same time on a Saturday evening, start with the overture, then the concert, then a symphony, and then let's see how many people are interested." (Poschner, quoted from Grubmüller 2017)

"Context" in art goes back to the beginnings of what in the 1930s was known as social history. Just as historiography no longer exclusively presents a list of rulers' genealogies or the course of wars and the conclusion of treaties, the work of art is now also given a social background. Considerations are emerging that seek to tie social content to works of art and, in doing so, take into account the audience the works of art are addressed to and the effects that could be achieved through them (Draxler 1994). At the beginning of the 1960s, Umberto Eco abandoned the autonomous work of art in his publication "Opera aperta" (Eco 1962) and defined the "open work" of art, which only emerges in the interaction between the work and the recipient. The structure of interpretation of the work of art remains incomplete and is co-constructed by the listener or viewer. In this sense, the audience becomes an actor. Bakhtin describes this process as follows:

> "The work and the world represented in it enter the real world and enrich it, and the real world enters the work and its world as part of the process of its creation, as well as part of its subsequent life, in a continual renewing of the work through the creative perception of listeners and readers." (Bakhtin 1982: 254)

In the following, a few examples will illustrate this way of working in *Musikvermittlung*:

Example I: Staging and contextualising

The Montforter Zwischentöne festival has been held in Feldkirch in Vorarlberg since 2015 and is curated by Folkert Uhde and Hans Joachim Gögl. They formulate their goal as "to establish a new festival form that combines everyday culture and music in formats that facilitate immediate aesthetic experiences" (Uhde/Gögl n.d.). Georg Friedrich Händel's "Messiah", which was performed in autumn 2016 as part of the focus on "Dying – On Letting Go", had several anchoring points to everyday culture and facilitated immediate aesthetic experiences: the audience could enter the hall via two entrances, one "for non-believers" and one "for believers". Visitors decided for themselves how they wanted to enter the concert hall. On their seats they found a card with questions to fill in about their own attitudes to the existential questions of the work. During the interval, the answers were evaluated and the results projected on the wall when they re-entered the hall. Three times during the concert, there was a live link to a reporter doing interviews. Hanno Settele, a former correspondent for ORF (state broadcasting company), was on the road to people and places, addressing the central questions of the work in a contemporary way. A comprehensive contextualisation of the oratorio therefore took place, with experts on everyday life topics, such as bullying, terminal care, poverty, birth and resurrection.

Example II: Moderation as contextualisation
The context of a work can also be opened up for the audience in conversation with the artists at a concert. This is done, for example, in the format "listening twice" (see also Petri-Preis in this volume). The method is simple, but all the more effective for that: a work (usually of contemporary art music) is first presented to the audience without any explanation or comments, followed by a discussion with the interpreters of the work, introducing its structure or the particularities of the stylistics, and discussing details of the rehearsal work and the musicians' personal references to the work in dialogue with the artists. This is followed by the second performance of the piece, so the listener has the pleasure of an intuitive perception and also a contextualised rendition in a concert.

Accordingly, practitioners of *Musikvermittlung* are looking for ways to put the repertoire of concert life into a context that, in Bakhtin's sense, connects the real world (current and historical) with the world represented in pieces of music.

"Shifting Walls or Tearing Them Down" - the Audience as Actor

Gerhart Hauptmann writes that in 1889 he wrote his play "Vor Sonnenaufgang" [Before Sunrise] "without even thinking of the audience, as if the stage did not have three but four walls" (Brauneck 1974: 163). A concert is not a play, but how many concerts have we experienced where there is an invisible wall between the stage and the audience? A key task of practitioners of *Musikvermittlung* is to find suitable moments in the concert to reduce or even eliminate this separation. There are now many examples of interaction between musicians and audience, two of which are mentioned here to illustrate the approach: *Im Klang* (at the Wiener Konzerthaus) and *Mittendrin* (at the Berlin Konzerthaus) are formats in which the audience takes a seat directly in the orchestra in order to immerse themselves in the orchestral sound at close quarters. Changing seats between movements is encouraged.

Why do practitioners of *Musikvermittlung* want to give the audience the chance to get so close to the action? Because music is an opportunity for communication, and through communication relationships are created between the musicians and the person in the nearest seat in the audience which are artistically refined in the concert through the music. Interaction in this sense does not mean taking part, but a special way of active listening on the part of the audience, which reaches a completely different intensity when sitting chair to chair with the orchestra's oboist or violinist, directly feeling the musician's body breathing, sweating, turning the pages, concentrating.

In 2016, the Ensemble Modern, together with three other contemporary art music ensembles (London Sinfonietta, Asko|Schönberg and Remix Ensemble), launched the "Connect" project in Frankfurt, commissioning new compositions that interactively involve the listeners in the action and already embed this in the work (see Toelle in this anthology).

> "I have long been a fan of collaborative theatre that interacts with the audience, creating theatrical experiences in which the audience become protagonists of the drama. Since I am also very interested in politically engaged music and music theatre, I am bringing together elements from both fields here." (Philip Venables quoted from Ensemble Modern 2018)

Here, the composer Venables hints at an attitude that will appear later in this article as "artistic citizenship". This artistic approach to interaction in the work itself is currently being taken up by numerous artists in the contemporary music and music theatre scene and is regarded as a field of experimentation.

However, interaction with the audience can also be incorporated directly into classical concerts. In the context of a concert with the four percussionists from the Graz Philharmonic Orchestra, something that has become standard in concerts for children took place to the delight of the adult audience: after the concert, those interested were invited to try out the timpani, marimba and drum themselves and to give free rein to their playing instincts and, above all, their curiosity.

Practitioners of *Musikvermittlung* want to involve the audience in the concert process more than before, to encourage them to participate actively and enable them to gain new perspectives on the musical activity, in order to initiate aesthetic experiences that also continue to have an effect after the concert.

"Giving the Parquet Floor a Fresh Shine" – Opening Up Classical Concert Repertoires for Young Audiences

Children's and youth concerts have become very differentiated since the early days of my career as a practitioner in *Musikvermittlung* in the concert business 25 years ago. Large orchestras regularly offer moderated, staged or choreographed concerts for schoolchildren and families. They find themselves in artistic dialogue with chamber music initiatives that stage perfectly rehearsed concerts in international cooperation. These lead children and young people into a different aesthetic world, where the boundaries between storytelling, theatre, dance, performance or concert blur in favour of a poetic *Gesamtkunstwerk*. Musicians work together with directors, scenographers and choreographers in intensive rehearsal phases and create touring concerts that have found their own booming market in Europe's major concert halls. In 1998, Anke Eberwein surveyed 76 professional German orchestras to ascertain which repertoire was played most often in their concerts for children. She came to the conclusion that "Peter and the Wolf" (1936) by Sergei Prokofiev, "Pictures at an Exhibition" (1874/1922) by Modest Mussorgsky, "The Moldau" (1874) by Bedrich Smetana and "The Carnival of the Animals" (1886) by Camille Saint-Saëns, i.e. predominantly compositions for children or programme music from the classical-romantic repertoire, had been most frequently performed in children's concerts since 1970 (Eberwein 1998: 72). This finding has changed significantly in the meantime: with the Tonkünstlerorchester Niederösterreich, Nicole Marte and Christoph Matl have shown that children under the age of ten can and will listen to an entire symphony by Gustav Mahler if it is contextualised accordingly.[3] Thus, in the course of the symphony, Gustav Mahler himself, a hunter and a female muse appear or emerge from the orchestra to lead the audience through Mahler's world of thought in search of the musical embodiment of a Titan, the description of nature and the impetus of springtime feelings. With Lilian Genn, the Vienna Symphony Orchestra embeds a classical orchestral repertoire by Franz Schubert or Wolfgang Amadeus Mozart in delightful stories

---

3   The Zentrum für Musikvermittlung has made a recording of the "Tonmahlerei" project by Nicole Marte and Christoph Matl, available online at: https://www.youtube.com/watch?v=oWKvwbopVJo [9.1.2021].

for children.[4] Likewise, concepts by Moritz Eggert and Heiko Hentschel[5], or Bernhard Gander and Axel Petri-Preis[6], show that there is no reason to shy away from contemporary music in children's and youth concerts if it is embedded in exciting storytelling. In painting and film workshops, writing workshops and workshops teaching composition, children and young people explore the nature of the works and the meaning that this music can have for them personally before attending the concert.

Up to this point, I have proceeded from my image of practitioners of *Musikvermittlung* as architects dealing with how an old house or concert can be renovated or filled with new life. Before I talk about the construction of a new house, I will give an overview of the formats in which *Musikvermittlung* appears today.

Formats – the Status Quo of *Musikvermittlung* in Concert Life

Musikvermittlung formats are continuously increasing in concert life: every orchestra and concert hall now has either a department, or at least one person, responsible for this area, and the Hamburg Elbphilharmonie even has around 20 people. New formats are developed here, and tried-and-tested touring projects are integrated into the houses' repertoire. In 2019, the German Orchestral Association even spoke of a tripling of music-educational workshop and concert activities between 2003/4 and 2017/18. (German Music Information Centre 2019). The main target groups are children, young people and families – although formats and projects for adults are on the increase.

Before the concert, musicians and practitioners of *Musikvermittlung* offer workshops and introductions to the special features of the works to be performed, to their instrument, or start longer participatory processes to provide their audience with low-threshold opportunities to make music

---

4   A recording of the "Mozart reist nach Prag" school concert by the Vienna Symphony Orchestra is available online at: https://www.youtube.com/watch?v=lfqV8nisIkU [9.1.2021].
5   A documentary on the Musiktheater im Revier Gelsenkirchen project "Teufels Küche" by Moritz Eggert and Heiko Hentschel can be seen online at: https://www.youtube.co m/watch?v=EyaxZAWhd7E [9.1.2021].
6   Axel Petri-Preis has made the concert "Monsters und Angels" with music by Bernhard Gander, available online at: https://www.youtube.com/watch?v=tiKs2etdiI4 [9.1.2021].

together with the orchestra (Wimmer 2018). Most of these offers are directed at a subsequent concert visit or dress rehearsal.

At the moment, *the concert itself* is probably where most experiments with communicative situations take place. Concerts for children already have a long tradition, but interdisciplinary approaches and performative settings are being developed in artistic teams in increasingly professional ways. Here, too, there is a new proximity to concert formats for adults that integrate contextualisation into the performance, or declare interaction with the audience as a conscious design element. *Concert design* and *new concert formats* serve as technical terms to describe this practice. Martin Tröndle created the term *concert studies* around this practice (analogous to *museum studies*) to bundle together theoretical approaches consisting of a mix of musicological interpretation research, cultural studies, cultural management, cultural sociology and *Musikvermittlung* (see Tröndle 2018).

"Then They Plan it Together with the Residents" – Participatory Formats and Community Music

In the second part of my contribution, in keeping with the image of building a new house, it is no longer about renovation but about the transformation of the music business. The second part of my metaphor does not concern the renovation of the regular music business from within, but its transformation: "When architects build a **new house**, they plan it together with the inhabitants and create places of communication, contemplation and retreat".

In 2018, the six nominees of the 13th "Junge Ohren Preis" [Young Ears Award][7] were chosen: orchestras and concert halls in Austria, Germany and Switzerland took part. What stood out was the following: four of the six nominated projects were no longer committed to the above-mentioned, by now established canon of *Musikvermittlung* formats, but the applicants saw the core of their work in a focus that was new for this sector: working in the community.

- The Hamburg Symphony Orchestra founded a community orchestra called the "Moving Orchestra", in which people of different ages and

---

7   The "Junge Ohren Preis" is a German-language competition for *Musikvermittlung* projects.

social backgrounds could make and invent music together with the orchestra.
- The Gewandhausorchester Leipzig started a district project that worked together with Leipzig institutions and local associations.
- In Nuremberg, a community opera based on the legend of the Pied Piper of Hamelin was created as part of the Bridging Arts Chamber Music Festival, with artists and amateurs aged from 7 to 83 taking part.
- The Lucerne Symphony Orchestra placed its entire *Musikvermittlung* work under the concept of inclusion. Since then, an inclusion advisory board has supported the musicians in testing concerts and projects for people with disabilities. In addition, there is a mobile music van with which the orchestra travels to markets, open air festivals or to neighbourhoods in deprived areas in order to seek contact with their audience on their own initiative.

Even if the fine distinction between participatory art projects and community art is not a major concern for practitioners in the field, and the terms have become colloquially ingrained in practice, it is worth briefly recalling here that there is a very significant difference in this approach. Francois Matarasso, an artist, writer and researcher, draws a clear distinction between "participatory art" and "community art": "Participation and community hold different visions of culture, democracy and human rights. At the risk of over-simplification, the first might be seen as a form of cultural democratisation (or giving people access to arts), while the second aspires to cultural democracy." (Matarasso 2019: 45f.)

In the projects described above, which were submitted for the "Junge Ohren Preis", the boundaries between participatory and community art are blurred, although in my opinion the pendulum is currently swinging more in the direction of participatory art, especially with regard to the motivation of the established orchestras and concert halls to initiate these projects in the first place: ultimately, high-culture institutions are increasingly concerned with providing access to *their* art for as many people as possible, providing barrier-free access – *giving people access to the arts*. Practitioners of *Musikvermittlung* are therefore increasingly planning projects for the diverse local inhabitants of a city or region, with the places of realisation as well as the outcome being completely open.

Participatory art requires a new attitude on the part of artists, which David J. Elliott et al. discuss under the term "artistic citizenship" (see Elliott/Silverman/Bowman 2016). The authors emphasise the need for the cultural sector not to pursue art exclusively as an end in itself, but also as a means of enlightenment, social interaction and empowerment of population groups that would otherwise have more difficult access to publicly funded (high) cultural institutions. "Artistic citizenship" in the understanding of Elliott et al. regards artists as members of society who are endowed with special abilities and talents and who can therefore have an integrative and transformative effect. However, this concept is to be understood more broadly, so that it includes all actors in the cultural sector who see art and their own actions as the key to the development of civil society.

This is where the first cornerstone of innovative and transformative concepts of the cultural enterprise as a whole can be found: "We can thus speak of innovation on an institutional level when the concept of a cultural organisation moves away from art and towards being a social enterprise" (Koch 2014: 189). This does not mean that art would be less important, but it points to a shift in perspective. Until recently, the focus of a cultural enterprise was primarily on the artistic programme, the artists themselves and the best possible production of concerts. The beginning of *Musikvermittlung* programmes and formats (from the point of view of the artistic directors) can also be understood from this perspective: children and young people should be given a playful introduction to cultural heritage, so that as adults they will want and be able to participate with pleasure in the conventional programme of a city's concert hall.

The programming itself remained immovable and intact at the centre. In the meantime, however, fundamental shifts have been taking place at many houses: the city is moving closer to the concert hall, and the concert hall in turn closer to the city's districts. The first beacons of this development were Sage Gateshead[8] in Newcastle and L' Auditori[9] in Barcelona. Built at the turn of the millennium, these new concert halls are no longer located in the bourgeois centres of cities but in originally socially disadvantaged districts. In their events and programming, they reflect the super-diverse structure of the population and organically integrate educational opportunities on a broad level into their identity as cultural institutions. The audience, in its variety and diversity, takes on a new meaning when one is referring to the interests and

---

8   Link to the Sage Gateshead webpage: https://sagegateshead.com/ [9.1.2021].
9   Link to the L'Auditori Barcelona webpage: https://www.auditori.cat/en/home [9.1.2021].

preferences of different population groups, as do the considerations of the organising team about how to cooperate with a city's social institutions and to carry out joint projects outside the concert hall. In this sense, both individual artists and institutions are currently setting out to transform concert life as a whole, and to place themselves more firmly at the heart of society than was previously the case: "If the high demands of 'culture for all' are to be realised in the form of real equitable access, and if classical cultural institutions are to be a living part of this social development, they will have to change further." (Brosda 2020: 133)

Musikvermittlung as an Innovative Factor in the Cultural Sector?

"Almost all innovations that are recommended or introduced into the organisational field today come from systems that are now perceived as external. The cultural education programmes, the new musical social forms in the fields of concert pedagogy and *Musikvermittlung* [emphasis added], probably still seem the least alien. The term "educational programmes" indicates that the idea comes from another system, albeit one related to the common ancestor of aesthetic education, that of education." (Koch 2014: 20)

When I look back at the development of *Musikvermittlung*, for me the most significant innovation, apart from the transformation towards the social, is that children have been integrated into the concert scene as an audience. In the meantime, they are a self-evident audience segment just like adults, who, however, have specific expectations of a concert. From early fairy-tale evenings with music at the beginning of the 20th century, artistically demanding and interesting concert formats have been developed and differentiated according to age groups, so that, in terms of quantity, they now account for a third of the total events in Viennese concert halls, and have become an indispensable part of the overall subscription package.

What are known as new concert formats for adults have a much harder time of it, and are still at the stage of invention and not yet of innovation, in the sense that an idea can be permanently established in the concert scene. It is obvious that much of the experimentation taking place in this field, whether at the Montforter Zwischentöne in Feldkirch, at the Podium Festival in Esslingen, at the Radialsystem in Berlin or at King's Place in London, has a lot to do with changes that also began in the sphere of children's concerts more than 30 years ago now: other arts come into play in addition to music, the audience is directly involved, the context of the music being played is dramaturgically integrated into the concert and not dealt with separately in a programme booklet. As in the early days of *Musikvermittlung*, both the term and the field of practice are spreading into several areas: people with expertise in various arts, dramaturgical contextualisation, cultural education, cultural management and cultural policy are called upon to work well together and develop the sector further.

The communicative mediation between different interests, people and artistic fields of practice has long since outgrown the infancy of a service for the cultural sector as such, and in this sense it no longer corresponds in any way to the image in the opening quotation to this article. This is a development that is not always desired, and which therefore brings forces of inertia into play.

Despite the diverse innovations and inventions mentioned above, "retrotopia" often still predominates in the classical concert scene, without a genuine desire for fundamental change:

- Many orchestral musicians would like all the outreach projects to enable children and young people to eventually go to the "real" classical concert – *Musikvermittlung* as a kind of preparatory listening school for the classical orchestral concert.
- Most artistic directors want young adults in the concert hall, who are indeed supposed to lower the age average in the audience but would have to come to terms with the 19th-century formats and put up with everything from the selection in the interval buffet to the uncomfortable cloakroom situation, which normally does not correspond to their attitude to life.
- Important artistic necessities for staged concerts, such as lighting and sound technology, or flexible use of space, are only marginally available in 19th-century architecture, and even if they are, they are difficult to incorporate into normal operations due to long conversion times and high costs.

Consequently, experimental concert formats remain limited to festival activities or to special concert venues that were not originally intended as such, like the Radialsystem in Berlin or the Kampnagl in Hamburg. So what would the vision of a concert hall look like from the point of view of *Musikvermittlung*?

A Contemporary Concert Hall

A city or a region needs a place that is open around the clock, because the population of a city wants to have different times to engage with art and culture: parents with small children in the morning, professionals immediately after office hours, senior citizens in the early evening, people interested in workshops at the weekend, young people late at night. The concert hall would have a coffee house, a bar and an interesting book and music shop, and provide spaces for intercultural choirs and amateur ensembles, as well as for digital developments in the sector. It would have sufficient space for interdisciplinary workshops and open its doors as a concert hall in the morning, at midday and in the evening in order to programme for a diverse and heterogeneous audience. There, everything we describe as *new concert formats* would simply be concert formats that contextualise the works artistically, historically or politically as a matter of course, invite the audience to interact and relate the arts to one another.

It would be a place where people create new ideas – after COVID-19 not only in live space, but also in virtual space. Where we can get into arguments about art, waste time on experiments and show our social colours.

It would be a place where cooperation is lived sustainably – with educational and social institutions as well as with international partners – and where a changing intercultural advisory board would keep an eye on the areas that need to be discovered artistically and that are relevant in the city or the region.

It would be a place where the artistic director and the *Musikvermittlung* manager make programmes together and interact with each other – and where, like an artistic research and development department, new formats and projects emerge and respond to the times – perhaps some of them will actually become innovations in the cultural sector.

Bibliography

Bakhtin, Mikhail (1982): Forms of Time and the Chronotype in the Novel, in: *The Dialogic Imagination*, Austin: University of Texas Press.

Brauneck, Manfred (1974): *Literatur und Öffentlichkeit im ausgehenden 19. Jahrhundert: Studien zur Rezeption des naturalistischen Theaters in Deutschland*, Stuttgart: Metzler.

Brosda, Carsten (2020): *Die Kunst der Demokratie: Die Bedeutung der Kultur für eine offene Gesellschaft*, Hamburg: Hoffmann und Campe.

Deutsches Musikinformationszentrum (2019): *Konzertstatistik*, [online] http://www.miz.org/downloads/statistik/78/78_Veranstaltungen_oeffentlich_fi nanzierter_Orchester.pdf [26.08.2020].

Draxler, Helmut (1994): Arbeit am Kontext: Ein Entwurf über die institutionellen Bedingungen "technischer Unfälle", in: Peter Weibel (ed.): *Kontext Kunst*, Cologne: DuMont Buchverlag, 201–205.

Eco, Umberto (1962): *Opera aperta*, Milano: Casa Ed. Valentino Bompiani.

Eberwein, Anke (1998): *Konzertpädagogik: Konzeptionen von Konzerten für Kinder und Jugendliche* (= Hildesheimer Universitätsschriften, Band 6), Hildesheim: Universität Hildesheim.

Ensemble Modern (2018): CONNECT – Das Publikum als Künstler: 10 Fragen an Philip Venables und Oscar Bianchi, [online] https://www.ensemble-m odern.com/de/mediathek/texte/2017-12-06/connect-das-publikum-als-k uenstler-10-fragen-an-philip-venables-und-oscar-bianchi [16.1.2021].

Elliott, David J./Silverman, Marissa/Bowman, Wayne D. (eds.) (2016): *Artistic Citizenship: Artistry, Social Responsibility, and Ethical Praxis*, New York: Oxford University Press.

Grubmüller, Peter (2017): "Videos, Streaming – wir sollten alle Kanäle nutzen", [online] https://www.nachrichten.at/kultur/Videos-Streaming-wir-sollte n-alle-Kanaele-nutzen;art16,2666020 [11.1.2021].

Haselbach, Dieter/Klein, Armin/Knüsel, Pius/Opitz, Stephan (2012a): *Der Kulturinfarkt. Von Allem zu viel und überall das Gleiche: Eine Polemik über Kulturpolitik, Kulturstaat, Kultursubvention*, München: Knaus.

Haselbach, Dieter/Klein, Armin/Knüsel, Pius/Opitz, Stephan (2012b): Die Hälfte? Warum die Subventionskultur, wie wir sie kennen, ein Ende finden muss, [online] https://www.spiegel.de/spiegel/print/d-84339528.h tml [4.10.2020].

Henschel, Alexander (2020): *Was heißt hier Vermittlung? Kunstvermittlung und ihr umstrittener Begriff*, Wien: Zaglossus e.U.

Koch, Klaus Georg (2014): *Innovation in Kulturorganisationen: Die Entfaltung unternehmerischen Handelns und die Kunst des Überlebens*, Bielefeld: transcript.

Matarasso, François (2019): *A Restless Art: How participation won and why it matters*, London: Calouste Gulbenkian Foundation.

McIntyre, Andrew (2020): Culture in Lockdown PART 3. COVID Audience Mindsets, [online] https://medium.com/@andrewmcintyre_71381/culture-in-lockdown-part-3-COVID-audience-mindsets-865e9c4ab1bd [3.10.2020].

Richter-Ibánez, Christina (2018): Wer sind die Übersetzer? Transkulturell Handelnde im Musikbetrieb, in: Dätsch, Christiane (ed.): *Kulturelle Übersetzer. Kunst und Kulturmanagement im transkulturellen Kontext*, Bielefeld: transcript, 67–79.

Tröndle, Martin (ed.) (2018): *Das Konzert^{II}. Beiträge zum Forschungsfeld der Concert Studies*, Bielefeld: transcript.

Uhde, Folkert/Gögl, Hans-Joachim (n.d.): Über die Zwischentöne, [online] https://www.montforter-zwischentoene.at/ueber-uns [11.1.2021].

Vertovec, Steven (2007): Super-diversity and its implications, in: *Ethnic and Racial Studies* Vol. 30, No. 6 (Taylor & Francis), 1024–1054 [10.4.2021].

Weber, Barbara Balba (2018): *Entfesselte Klassik. Grenzen öffnen mit künstlerischer Musikvermittlung*, Bern: Stämpfli Verlag.

Wimmer, Constanze (2018): Einen Sehnsuchtsort der Wahrnehmung öffnen. Musikvermittlung im Konzertbetrieb, in: transcript, Martin (ed.) (2018): *Das Konzert^{II}. Beiträge zum Forschungsfeld der Concert Studies*, Bielefeld: transcript, 197–214.

Biographical note

Constanze Wimmer is professor for Audience Engagement at the University of Music and Performing Arts in Graz. She studied musicology, journalism and arts management, and holds a PhD in music pedagogy from the University of Music and Performing Arts Vienna. She has worked in the fields of audience engagement, audience development and musical dramaturgy. As a project developer, she collaborates with numerous international orchestras, concert halls and festivals. Since spring 2020 she holds the position of Vice Rector for Academic and International Affairs at the University of Music and Performing Arts in Graz.

The Promotion of Pleasure in Individual Perception
Musikvermittlung as a Key Agenda in Concert Life

Matthias Naske

It happens to many people at some point in their lives: music takes one captive. For every one of us, this beginning is connected with a different moment and with another situation. It is a deeply individual moment, one in which a musical event speaks directly to a person for the first time, so that he or she is moved by it. Whether it is in the early days of childhood, on the lap of a parent or grandparents, the first experience of singing and/or dancing together, in a sacred space or out on the street. Eventually, the day arrives when one experiences a first concert within a framework specially designed for it, within the specific situation of one's attention being drawn to the musical event. Whether, in the process, one understands an inherent structure, message or other quality in the music is an open question. Furthermore, this understanding has boundless multi-layered facets and will accompany someone who is open to it as a secret of deep longing throughout their life.

One element of concerts, and therefore also of the work of a concert organiser, which has long fascinated me is the dimension of precisely how the shared collaboration of many people creates the possibility of a deeply individual perception of an artistic event. Musical pieces or works take a variety of objective forms and structures. The dimension which moves the individual listener is connected to the world of objects and structures, and yet it is utterly individual. A collective accomplishment renders an individual disposition possible, evoking its full impact within the listener.

From the perspective of reception, it is always essentially a matter of perception. That is also the reason why the perception of music is to be understood as an act of communication. *Resonance* is the key concept needed to describe this process.

Let us envision the situation of a concert: the event is characterised by the fact that the people in the audience give their attention to other people on the stage. Visitors to a concert therefore direct their attention towards what is happening on the stage. From there, the musicians transmit information to the audience. The resulting exchange via form and content is nothing other than communication. In a concert, this is sometimes conveyed by words, although often it is non-verbal. Decisive for the communicative process here is the artistic quality, authenticity and immediacy of the composition and the performance, although of equal significance is the attention directed towards the artistic happening by the listeners. A successful concert is a successful communicative process, a direct, unique exchange between people which is at once individual and social. Whether a concert is a success or not is therefore not only decided on the stage.

If we understand this exchange process as being a central element of a concert, then it becomes obvious that all the elements which support the audience in connecting the dialogical process of perception with an open attitude are of immediate and particular value. This is why I understand *Musikvermittlung* as the *promotion of individual pleasure in the perception of music*. Over all the years, actually decades, in which I have been lucky enough to work for ensembles, orchestras and concert halls, I have found confirmation that *Musikvermittlung* should be given a significant role and have central importance in every cultural institution which stages concerts. Based on excellent concert planning, it is a key function for the sustainable stimulation of as many people as possible to take a continuously growing interest in and an openness towards music as an art form.

In the given context, one author from whom I have received many valuable impulses for my work is the philosopher and author Günther Anders (1902-1992), born in Breslau as Günther Siegmund Stern). After studying philosophy under, among others, Ernst Cassirer, Martin Heidegger and Edmund Husserl, Anders earned his doctorate in 1924, under Husserl. One noteworthy aspect of his personal biography is that, from 1929 bis 1937, Günther Anders was married to Hannah Arendt. In the late 1920s, Anders worked on "Philosophische Untersuchungen über musikalische Situationen" ("Philosophical Investigations into Musical Situations"). In this paper, Anders undertakes the attempt to devise a philosophy of music which has as its starting point neither the objective formal language of this art form, nor the subjective dimension of the recipient. Günther Anders views the central communicative event as guided subjectivity and demonstrates, via phenomenological contemplation of the situation, the significance of *Lauschen* (= listening carefully, but also eavesdropping), i.e. attention as guided subjectivity directed towards the musical event (Liessmann 2003: 6ff.). This is precisely the aspect that concerns *Musikvermittlung*. In his journey through 2,000 years of European cultural history, Jürgen Wertheimer refers, within the context of the ideas of John Locke, to studies in the psychology of perception which in the 21st century empirically prove what the English philosopher speculatively concluded in the 17th century: that perceptual patterns guide our sense impressions, i.e. ideas determine what and how we perceive. Reflection about perceptual patterns produces changes even down to the definition of what we accept or dispute as reality (Wertheimer 2020: 295).

One key to ensuring the sustainable success of a cultural institution is to align the artistic offering, i.e. the concert and event planning, with the needs and cultural aspirations of the potentially responsive people. The permeability necessary for this can be measured by whether the people working for the organisation are able to grasp the respective concrete social, cultural-political and socio-political challenges and potential, and to develop the corresponding artistic ideas. A good part of the *craft* of event organisation consists in securing the right ideas through functional structures and initiating their realisation. In view of the heterogeneity of the living conditions and realities which characterise our present-day life, cultural institutions must face up to the respective social constellations which have an impact locally, regionally und supra-regionally, and seek to provide answers in an organisationally functional form. It is obvious that, in doing so, these answers will turn out to be very varied. Nevertheless, those who are open and mentally agile can and should learn from the respective best examples, even those far beyond national borders. An orchestra or a concert house will then bring itself into the life of a society in a sustained and lively manner when it is in a position to offer programmes which correspond artistically and concretely to the variety of cultural dispositions. In designing a programme, it is necessary to challenge the fine interplay between expectation and fulfilment, and also to continuously challenge the stimulation of expectation and the fulfilment of wishes, and to consistently take delight in transforming them afresh into concrete projects. Being open to understanding artistic planning as a dialogical process brings vitality and the chance of sustained success to the organisation.

In this spirit, no less than 600 activities involving *Musikvermittlung* took place at the Wiener Konzerthaus during the last complete season before the Corona crisis, i.e. in the 2018/19 season. Of the approximately 940 events which were held during that season, the majority of the concerts therefore included offerings which catered to the desire to perceive an artistic happening in very different forms, or which were geared to this to a finely differentiated degree.

In an EU-funded participatory project entitled "Orfeo & Majnun", involving various municipal districts of Vienna, the *Musikvermittlung* Team at the Wiener Konzerthaus, led by Katja Frei, succeeded in connecting some 3,000 participants emotionally with given artistic themes. In close cooperation with Basis.Kultur.Wien, the Caritas-supported socio-cultural initiative Brunnenpassage, and numerous local cultural organisations and district initiatives, the parallels and contemporary relevance of the ancient Greek myth of Orpheus and Eurydice and the story of Leila und Majnun, which is widely popular in Arab countries, were given various artistic treatments. In this way there arose over many months the largest participatory project to date in the history of the Wiener Konzerthaus. An important aspect of this project was that its aim was to increase cultural participation through professional stimulation and regular, confidence-building activities outside of the cultural organisation.

Another event format, first introduced by the Wiener Konzerthaus in the same season, bears the title "klangberührt". In this production, conceived as a multipart concert series, the attempt is made to design a social space which makes it possible both for people with a variety of disabilities and for those without disability to have a common experience of music. Moderating the events is Lilian Genn, whose expertise in *Musikvermittlung* enables her to support the musicians and ensembles, changing from concert to concert, with a compact and sensitive response to the specific situation. In this way, the audience experience of artistic excellence is facilitated by making a connection to the musical happening that immediately follows in the programme. With this series of events, the Wiener Konzerthaus opens up towards persons who, in its traditional way of operating, are often excluded from a direct encounter with (live) music. Many of the musicians who declare themselves willing to perform in this format are used to appearing on stages around the world, but are still impressed by the intensity of the communication between the audience and the performers in this special concert series. The visitors, too, whether they experience the event alone or accompanying disabled people, show that they are deeply moved by the authenticity and power of the situational energy. Yet this series of events makes use of only a negligibly small part of the far greater performance space of a concert house.

To constantly explore these performance spaces with an open mind is one of the most valuable attitudes and is thoroughly in keeping with *Musikvermittlung* in the true sense of the word. According to my observations, economic limitations are frequently adduced as an explanation for why one or another idea for expanding or differentiating the repertory season cannot be realised. Yet in the final analysis, it is the quality of vitality in an organisation which is decisive in repeatedly allowing openness, change and further development. Every connection to people who were previously not in the focus of the respective institution expands the horizon and opens up new possibilities and chances.

The immediate experience of a musical work contains within itself, among many codified or even completely concrete narratives, also the element of an artistically condensed present moment. Music brings to life the creative ideas which a composer was able to mould as a child of his or her times. In this way, musical works, of course particularly ones that are radiant with great originality, build bridges and make it possible to undertake intellectual time travel between various epochs. Through the performance of an artistic concept, often one deriving from days long past, a narrative is evoked which is able to transcend times, cultures and identities to resonate within the listener. The multi-faceted nature of this process constitutes a significant part of the fascination which characterizes the concentrated act of listening to music in communication spaces which are ideally suited to it. Due simply to the desire for resonance and the necessity for resonance spaces, direct encounters with music will continue to have special value in people's lives. A value which should be matched by the multifaceted and diverse culture of the respective spaces.

Musikvermittlung, in the true and most essential meaning of the word, should skilfully lend its support to people, and repeatedly give music more space in the lives of as many as possible.

Bibliography

Anders, Günther (2017): *Musikphilosophische Schriften: Texte und Dokumente* (edited by Reinhard Ellensohn), München: C. H. Beck.
Liessmann, Konrad Paul (2003): Die Kunst des Hörens. Über den Umgang mit Musik, in: *Österreichische Musikzeitschrift*, Vol. 58, No. 8-9, 6–12.
Wertheimer, Jürgen (2020): *Europa. Eine Geschichte seiner Kulturen*, München: Penguin Verlag.

Biographical note

Matthias Naske holds the position of the Artistic Director and CEO of the Wiener Konzerthausgesellschaft as well as president of the Wien Modern Festival since 2013. The Wiener Konzerthausgesellschaft, operator of the Wiener Konzerthaus ever since it was first inaugurated in 1913, has always been – and still is today – a private, non-profit association with a self-financing level of 88 % of the total budget. Matthias Naske is a member of the Executive Board of Camerata Salzburg as well as being Vice-President of the Board of Trustees of the Alban Berg Stiftung. Furthermore he is a member of the International Board of Teodor Currentzis's ensemble MusicAeterna, based in St. Petersburg, and chairman of the advisory board of MICA (Music Information Centre Austria).

Musikvermittlung as Everyday Practice
The Cello Quartet *Die Kolophonistinnen*

Sarah Chaker

Artists
Hannah Amann, cello
Marlene Förstel, cello
Elisabeth Herrmann, cello
Theresa Laun, cello

Programme
Andreas Lindenbaum: "Streich für vier Cellistinnen" (2011)

Saverio Mercadante (1795-1870): "La Poesia" (undated)
Wilhelm Fitzenhagen: "Ave Maria" op. 41 (1896)
Georg Goltermann (1824-1898): "Serenade" op. 119 (undated)

Johann Strauß Snr./Leonhard Roczek (arranger): "Radetzky March" op. 228 (1848)
Johann Strauß Jnr./Leonhard Roczek (arranger): "Wiener Blut" op. 354 (1873)

Performative concepts
Die Kolophonistinnen & Axel Petri-Preis

The Quartet's Approach to *Musikvermittlung*

For the Austrian cello quartet Die Kolophonistinnen, which is as young as it is successful, *Musikvermittlung* is not something exceptional, but rather quite natural, an essential part of their everyday professional practice, playing a significant role in determining the planning and design of their programme.[1] The quartet decides its respective programme for an event from case to case, independently and in agreement among themselves, in accordance with the respective framework, i.e. the venue, and with the desired character of the event playing an essential role in the choice of pieces and suitable *Musikvermittlung* concepts. In general, the quartet favours the combination of different, not overly long pieces, since in their experience this is a very good way to help maintain the listeners' excitement. In this respect, according to Förstel, *Musikvermittlung* plays an important role, since it is especially suitable for generating and holding attention in alternative performance concepts. Furthermore, as they themselves admit, the musicians very deliberately attempt to use the conceptualisation of their programme to shape and modulate emotions via the music.

The amount of original music available for four cellos is negligible and generally, due to the unusual instrumentation, tends to be less well known. Besides the attempts by the quartet to unearth and rehearse further original music, arrangements play an important role, when aspects of *Musikvermittlung*, in the sense of presentation practice and performance, very frequently have to be taken into consideration from the outset: "Then there are pieces which we definitely want to play, and these are then arranged by someone, either [it's done by] one of us or, for instance, Leo [Roczek]" (Förstel 2021). In doing so, however, the ensemble at present proceeds, much to their own regret, and as they remark in a quite self-critical way "rather from feeling [...] than from specific training" (ibid.), also because *Musikvermittlung* does not at present play a role in the context of their artistic training at university: "Everything that we know about *Musikvermittlung* comes from outside, has been learned externally or through participating in a course" (ibid.). For that reason, additional access to the field of *Musikvermittlung* as part of artistic-university studies would be "very helpful" (ibid.), on the one hand, because they "are of course also further artistic training" (ibid.), and on the other because it can be foreseen that the field of *Musikvermittlung* will become even more important in future.

---

1   The information in this article derives, on the one hand, from details provided by the musicians during our lecture series in December 2019, on the other hand it is based – and this concerns above all the original quotations in this article – on an interview which Sarah Chaker conducted with Marlene Förstel on August 16th 2021.

In response to the question of how it has come about that *Musikvermittlung* plays such an important role in the work of the quartet, even though the research, conceptualisation etc. that is involved demands considerably more effort and expense in comparison with traditional performance contexts, the musicians affirm that they "just didn't know anything else. We began [with this kind of performance practice] at the age of 14; at that time we had hardly any concert experience at all" (ibid.). The BePhilharmonic Strauß Music Contest of the Vienna Philharmonic Orchestra, which was the quartet's first large-scale competition, in which they achieved great success with a Strauss arrangement by Leonhard Roczek, proved in retrospect to be indicative of the ensemble's future direction as far as their programme is concerned: since then, formats related to *Musikvermittlung* have constituted a standard component of their performance culture. Among cello quartets, the Kolophonistinnen have thereby successfully established a stand-out feature for themselves in their live performances, and the reactions to this by their colleagues are described in thoroughly positive terms: "Most of them encourage us and like what we do. They also find our built-in gags funny. However, if people don't know us yet or haven't been to one of our concerts, it can be that they underestimate us because of the unusual line-up or the wide-ranging selection of pieces. They are definitely very difficult pieces, technically." (ibid.) *Musikvermittlung* and the alternative performance concepts associated with it, which could possibly disturb the "church service" (see Schulze 2009: 46ff.), therefore still seem to pose a certain risk especially for female musicians, insofar as they are all too quickly suspected of wanting to use performance elements to compensate for a lack of quality.

One particular reason why *Musikvermittlung* also seems to be of great importance to the Kolophonistinnen is because it makes a special kind of collaboration and concert performance possible, one which the quartet experiences as particularly fulfilling – especially in direct comparison with the more traditional settings, which the musicians are also musically involved with individually. In general, *Musikvermittlung* ensures "a better understanding on all levels" (Förstel 2021) – on the level of the artists during the development and appropriation of the piece, as well as on the level of the listeners, who in their turn, through the performance, can experience and understand the quartet's approach to the piece and the process of appropriation that it has undergone. It is through *Musikvermittlung* that a certain piece first really becomes "one's own", or "one of ours" (ibid.). Through an open and playful approach to a work, through working on and developing suitable performances together, one can furthermore "put much more of one[self] into it" (ibid.). In this way, one also gets to know a piece "completely differently" (ibid.).

The audience also plays an important role in the quartet's considerations, as Marlene Förstel points out: generally, in music, it is always a matter of wanting to pass something on. However, to do that, one first has to practically "mediate it for oneself" (ibid.). In the process of doing so, one thinks about it and considers how the reproduction of a piece of music could best be achieved, although with regard to the listeners, one "always [has] something a bit freer and more modern in mind, moving away from this 'just sit up straight, and one has to pay attention and be quiet', und so on. I just find it so much more pleasant, when there's a bit of freedom in the audience" (ibid.). The fact that the audience's reactions are not clearly predictable and that they react differently to what is performed each time means that the performances remain exciting for the musicians, although the ensemble format obviously favours experimentation with new performance practices: "With four of us, each one is brave enough, because we have one another." (ibid.)

Concepts Presented during the Lecture Series

For our lecture series, the Kolophonistinnen, together with Axel Petri-Preis, elaborated a multifaceted programme in the run-up to the event, which was organised in such a way as to show the audience which was present a variety of approaches to and possibilities of *Musikvermittlung* in direct comparison.

The programme began with Andreas Lindenbaum's "STREICH für vier Cellistinnen", dating from 2011, which is as short as it is physically performative, and sonically interesting with regard to the use of the instruments. It has since become part of the quartet's standard repertoire – a recording of the piece from the Schubert Hall of the Wiener Konzerthaus, as part of the Musica Juventutis programme, can be listened to and viewed under the following QR-code below.

Listening and watching are firmly intertwined in this piece. The kind of performative execution and presentation required is exactly stipulated by the composer in the form of directorial-like instructions, which are inscribed in the composition – so that it constitutes a *Musikvermittlung* composition *per se*. However, this leaves the musicians comparatively little interpretative leeway as performers, even if the interplay has to be tested and rehearsed in a completely new way. It is exciting for the audience to follow the purposeful staging of interaction, as the bodies of the musicians, using their cellos und cello bows like tools, are brought into harmony and counter-harmony with the sound. Within the framework of the lecture series, the concert hall was, at the suggestion of Axel Petri-Preis, additionally bathed in blue light, in order to further emphasise the machine-like nature of the performance.

According to Marlene Förstel, experience has shown that listeners and spectators react to this piece in very different ways, although in the meantime it has become a fixture in the Kolophonistinnen's programme, and especially in children's concerts – "because the children find it funny. I always found it a very exciting piece, but I would never have had the idea that it was funny" (Förstel 2021). Many adults, however, approach Lindenbaum's composition in a rather intellectual manner: "everyone in the audience is very concentrated during this piece because they want to understand it" (ibid.). So even though an open approach to music and an appetite for and pleasure in the alternative use of musical instruments seems to have been unlearned in the course of socialisation, Lindenbaum's piece is suitable for focusing the concentration and attention of all present – and thus it has a good chance of succeeding (regarding attention as a kind of glue "that holds the concert event and the audience together", see Tröndle 2009: 26f.).

As part of the lecture series, the quartet played the compositions by Mercadante, Fitzenhagen and Goltermann with different light settings and spatial positioning. For Fitzenhagen's "Ave Maria", the musicians were spread out in the four corners of the hall, which was bathed in complete darkness for this piece. Further, the audience was asked to put on sleeping masks, which had already been placed on the chairs for the purpose. By deliberately blanking out everything visual, undivided attention was given to what could be heard and felt, thus also providing a contrast to the Lindenbaum piece performed at the beginning of the programme. For the musicians, the darkness, and the fact of being positioned at a distance to one another in the room, created the special challenge of finding a way to play together by concentrating on each other as much as possible, even though they were virtually "blind". During Goltermann's "Serenade", the musicians then began singing and slowly moving towards each other with their instruments, until they finally came together again in the front third of the hall.

Fig. 1: Die Kolophonistinnen performing at the lecture series at the mdw, December 2019

Source: private

Finally, the Kolophonistinnen performed two arrangements of the famous pieces "Radetzky March" (Johann Strauss the Elder) and "Wiener Blut" ["Viennese Blood"] (Johann Strauss the Younger), which Leonhard Roczek was specially commissioned by the Kolophonistinnen to create for the ensemble's instrumentation. According to Förstel, Roczek, himself a cellist, paid particular attention to giving the four cellos equal opportunities to play, so that "each cello part becomes the centre of focus at some point in the piece" (Förstel 2021). The interventions in the originals vary in intensity – the "Radetzky March", for example, begins in a minor instead of a major key, which gives the mood of the piece a completely different colouring. Moreover, the arrangements contain frequent references to films or film music and so to popular culture: "Star Wars", for instance, is quoted in the "Radetzky March", and Roczek integrated a middle section into the arrangement of "Wiener Blut" which, although it is not a direct quotation, is strongly reminiscent of film music in its compositional structure. Furthermore, the arrangements contain theatrical and choreographic elements, for example when dialogues between the musicians are developed and integrated into the piece, or when, as in "Wiener Blut", a scene with a dispute and thus an interaction is set in motion by one of the cellists hitting another on her instrument with her bow, which is accompanied in the composer's instructions by "look angry".

As their performance during our lecture series demonstrated, the Kolophonistinnen have practically no fear at all of engaging with new and unusual performance concepts and contexts. Not to be underestimated is the shared courage and strength which the young female musicians summon up each day in order to once again swim against the tide in the field of classical music, with its handed-down performance practices and mostly rather traditional understanding of roles and gender concepts. Perhaps, due to their alternative and playful approaches to music, they have to experience and process not only approval but also rejection, nevertheless remaining curious and creative. The innovative potential of *Musikvermittlung* can only unfold with and through such female musicians, which is why appropriate support and promotion of it must be more firmly anchored at the institutional level during the years of (higher) music education and also later on in professional life.

Bibliography

Förstel, Marlene (2021): Qualitative interview [via Zoom] concerning *Die Kolophonistinnen and Musikvermittlung*, conducted by Sarah Chaker. Vienna: 16.8.2021.

Schulze, Gerhard (2009): "Die Erfindung des Musik Hörens". In: Tröndle, Martin (ed.): *Das Konzert. Neue Aufführungskonzepte für eine klassische Form*. Bielefeld: transcript, 45–52.

Tröndle, Martin (2009): "Von der Ausführungs- zur Aufführungskultur". In: Tröndle, Martin (ed.): *Das Konzert. Neue Aufführungskonzepte für eine klassische Form*. Bielefeld: transcript, 21–41.

QR-code: Die Kolophonistinnen, performing Andreas Lindenbaum's "STREICH für vier Cellistinnen" at the Wiener Konzerthaus in 2019; source: YouTube [online: https://www.youtube.com/watch?v=qjr4c_LzJGA].

Biographical notes

The cello quartet **Die Kolophonistinnen** was founded in 2014. The quartet was able to celebrate its first great successes in the competitions Prima la Musica and at the BePhilharmonic Strauss Music Contest of the Vienna Philharmonic. As prize winners, they were able to perform at the dress rehearsal of the 2016 Summer Night Concert and in the film shown worldwide during the intermission of the 2017 New Year's Concert of the Vienna Philharmonic, which is broadcast worldwide. Within the framework of the Musica Juventutis competition, the quartet were awarded a performance at the Wiener Konzerthaus in November 2018. Since autumn 2018, they have been members of the Live-Music-Now Yehudi Menuhin Organisation. The Kolophonistinnen performed outside of Europe for the first time in January 2019, when they embarked on a two-week tour of Chile. In February 2019, they won 2nd prize at the Fanny Mendelssohn Förderpeis [Sponsorship Prize] in Hamburg. The following year, the quartet released their debut CD "Heldinnenleben" (Gramola). The Kolophonistinnen have given concerts in the Glass Hall of the Musikverein Wien, the Schubert Hall of the Wiener Konzerthaus and the Stefanien Hall of the Musikverein Graz. More information is available on their website: http://www.diekolophonistinnen.at/.

Hannah Amann (born in 2001 in Vienna) is currently studying with Stefan Kropfitsch at the mdw – University of Music and Performing Arts Vienna. She has performed both as a soloist and as a chamber musician at the Wiener Konzerthaus, the Musikverein Klagenfurt and the Palace of Justice in Vienna. Within the framework of the summer academy in Radolfzell, she received a sponsorship award from Gustav Rivinius. In spring 2021, she won 1st prize at the international competition Musica Goritiensis in Gorizia, Italy.

Marlene Förstel (born in 2000 in Lower Austria) is currently studying with Reinhard Latzko at the mdw – University of Music and Performing Arts Vienna. She has won several prizes in the Austrian Prima la musica competition. In April 2018 she won her category in the international Svirel competition in Slovenia. Her solo performances include appearances at the Festspielhaus St. Pölten (2016), at the Palace of Justice in Vienna with the Franz-Schmidt-Kammerorchester (2018) and in Slovenia with the Slovene-Philharmonic-Chamber Orchestra (2019).

Elisabeth Herrmann (born in 2001 in Vienna) is currently studying with Stefan Kropfitsch at the mdw – University of Music and Performing Arts Vienna. She plays as both a soloist and a chamber musician in chamber music ensembles at Vienna's concert houses, including the MuTh, the Wiener Konzerthaus (Musica Juventutis prizewinner 2019) and the Musikverein Wien. In addition to her studies in Vienna, she is a pupil of Sol Gabetta in a master class at the Musikakademie Basel.

Theresa Laun (born in 2001 in Vienna) is currently studying with Reinhard Latzko at the mdw – University of Music and Performing Arts Vienna. Active as both a soloist and a chamber musician, she has performed at the Palace of Justice in Vienna with Franz-Schmidt-Kammerorchester, at the Mozart House, at the Wiener Konzerthaus, at the Biennale Horn and elsewhere. She is a prizewinner of the Musica Juventutis competition, and as such will make her debut in a performance at the Schubert Saal of the Wiener Konzerthaus in spring 2022.

Practical Intelligence and the Limitations of Practitioners
Multiple Forms of Knowledge, and Their Significance in Music and *Musikvermittlung*

Tasos Zembylas

In this chapter I argue that knowledge in the broadest sense of the word is not only pivotal for any practice, but it is also the motor for innovation. Traditionally, academic scholars tend to overvalue the role of theory, as if theory could lead to practice. The concept of knowledge that I will present here goes far beyond academic epistemes. Knowledge in my understanding – in alignment with John Dewey (1916; Dewey/Bentley 1949), Gilbert Ryle (1949), Ludwig Wittgenstein ([1953] 1999) and Michael Polanyi (1958, 1966) – is constitutively interwoven with practices. Theoretical analyses of knowledge can be insightful, but they cannot shape or replace the practice as such. In order to become a good practitioner in *Musikvermittlung*, one does not have to read this research, yet reading it may support critical reflection on practice. Since the practice of *Musikvermittlung* consists of doings and sayings, the capacity for critical reflection is an inherent part of the professional practice.

As other contributors to this anthology highlight, there is a great variety of formats and situations[1] where *Musikvermittlung* activities take place (see also Allwardt 2012: 3f.). In the following analysis, however, I refer primarily to formats of *Musikvermittlung* that have been established in concert halls and festivals of classical and contemporary art music[2] which address adult audi-

---

1   Alternative formats have emerged in the last few decades, after an explicit critique of the traditional practice of *Musikvermittlung*, which was accused of mediating a narrow and normative concept of music and disseminating certain social biases against the musical cultures of lower social classes and marginalised groups ("sub-cultures").
2   "Art music" is aligned with a normative assumption about the aesthetic value of certain music and implies a devaluation of other musical practices that are not included within

ences. By focusing on this particular format, it is easier to relate the practice of *Musikvermittlung* to the main subject of my contribution, which is the role of multiple forms of knowledge in this practical field.

Formats of *Musikvermittlung* that contemporary audiences experience in many concert halls and festivals emerged from a particular historical tradition. In Europe, the performance of sacred music, and later of art music, was developed in such a way that it mainly cultivated spectatorship and listenership rather than active audience involvement, such as joining in by singing, clapping as rhythmic accompaniment, dancing, and spontaneous public responses to the music – although exceptions were permissible, for example in dance halls, or during particular ceremonies and celebrations in which the attendees were not always sitting in a contemplative modus. Furthermore, audiences generally experience art music produced by professionals, which is planned and managed by organisations such as concert halls, opera houses and festivals that sell tickets, thereby establishing an economic relationship between music, musicians and consumers.

Musikvermittlung professionals work with certain resources and in given settings; they are therefore affected by various formal and informal constraints according to the particular working conditions. Within this context, *Musikvermittlung* can best be understood as an attempt to promote cognitive access and enhance aesthetic experiences, often by providing audiences with cultural knowledge and facilitating musical listening.[3] Yet in almost all its manifestations it does not have any 'revolutionary' aspirations to transform the dominant practice of listenership (i.e. sitting in a silent and contemplative modus) within the realm of classical and contemporary art music and its institutions.[4]

---

this concept. Without ignoring the social and political critique of this conception, I have nevertheless used it because it is generally understood to refer to a certain musical genre. Yet the concept has a relatively open meaning, since its boundaries to other musical genres are in certain contexts permeable.

3   On a practical level, the goals of *Musikvermittlung* are diverse (Wimmer 2010: 91–93, 110) and reflect the heterogeneity of its addressees, and the various organisational directives and the demands of stakeholders.

4   There exists a rich critical discourse on the format, conventions and rituals of classical concerts – e.g. Martin Tröndle (2018).

Why *Musikvermittlung*?

Classical formats of *Musikvermittlung* presuppose that music is not an artistic practice or a cultural good that audiences can take for granted. Music in its vast phenomenological variety of practices and formal developments includes very different musical languages – in the terminology of Ernst Cassirer ([1923] 1955) different "symbolic forms" – that appear in very diverse social and cultural situations. Accordingly, the basic justification of *Musikvermittlung* is that music needs mediation[5]: firstly, because it is already mediated by different materials, systems of meaning, technologies, discourses and cultural practices; and secondly, because it demands certain basic competences for practicing certain activities, for example listening, singing, dancing, playing and creating music, coding and decoding, understanding, appreciating, talking about music and so on. From this point of view, the fundamental questions of *Musikvermittlung* revolve around its objectives, and the identification of methods and competences that enable people – those who are not involved in the creation and realisation of an artistic work[6] – to gain rich and meaningful aesthetic experiences and occasionally new aesthetic insights. The adjective "new" assumes an indeterminate corpus of previous understandings, presuppositions and cultural beliefs that lead people to remain attached to certain images or ideas about music and particularly about art music (Wittgenstein [1953] 1999: § 109, 115, 309). Such images are, for example:

---

5   In Georg Wilhelm Friedrich Hegel's "Phenomenology of Spirit" ([1807] 2018) the concept of mediation refers to the transmission of Spirit in its different historical stages through manifold artistic forms. Any manifestation of the Spirit needs a medium and therefore mediation is a priori. Two hundred years later, one need not be a Hegelian to establish a relation between medium, form, meaning and understanding – see Niklas Luhmann ([1995] 2000), and for explicit reference to music see Wilfried Gruhn (2005).
6   Roland Barthes ([1967] 1977) proclaimed the "death of the author", which also seeks "to restore the place of the reader" (Barthes [1967] 1977: 143). This specific argument denies the relevance of authorial intentions and consequently ascribes to the audience an active role in constituting meaning. Since reading or listening to music is not a merely physiological but a profoundly cultural activity, I would like to underline that becoming a reader or a listener demands cultural education, i.e. extended knowledge and practical experience. People are usually familiar only with limited kinds of music and only after experiencing unfamiliar music practices do they become aware of what it takes to become a competent listener.

- a somewhat static, work-centred perspective associated with certain dogmatic beliefs, e.g. faithfulness to the work of art, its original meaning, artistic essence or truth;
- a pre-social, and philosophically-speaking an idealistic idea, about the special status of art based on weighty metaphysical assumptions, e.g. the idea of genius, of autonomous, self-sufficient works of art, or of timeless masterpieces;
- a deep-seated conviction about the superiority of one's own culture, and more specifically about the European art music tradition.

If *Musikvermittlung* is to be enhancing and inspiring for us, its addressees, it should encourage us to change ourselves by expanding our cognitive and experimental capabilities and, as a result, intensify our aesthetic experience and reflection. This transformative process makes, according to Dewey ([1934] 1939: 35–57), the difference between a full experience and a mere impression. While a mere impression is rather superficial, a full experience is associated with learning which gives meaning to experience. Aisthesis, that is to say sensations and emotions, are central components of experience: "The esthetic", Dewey ([1934] 1939: 48) writes, "is no intruder in experience from without [...but rather] the clarified and intensified development of traits that belong to every normally complete experience." Thus *Musikvermittlung* that deals with aesthetic experience goes beyond learning *about* music. It addresses our understandings, tastes, identities, and emotional capabilities. Perhaps some practitioners in the field of *Musikvermittlung* believe that this assertion is exaggerated. Maybe – but I would nevertheless like to argue that placing such high expectations on *Musikvermittlung* can set a creative challenge to overcome established professional routines and invent new practical approaches for its audiences.

Music and *Musikvermittlung* as Socially Organised Related Practices

As mentioned above, aesthetic experiences are not unmediated and self-evident. The same holds true for artistic practices and artworks. These are always all mediated in multiple ways – materially, practically, immaterially, symbolically, culturally, socially, historically, etc. (Born 2005: 7f.; Cook 2013). Antoine Hennion elaborated this thesis as follows: "[T]aste, pleasure and meaning are contingent, conjunctural, and hence transient; and they result from specific yet varying combinations of particular intermediaries, considered not as the neutral channels through which predetermined social relations operate, but as productive entities that have effectivities of their own." (Hennion 2003: 84) This perspective can also be widened in an anthropological sense: individuals who are creating or experiencing an artwork (in the broadest sense of this term, including a wide range of cultural goods) are always embedded in particular situations, moods and forms of life (DeNora 2000: 40ff.; for a more general account of situatedness, see Schatzki et al. 2001). Therefore creating art, presenting art, perceiving art with all your senses, communicating art, reflecting, discussing with others and evaluating are activities built on knowledge and practical experiences – which is generally called enculturation. These requirements, however, are barely perceptible. Wittgenstein reflects on this when he asks:

> "[H]ow can it be explained what 'expressive playing' is? Certainly not by anything that accompanies the playing. – What is needed for the explanation? One might say: a culture. – If someone is brought up in a particular culture – and then reacts to music in such-and-such a way, you can teach him the use of the phrase 'expressive playing'." (Wittgenstein 1970: §164, see also §157–172)

To understand what expressive playing means requires a kind of knowledge or, with reference to musicians, a practical artistic skill that entails collectively shared criteria (Wittgenstein, [1953] 1999: §150, 182, 238, 269; Becker 1982: 40–67; Crispin/Östersjö 2017: 288–305). The knowing person must be embedded in and participate in a social world in order to appreciate different contexts of sense-giving and valuation, and to carry out practices himself or herself in a certain way (e.g. playing music expressively). Theoretical knowledge, as well as practical knowing in music – or to use Ryle's (1949: 27ff.) terminology, to "know that" and to "know how" – therefore presuppose a community of cultural practice that cultivates a certain musical tradition. All the various forms of knowledge are constitutively interwoven with practices, specifically with doings and sayings (Wittgenstein, [1953] 1999: §6, §19; Taylor 1995: 7). Yet the production and reproduction of a musical practice are largely discreet, because the where, how and when (i.e. the place, the medium and the time) through which we acquire knowledge and abilities can barely be fully identified. The history of practice is thus a tacit history, in the sense that practice has many aspects that lie beyond the reach of individual awareness, and also beyond what can be verbally articulated. Wittgenstein regards this practical background, constituting human agency and intelligibility, as a non-analysable whole. It was Pierre Bourdieu's great achievement to elaborate the concept of habitus[7] in order to make the practical background of human agency accessible for sociological analysis.

In the same way as music, *Musikvermittlung* is a socially organised practice and most *Musikvermittlung* activities take place in specific organisational environments and are pre-structured by higher-chain cultural-managerial decisions (e.g. the music programme; the duration of a *Musikvermittlung* unit; the spatial and material conditions in which an event takes place; the number and selection of participants). What *Musikvermittlung* conveys (for example, the creative process of a musical work, the context of its creation, the aesthetic form and the formal relations of its elements, the art of presentation or performance practice of a work, as well as the sensual perception, reflection and evaluation of musical achievements) has – epistemologically speaking – a "tacit dimension", to borrow a term from Polanyi (1966). This "silent" dimension of musical knowledge often escapes our awareness, and it seems reasonable to assert that practitioners of *Musikvermittlung* "know more than [they] can tell" (Polanyi 1966: 4). In fact, communication about music "displays a knowledge that we cannot tell" (Polanyi 1966: 5).[8]

This brings me to the difference between "knowledge" and "knowing", and their dynamic relationships in music in general, as well as in *Musikvermittlung* in particular.

---

7   The critique of Bourdieu's concept of habitus for its deterministic traits is controversial, but not completely unwarranted. In early publications (e.g. Bourdieu [1972] 1977) Bourdieu introduces habitus as an explanatory concept to refer to regularities and the reproduction of social order. In later works he interprets this concept slightly differently:"The habitus goes hand in glove with vagueness and indeterminacy. As a generative spontaneity which asserts itself with an improvised confrontation with ever renewed situations, it obeys a practical inexact, fuzzy sort of logic, which defines one's normal relation to the world." (Bourdieu [1987] 1990: 77–78, cited after Bouveresse 1999: 62.)

8   Although Bourdieu does not refer to Polanyi, he arrives at a similar conclusion when he writes: "It is because subjects do not, strictly speaking, know what they are doing that what they do has more meaning than they know." (Bourdieu [1972] 1977: 79)

Knowledge and Knowing

The term "knowledge" (or again in Ryle's words to "know that") is traditionally understood as a justified true belief, and that is why this meaning has been linked to the concept of scientific knowledge. In contrast, "knowing" (or in Ryle's terminology to "know how") signifies "something we do", as Dewey (1916: 331) puts it. It has no content that can be distinguished from action. Therefore knowing is always implicit in action (Ryle 1949: 57, Schön 1983: 56, for an overview see Neuweg 2004). However, both "knowledge" and "knowing" are theoretically complex, since they are closely associated and discussed with other concepts, e.g. the mind, experience, body, language, institutions, norms, power, ideology, paradigms, styles of thinking, communities of practice, etc. This means that using the terms "knowledge" and "knowing" – as here in the context of *Musikvermittlung* and musical practice – should incorporate these numerous facets.

In everyday life, knowledge is made manifest by being able to verbalise what one knows, make certain justified assertions, claim that an utterance is true (Wittgenstein, [1953] 1999: §78). An assertion and a claim to truth can be criticised as true or false, as right or incorrect, and as warranted by facts or unwarranted. Knowing, however, can only be demonstrated when you perform something well, when you are better or more adept at dealing with certain tasks and problems than others. True and false are not appropriate evaluative categories for knowing; therefore other criteria of practical success or failure have to be used. It should be noted that theories of truth, as well as regimes of competence and further associated criteria of success, are volatile and socially contestable (Selinger/Crease 2006). What I want to emphasise here is that knowledge and knowing are fundamentally different. Accumulated knowledge leads to connoisseurship and scholarship. Accumulated knowing leads to mastery in the sense of "skilled action, [and] ability in execution" (Dewey [1934] 1939: 47). These considerations mark the distinction between an epistemology of propositional knowledge and the epistemics of practical knowing. In both cases the nature of claims, demonstrations, justifications and evaluations differ significantly.

Musikvermittlung as a cultural practice implicates both knowledge and knowing. Since *Musikvermittlung* presupposes connoisseurship – but not necessarily scholarship – it involves propositional knowledge (first and foremost broad historical and musicological knowledge), but also knowledge about the performing musicians. *Musikvermittlung* also requires practical knowing on several levels. At least some practical understanding of musical creation and musical performance are necessary to convey understanding and stimulate aesthetic experiences. Moreover, some practical insights are needed, such as to how to address, motivate, integrate, and stimulate different participating social groups in *Musikvermittlung* activities. *Musikvermittlung* can therefore be performed well or not, that is to say its practice can be improved up to a level of proficiency and mastery. Furthermore, since *Musikvermittlung* stimulates feelings and imagination, and supports interaction and dialogue with participants, it has an ethical dimension (Bowman 2016). Consequently, professional competence and mastery should not be understood merely in a 'technical' sense, but should also encompass the concept of practical wisdom (phronesis), i.e. a genuine interest in the well-being of people.

Multiple forms of knowledge and knowing in musical professions

As argued above, all kinds of musical practices, as well as the practices of *Musikvermittlung*, require knowledge and knowing (see also Rink et al. 2017; Cook 2018). I will now elaborate on this, exploring concrete examples and multiple forms of knowledge and knowing in various musical professions.

Musical practices are anchored in shared cultural traditions, collective experiences, habitualised ways of thinking and evaluative patterns. This does not mean, however, that this anchoring has a determining effect in the strictest sense. Indeed, the actions of a musician are formed in the respective specific situation (Joas 1996: 160f.). In the action process, there is a dynamic interplay between already acquired knowledge and a situational knowing *in actu*. I therefore use two different epistemic concepts that are both relevant to musical professions: forms of artistic practical knowing and forms of propositional knowledge.[9]

Both artistic practical forms of knowing and propositional forms of knowledge can be further differentiated. With reference to artistic practical forms of knowing there are three distinct forms:

---

9   These basic concepts emerged from two empirical research projects that were published a few years ago – see Zembylas/Niederauer (2018); Zembylas (2014); Zembylas/Dürr (2009).

- Knowing the working process
- Situative knowing
- Body knowing

Knowing the working process

Experienced artists usually heed those aspects that are conductive or detrimental to their own productivity. This practical knowing and awareness of the conditions and peculiarities of creative work processes is personal, meaning that in contrast to theoretical knowledge, it is not easily transferable but rather bound to the person who has had the relevant experiences (Polanyi 1958; see also the concept of intransitive understanding in Wittgenstein [1969] 1980, part III, § 37, 77ff. and Johannessen 1994: 240ff.). A further kind of knowing the working process, which is cumulatively generated on the basis of experience, is the technical-practical knowing of how to handle musical instruments and equipment, how to grasp their maximum performance spectrum, their "affordances"[10] and how to use them judiciously in specific cases to achieve certain results. This knowing is not merely theoretical and propositional – even if some technical instructions exist. Trying out, experimenting and playing around are prototypical ways of generating technical-practical knowing. Hence, knowing the working process ultimately leads to familiarity with several working steps and tasks, and bestows a subjective certainty with regard to creative challenges. Familiarity and subjective certainty in the working process are not primarily conceived here as psychological concepts, but arise from the tacit dimension of all knowledge and knowing (Polanyi 1966: 195f.; Collins 2010: 6).

Situative knowing

Acts of perception that appear to be meaningful lead to situative experience *in actu*. The sensual feeling of the instrument while playing, as a result of tac-

---

10   James J. Gibson (1979) introduced the term "affordance" to refer to the situational action-stimulating effect of objects. He thus pleaded for an activist interpretation of the relationship between people and objects. James G. Greeno (1994: 338) links "affordance" with "abilities" and points out that affordance is not something given, but rather arises interactively and is shaped by the abilities of those acting. Furthermore, when dealing with an object, not only is already existing knowledge used, but new knowledge can also emerge.

tile, proprioceptive and kinesthetic perception, as well as the hearing of its sounds, are meaningful and action-guiding events (Leman/Maes 2014: 83f.). The meaning of perception is integrated into the action, which is why Donald Schön (1983) spoke of "knowing-in-action". However, the significance of sensual-situational perception does not negate the relevance of reflexive, discursive and intellectual components in composing or playing music. Perceptual judgements are only possible on the basis of a certain practical, cultural and epistemic background – think of the Wittgenstein quotation above. Musicians often say, with reference to their perceptual impression and perceptual judgement, e.g. when a sequence of music sounds sad, or humorous or wrong, that "you hear it" or "you feel it". Interestingly, they often refer to a generalised subject – "one hears it" – and avoid the first person "I". If we confront musicians with this observation, they refer to the immediacy of the judgement (Zembylas/Niederauer 2018: 91f.; Zembylas/Dürr 2009: 68, 97f., 108f.). Their perception and judgement formation are intuitive, sentient and not primarily analytic-reflexive. Allan Janik correctly argues that this immediacy results from practical experience: "Learning to see is thus learning to judge 'at a glance' that this complex before me is a significant unity, a Gestalt. This is a matter of judgement [...]. 'Seeing' in such situations is anything but a matter of perceiving discrete sense data, collecting them and then synthesising them." (Janik 1994: 41f.). According to Polanyi (1966: 44), it is essentially an act of tacit integration of discreet particulars leading to a focal whole.

Body knowing

The body is an organism able to generate knowing. It is a synaesthetic and an action-oriented entity. It creates basic ideas of space and time and provides existential certainty (see also the concept of somaesthetics, Shusterman 2000: 137ff.; Shusterman 2008). Furthermore, the human body – certainly also the bodies of many other animals – can be trained to cope with complex tasks. This multi-functionality is often understood as "embodied intelligence" (see Lakoff/Johnson 1999; Shapiro 2014). The attribute "intelligent" is justified, because the body, despite all the training and drilling, can do more than just reproduce what it has practised; under certain conditions the body can be creative. For this, artists have to adjust their body to a certain mood. These are subtle adjustments: the body tension achieved when one works standing; the body relaxation when lying down comfortably; stimulation through the enjoyment of chocolate, coffee or a glass of wine, etc. The body is prepared, so to speak, to act as a catalyst for ideas.

The corporeal response to perceptions and situations – such as goose bumps, palpitations or smiles – contains evaluations and judgements. In this sense, such resonances can be interpreted as physically-intelligible responses to the environment, i.e. to situations, objects and persons. Furthermore, the body generates knowing because it is constantly learning. Pianists, for example, speak of the knowledge of their fingers when they sit at the piano and their fingers tell them whether a sequence of notes feels good or whether a certain passage is playable (Sudnow 2001: 71f., 79). In no art form – not even in literary writing – is the body mute or absent. A bodiless aesthetic experience is a contradiction in terms.

With reference to propositional forms of knowledge, I also distinguish between three distinct forms:

- Scholarly knowledge
- Local knowledge
- Formal, technical knowledge.

Scholarly knowledge

The term scholarly knowledge refers to the theoretical, concept-based and scientific production of knowledge. The majority of musicians in the field of European art music have a profound knowledge of the historical and contemporary repertoire of their music culture; they are well-informed about music-related discourses, and deal with a wide range of texts from different fields such as music analysis, music theory, aesthetics, psychology of perception, etc. Their explicit knowledge is not only theoretical and formal, but often also practically relevant in several respects. For many musicians, non-musical works, including scholarly texts, are inspiring, i.e. they trigger thoughts and ideas, which flow into their creative work. Thus, scholarly knowledge, among others, provides a semantic framework through which, for example, structural relationships between individual tones acquire a certain meaning, or musical quotations and stylistic elements are associated with certain aesthetics. Nevertheless, scholarly knowledge is not genuinely practical because it is not an immediate condition for artistic agency (Duguid 2005: 114).

Local knowledge

Under the category of local knowledge – also called context knowledge – I subsume knowledge of the local music business, music agencies, music publishers and funding organisations, the activities of other colleagues, of festivals and so on. Such knowledge also influences practical and creative action. Local knowledge is explicit, but differs from systematic scholarly knowledge because it primarily arises in everyday life rather than academic scholarly contexts. Practitioners do not judge its validity and relevance on the basis of the categories true/false, but mostly on the basis of their own involvement, interests and collectively established regimes of competence (Wenger [1998] 2002: 136f.). Local knowledge accompanies the everyday life of the artists, shapes their identity and consolidates their membership in a professional community of practice (Szivos 2014).

Formal, technical knowledge

Formal, technical knowledge refers to knowledge about the formal characteristics and functioning of instruments, devices, software etc. This knowledge is largely propositional, since there are relevant descriptions and instructions about it. Yet this formal knowledge alone does not ensure technical practical competence. Nevertheless, formal technical knowledge is important, for example, when composing, in order to be able to use the sound and technical potential of the instruments in a differentiated way, to consider the perspective of the performing musicians when writing, to integrate room acoustic elements or to communicate with other specialists, such as sound engineers.

A Holistic Understanding of Knowledge and Knowing

I am advocating a holistic understanding of the multiple forms of knowledge and knowing. All the various forms mentioned above should always be considered in their synergy and interdependence. Within some activities, certain forms of knowledge and knowing seem to dominate (see Polanyi's remarks on focal and subsidiary awareness, Polanyi 1958: 57–59). Despite this dominance, however, other forms are not eliminated but are always co-present. We should therefore understand the various forms of knowledge and knowing not as opposing but as complementary components that constitute artistic or aesthetic agency.

It seems important to emphasise the synergy of the various forms of knowledge and knowing. From an anthropological perspective, humans are, in addition to their practical anchoring in the world, deeply shaped by symbolic forms that human cultures have created and that are continuously used. Thus human understanding (e.g. of music) is their way of being in and making sense of their sensual experience (Johnson/Larson 2003: 78). It is indeed hardly possible to draw a sharp line between people's implicit access to their own aesthetic and meaningful experiences and their explicit understanding of them (e.g. of music) (Taylor 2006: 32). Similarly, analytical cognitive processes cannot be clearly demarcated from synthetic cognitive processes, nor can general propositional knowledge be entirely distinct from inarticulate sensual-practical knowledge (Lakoff/Johnson 1999: 19f.). Therefore I would like to argue first, that the general propositional knowledge of artists is not only theoretical and abstract, but is intrinsically interwoven with other – sensual and motor – skills. Second, the change between a flow of action and a conscious distancing from material or work, i.e. between intuitive and reflexive working methods, is a typical characteristic of complex artistic activities.

Extending the Theoretical: Some Consequences for the Practice of *Musikvermittlung*

The analytical differentiation between knowledge and knowing has an impact on the discussion of *Musikvermittlung*. In conclusion, I want to propose three distinct considerations:

The first concerns a (de)mystification of acts of music-making and creation, especially in the context of classical art music. Many creativity psychologists emphasise the importance of talent and giftedness (e.g. Weisberg 2006: 769f.). Both concepts are legitimate, but they should not be understood as an innate disposition or personality trait that relativises the central importance of learning. Until now, talent and giftedness have been central but highly problematic categories used by professionals in music universities, concert halls and festivals to legitimise their selection process of students and young artists, and ultimately offer a widely accepted explanation for artistic success. Yet the simplistic and at the same time opaque meaning of both terms ignores the social and competitive character of artistic professions and naturalises artistic success. Thus both these terms – talent and giftedness – often have an ideological impact, since they promote a pre-social and inscrutable conception of artistic practice. Specifically, I suggest that in conversations and when working with musicians, practitioners in the field of *Musikvermittlung* should convey an understanding of artistic creative work by focusing on musicians' working conditions, everyday practices, collaborations and experiences.

The second consideration relates to non-propositional understanding. Non-propositional understanding is internally related to the limits of verbalisation, i.e. the limits of the ability to make sensual-sensing experiences as well as bodily sensations explicit. Since sensual-sensing experiences are not directly linguistically explicable, they can only be conveyed by resorting to analogies and metaphors. In order to understand this in concrete terms, I invite the reader to closely observe the linguistic and non-linguistic communication between a conductor and musicians during rehearsals. Our communicative counterpart can only understand the analogies and metaphors that we use (e.g. "a soaring melody", "the percussion should sound stormy, violent, dangerous", "the scream cut through the air"), if he or she understands the hint or nod that a linguistic picture contains (Lakoff/Johnson 1980: 115f.; Johnson/Larson 2003: 66-78). Since practitioners in *Musikvermittlung* "can know more than [they] can tell" (Polanyi 1966: 4), they are constantly facing communicative challenges and limitations (Wittgenstein [1953] 1999: §78). Consequently (as many practitioners do already), they elaborate further means of non-linguistic aesthetic communication and interaction appropriate to the different groups of *Musikvermittlung* addressees (see also Smilde et al. 2019: 119f.).

The third consideration concerns the deconstruction of claims of knowledge and competence. Deconstruction has two meanings here: it is used to analyse the construction principles of an entity; it is also critical and means the unmasking of unwarranted assertions. I have no doubt that practitioners in *Musikvermittlung* have a broad knowledge of music and many years of practical experience in their field; some of these professional experiences form habits and work routines. Intelligent routines are indispensable, but they must remain modifiable if a professional situation demands it. Otherwise, a situation can arise whereby practitioners become prisoners of their own realm of experience. The deconstruction of claims to knowledge and competence can therefore be twofold. One can take a closer look at the discourse features of one's own descriptions and comments on music. Do we sometimes use, for example, a transfiguring and celebratory discourse with music? And which criteria of quality or excellence are implicit in our statements? The point is to create spaces for a critical distance from dominant cultural theories and one's own musical preferences. And there is a self-reflective dimension here: do I tend to present my own judgements and preferences as universally valid? Do I tend to privilege European art music? And how do I deal with music from other musical (sub)cultures that I am not familiar with? Nevertheless, the questioning of beliefs and certainties is not an end in itself, but rather makes productive scepticism effective. A willingness to criticise and negotiate social and cultural meanings and valuations is a central component of any lively search for new aesthetic insights and experiences.

In the title of this chapter I refer to the intelligence and limitations of practitioners, implying that practitioners in *Musikvermittlung* acquire continuously new learning experiences in the course of their professional life, which can lead to a new orientation of their practice. By re-examining their understanding and methods, their professional skills expand. This process implies, as Schön put it, reflection-in-action and reflection-on-action (Schön 1983: 26–29; also Polanyi 1966: 19). The first is largely implicit, the second explicit, and both represent the two ends of a continuum of reflective practice. Since the agency of practitioners is shaped not only by their knowledge and capabilities, but also by professional constraints, their practice is structured by internal and external limitations – e.g. what they do not know or are not able to perform, and what managerial decisions, institutional structures and limited resources impact on their actions. Both their practical intelligence, as well as their practical limitations, are constitutive for the development of their practice.

This anthology addresses the innovative potential of *Musikvermittlung*. If we take situatedness and contextuality in the practice of *Musikvermittlung* seriously, then we can address two aspects of innovative potentials. The first concerns the contents and methods of *Musikvermittlung* as regards the variety of addressees, the modes of reflective dialogue and participation, and the ways of creating shared experiences and of negotiating meanings.[11] The sec-

---

11 Constanze Wimmer (2010: 100–115) discusses the quality of contents, as well as of applied methods, in the offerings of *Musikvermittlung*. Her approach is practice-oriented and surely fruitful for practitioners and cultural organizations. My remarks in this chapter are indirectly related to her discussion of quality, though they are set on a more general and philosophical level.

ond relates to the organisation of *Musikvermittlung*. As a rule, the majority of *Musikvermittlung* activities in the field of classical and contemporary art music are one-off events (usually lasting around one hour) with participants that professionals meet only once. Due to this lack of continuity, it is virtually impossible to think about a systematic development of aesthetic capabilities. Yet unless there is continuity when engaging in arts, and unless there is an expansion of one's own capabilities, it is extremely unlikely that aesthetic experiences can trigger a transformative process. In order to conceive and stimulate the innovative potential of *Musikvermittlung*, we should also question the current corseting of its implementation, so as to negotiate new and better conditions for it to develop and flourish.

Bibliography

Allwardt, Ingrid (2012): Musikvermittlung, [online]: http://www.miz.org/static_de/themenportale/einfuehrungstexte_pdf/archiv/allwardt_2012.pdf [17.06.2019].

Becker, Howard S. (1982): Art Worlds, Berkeley: University of California Press.

Barthes, Roland ([1967] 1977): The Death of the Author, in ibid.: *Image-Music-Text*, London: Fontana Press, 142–148.

Born, Georgina (2005): On Musical Mediation: Ontology, Technology and Creativity, in: *Twentieth-Century Music*, Vol. 2, 7–36.

Bourdieu, Pierre ([1972] 1977): *Outline of a Theory of Practice*, Cambridge: Cambridge University Press.

Bourdieu, Pierre ([1987] 1990): *In Other Words: Essays Towards a Reflective Sociology*, Cambridge: Polity Press.

Bouveresse, Jacques (1999): Rules, Dispositions and Habitus, in: Schusterman, Richard (ed.), *Bourdieu: A Critical Reader*, Oxford: Blackwell, 45–63.

Bowman, Wayne D. (2016): Artistry, Ethics and Citizenship, in: Elliot, David J./Silverman, Marissa/Bowman, Wayne D. (eds.), *Artistic Citizenship: Artistry, Social Responsibility, and Ethical Praxis*, New York: Oxford University Press, 59–80.

Cassirer, Ernst ([1923] 1955): *The Philosophy of Symbolic Forms. Vol. I: Language*, New Haven: Yale University Press.

Collins, Harry (2010): *Tacit and Explicit Knowledge*, Chicago: University of Chicago Press.

Cook, Nicholas (2013): *Beyond the Score: Music as Performance*, Oxford: Oxford University Press.

Cook, Nicholas (2018): *Music as Creative Practice. Studies in Musical Performance as Creative Practice*, New York: Oxford University Press.

Crispin, Darla/Östersjö, Stefan (2017): Musical Expression from Conception to Reception, in: Rink, John/Gaunt, Helena/Williamon, Aaron (eds.), *Musicians in the Making: Pathways to Creative Performance*, Oxford: Oxford University Press, 288–305.

DeNora, Tia (2000): *Music in Everyday Life*, Cambridge: Cambridge University Press.

Dewey, John (1916): An Added Note as to the 'Practical', in: ibid. *Essays in Experimental Logic*, Chicago: University of Chicago Press, 330–334.

Dewey, John ([1934] 1939): *Art as Experience*, New York, Capricorn Books.

Dewey, John/Bentley, Arthur (1949): *Knowing and the Known*, Boston: The Beacon Press.

Duguid, Paul (2005): "The Art of Knowing": Social and Tacit Dimensions of Knowledge and the Limits of the Community of Practice, in: *Information Society*, 21, 109–118.

Gibson, James J. (1979): *The Ecological Approach to Visual Perception*, Boston: Houghton Mifflin.

Greeno, James G. (1994): Gibson's Affordances, in: *Psychological Review*, 101(2), 336–342.

Gruhn, Wilfried (2005): Understanding Musical Understanding, in Elliott, David J. (eds.), *Praxial Music Education: Reflections and Dialogues*, Oxford: Oxford University Press, 98–111.

Hegel, Georg Wilhelm Friedrich ([1807] 2018: *Phenomenology of Spirit*, Cambridge: Cambridge University Press.

Hennion, Antoine (2003): Music and Mediation: Towards a New Sociology of Music, in: Trevor, Herbert/Clayton, Martin/Middleton, Richard (eds.), *The Cultural Study of Music*, London: Routledge, 80–91.

Janik, Allan (1994): *The Concept of Knowledge in Practical Philosophy*, Innsbruck: Brenner Archiv, unpublished manuscript.

Joas, Hans (1996): *The Creativity of Action*, Chicago: University of Chicago Press.

Johannessen, Kjell (1994): Philosophy, Art and Intransitive Understanding, in: Johannessen, Kjell/Larsen, Rolf/ Åmås, Knut O. (eds.), *Wittgenstein and Norway*, Oslo: Solum Forlag, 217–250.

Johnson, Mark/Larson, Steve (2003): "Something in the Way She Moves" – Metaphors of Musical Motion, in: *Metaphor and Symbol*, 18(2), 63–84.

Lako, George/Johnson, Mark (1980): *Metaphors We Live By*, Chicago: University of Chicago Press.

Lako, George/Johnson, Mark (1999): *Philosophy in the Flesh: The Embodied Mind and Its Challenge to Western Thought*, New York: Basic Books.

Leman, Marc/Maes, Pieter-Jan (2014): Music Perception and Embodied Music Cognition, in: Shapiro, Lawrence (ed.), *The Routledge Handbook of Embodied Cognition*, London: Routledge, 81–89.

Luhmann, Niklas ([1995] 2000): *Art as a Social System*, Stanford: Stanford University Press.

Neuweg, Hans Georg (2004): Tacit Knowing and Implicit Learning, in: Fischer, Martin/Boreham, Nicholas/Nyhan, Barry (eds.): *European Perspectives on Learning at Work: The Acquisition of Work Process Knowledge*. Luxembourg: Office for Official Publications for the European Communities, 130–147.

Polanyi, Michael (1958): *Personal Knowledge: Towards a Post-Critical Philosophy*. London: Routledge.

Polanyi, Michael (1966): *The Tacit Dimension*, London, Routledge.

Rink, John/Gaunt, Helena/Williamon, Aaron (eds.) (2017): *Musicians in the Making. Pathways to Creative Performance*, Oxford: Oxford University Press.

Ryle, Gilbert (1949): *The Concept of Mind*, London: Hutchinson.

Schatzki, Theodore/Knorr Cetina, Karin/Savigny, Eike von (eds.) (2001): *The Practice Turn in Contemporary Theory*, London: Routledge.

Schön, Donald (1983): *The Reflective Practitioner. How Professionals Think in Action*. Aldershot: Ashgate.

Selinger, Evan/Crease, Robert (eds.) (2006): *The Philosophy of Expertise*, New York: Columbia University Press.

Shapiro, Lawrence (ed.) (2014): *The Routledge Handbook of Embodied Cognition*, London: Routledge.

Shusterman, Richard (2000): *Performing Live: Aesthetic Alternatives for the Ends of Art*, Ithaca: Cornell University Press.

Shusterman, Richard (2008): *Body Consciousness: A Philosophy of Mindfulness and Somaesthetics*, Cambridge: Cambridge University Press.

Smilde, Rineke/Heineman, Erik/de Wit, Krista/Dons, Karolien/Alheit, Peter (2019): *If Music be the Food of Love, Play on: Meaningful Music in Healthcare*, Utrecht: Eburon.

Sudnow, David (2001): *Ways of the Hand. A Rewritten Account*, Cambridge: MIT Press.

Szivós, Mihály (2014): A Practice-Oriented Classification of Tacit Knowledge for the Research into Creativity and Innovation, in: *Polanyiana*, 1–2 (23), 21–30.

Taylor, Charles (1995): Overcoming Epistemology, in: ibid. (ed.), *Philosophical Arguments*, Cambridge (MA): Harvard University Press, 1–19.

Taylor, Charles (2006): Merleau-Ponty and the Epistemological Picture, in: Carman, Taylor/ Hansen, Mark B. N. (eds.), *The Cambridge Companion to Merleau-Ponty*, Cambridge: Cambridge University Press, 26–49.

Tröndle, Martin (ed.) (2018): *Das Konzert^{II}. Beiträge zum Forschungsfeld der Concert Studies*, Bielefeld: transcript.

Weisberg, Robert W. (2006): Modes of Expertise in Creative Thinking: Evidence from Case Studies, in Ericsson, Anders K./Charness, Neil/Feltovich, Paul J./Hoffman, Robert R. (eds.), *The Cambridge Handbook of Expertise and Expert Performance*, Cambridge: Cambridge University Press, 761–787.

Wenger, Etienne ([1998] 2002): *Communities of Practice: Learning, Meaning, and Identity*, Cambridge: Cambridge University Press.

Wimmer, Costanze (2010): *Exchange – Die Kunst, Musik zu vermitteln. Qualitäten in der Musikvermittlung und Konzertpädagogik*, Salzburg, Stiftung Mozarteum, https://www.kulturmanagement.net/Themen/Exchange-Die-Kunst-Musik-zu-vermitteln,837 [19.7.2020].

Wittgenstein, Ludwig (1970): *Zettel*, Berkeley: University of California Press.

Wittgenstein, Ludwig ([1969] 1980): *Philosophical Grammar*, Oxford: Blackwell.

Wittgenstein, Ludwig ([1953] 1999): *Philosophical Investigations*, Oxford: Blackwell.

Zembylas, Tasos/Dürr, Claudia (2009): *Wissen, Können und literarisches Schreiben. Eine Epistemologie der künstlerischen Praxis*, Wien: Passagen Verlag.

Zembylas, Tasos (2014): Forms of Knowing in the Literary Writing Process, in: ibid (ed.), Artistic Practices. *Social Interactions and Cultural Dynamics*, London: Routledge, 112–131.

Zembylas, Tasos/Niederauer, Martin (2018): *Composing Processes and Artistic Agency: Tacit Knowledge in Composing*, London: Routledge.

Biographical note

Tasos Zembylas has a PhD in Philosophy from the University of Vienna. He has been the Professor for Cultural Institutions Studies at the mdw – University of Music and Performing Arts Vienna since 2003. In 2009 he was Visiting Professor at the Zeppelin University in Friedrichshafen, Germany. His research specialisations include the sociology of artistic practices, the institutional analysis of art worlds, and public cultural funding policies.

Engaging with New Audiences
Perspectives of Professional Musicians' Biographical Learning and Its Innovative Potential for Higher Music Education

Rineke Smilde

Music can touch people deeply, and lead to well-being as an all-encompassing word for everything that makes life worth living, or at least can make it liveable. Musicians can play an important role in these processes, not as pseudo-therapists, but from their own artistic identity, with an approach in which they profoundly understand the social contexts to which they respond. In essence, this is about connecting as a musician with those who, due to whatever circumstances, are vulnerable, and/or those who cannot easily come into contact with live music.

This requires new qualities and skills from such "new audience musicians" who want to engage with people in contexts beyond the concert hall, jazz club or church, like schools, hospitals, nursing homes, prisons, or e.g. the corporate world.

Underpinning engagement with those new audiences is first and foremost a set of values that implies that music can work as a catalyst for interactive communication between various groups of people from different cultural and social contexts, and can bring about social change, no matter how small (Smilde 2018: 673). The point of departure is the idea that artistic processes can have a transformative potential which can bring about a sense of community, inclusion and collective identity.

In this chapter, research into musicians' engagement with new audiences will be explored through examples in the field of music and healthcare. I will do that from a biographical perspective, where the musicians' personal and professional development is strongly influenced by their experiences in their artistic practice. Here, biographical learning processes are at the core of what we might term, musicians' "professional performance" (Lombarts 2010).

Two examples are discussed in this light: research into the programme "Music for Life", on music and dementia, taking place in elderly care homes, and the project entitled "Meaningful Music in Healthcare", which focuses on music in the hospital. After that, the text will address what everything that has been learnt means for learning and teaching in higher music education, embracing the idea of engaging with new audiences and the potentials of *Musikvermittlung*.

Learning Processes of New Audience Musicians

Before delving into these two examples, I will first elaborate on new audience musicians and their learning processes as a theoretical underpinning of the two examples.

Musicians who engage with audiences beyond those in the traditional concert hall need more than only their artistic skills. They are required to be innovative, entrepreneurial, responsive and communicative, to be able to create sustained partnerships, and collaborate with an eye for the contexts they relate to (Smilde 2009, Bennett 2012). They must be reflective, aware of what is needed in order to generate their work and to produce it with high quality. This includes an awareness of their own individual needs for learning and development (Smilde 2018: 674-5). In short, they need to be "lifelong learners", in the holistic definition of Peter Jarvis:

> "The combination of processes throughout a lifetime, whereby the whole person – body (genetic, physical and biological) and mind (knowledge, skills, attitudes, values, emotions, beliefs and senses) – experiences social situations, the perceived content of which is then transformed cognitively, emotively or practically (or through any combination) and integrated into the individual person's biography, resulting in a continually changing (or more experienced) person." (Jarvis 2006: 134)

Musicians who want to connect to new audiences must be able to respond artistically and reflexively to changing social contexts, read their audience, be able to step out of their comfort zone and reflect on their learning processes. That requires, in other words, lifelong learning. Biographical learning is at the core of such lifelong learning processes. There is no biography without learning, and no learning without biography. Biographical learning includes people's experience, knowledge and self-reflection, and learning about transitions in their lives; in short, everything people have learned throughout their lives and have absorbed into their biographies (Smilde 2009: 16). From biographical learning a new understanding of people's learning processes can emerge, both in terms of emotion and cognition. A biographical approach to learning has the capacity to change both the learner and their environment, and that is the social context in which the learning takes place (Smilde 2009: 16).

Another important concept within these lifelong learning processes is the social learning, the learning as participation, which can take place within a "community of practice" (Lave/Wenger 1991, Wenger 1998, 2009). Within his definition of a community of practice, Etienne Wenger (2009: 211) distinguishes four interconnected components. These are Meaning ("a way of talking about our (changing) ability [...] to experience our life and the world as meaningful"); Practice ("a way of talking about the shared historical and social resources, frameworks and perspectives that can sustain mutual engagement in action"); Community ("a way of talking about the social configurations in which our enterprises are defined as worth pursuing and our participation is recognisable as competence") and Identity ("a way of talking about how learning changes who we are and creates personal histories of becoming in the context of our communities"). A community of practice integrates these components. In a community of practice, the concept of "peripheral participation" (Lave/Wenger 1991) is pivotal, where the learner learns through participation, starting in a peripheral position, gradually reaching a more central position, and finally achieving full membership of a community.

Music and Dementia

The research project "Music and Dementia" took place between 2009, when we[1] started with a first sensitisation of the field, and 2014, when our publication "While the Music Lasts" appeared, presented at our second dissemination symposium. It was a project which showed to what extent participatory music workshops with people with dementia and their caregivers can enhance the quality of life and work, and in which the learning processes of all involved

---

1 The research was conducted by Rineke Smilde, Kate Page and Peter Alheit.

(eight people living with dementia, five caregivers and three musicians) were found to lead to (small-scale) social changes.

We conducted ethnographically informed research into the programme "Music for Life", which is managed by Wigmore Hall in London, in collaboration with the organisation Jewish Care. "Music for Life" consists of a series of interactive creative music workshops in various care homes and centres for day-care for people living with dementia. Professional musicians with a portfolio career (Smilde 2009), where they combine several forms of professional activity, like playing in an orchestra or ensemble, or teaching, take part in "Music for Life", after receiving a training from Wigmore Hall.

In the "Music for Life" programme, held over an eight-week period, three of these musicians work together with a group of eight residents and five members of care staff and use improvisation as a kind of catalyst to bring about communication in the broadest sense of the word. The musicians use an array of verbal and non-verbal cues to connect to residents and their caregivers as a group (Smilde/Page/Alheit 2014: 27). In these interactive creative music workshops, the musicians need, as they call it themselves, a 360-degree radar: a great sensitivity for the group they are working with. That is also apparent in their improvisations with the residents and caregivers, which for that reason we have called "person-centred" or "applied" improvisation in our research. We defined this as "a variety of approaches that seek to tune in to the group in order to create music that authentically reflects the members of the group, with musicians drawing upon a body of shared repertoire and approaches" (Smilde/Page/Alheit 2014: 27).

A strong impact of this programme, as found by (unpublished) evaluations previously conducted by Wigmore Hall, can be that caregivers come to realise that a resident has a biography and that a person's observable behaviour can be a manifestation of the condition of dementia and does not necessarily reflect the person themself. That awareness can lead to an improved interaction and relationship between caregivers and residents. The projects are therefore about "finding the person behind the dementia" (Smilde/Page/Alheit 2014: 27, see also Kitwood 1997).

There is a considerable amount of research that shows that musical communication is beneficial for people with dementia, and that they can be reached through music, even in the later stages of dementia, when verbal communication is no longer possible. Oliver Sacks wrote: "Once one has seen such responses, one knows that there is still a self to be called upon, even if music, and only music, can do the calling" (Sacks 2008: 385). Sacks talks about the "I" that can always be appealed to and that is exactly the core value of this practice.

After preliminary research, where we observed various "Music for Life" workshops and held interviews with musicians and caregivers in order to familiarise ourselves with the field, we researched during eight successive weeks the workshops of a particular "Music for Life" project as it had been organised in a care home in London. Here we gathered data using participant observation and narrative expert interviews with the three musicians (an oboist, a cellist and a harpist), as well as with the staff development practitioner. We also held three group interviews with the group of musicians, before, during and after the project. In addition, the musicians and staff development practitioner kept a reflective journal which they handed in every week, after the sessions. We then analysed the data, using grounded theory (Charmaz 2006).

When looking at the learning processes of the musicians in this practice, it showed that the musicians' ability to reflect on their practice, and on the roles they have and respond to, is key. Critical reflection, as it is defined by Donald Schön (1983, 1987), can give a practitioner the opportunity to make a new sense of situations. The musicians therefore had to be, as Schön (1983, 1987) terms it, "reflective practitioners", reflecting "on" their action as well as "in" their action, in the latter case drawing on implicit or tacit knowledge (Polanyi 1966). When the musicians reflected, their implicit knowledge gradually became explicit, and as of then it could lead to insight, enabling an increasing awareness of the emotional and implicit, as well as the cognitive and explicit, to emerge (Smilde/Alheit 2016: 285). That is clearly a part of the concept of lifelong learning, where one can get to know what one implicitly knew before, and where one is learning from oneself, through critical reflection.

Mindful of what Jarvis (2006: 134) calls the "continually changing (or more experienced) person" within the concept of lifelong learning, we were able to become aware of the transformative processes the musicians went through. That is where the biographical learning comes in: it includes learning about transitions.

For musicians and caregivers alike, such "learning in transition" (Alheit 1994) underpinned this practice. When, for instance, a caregiver has changed her attitude to a resident as a result of an awareness or new insight created by interaction through music, she has learnt in transition. This transitional learning is self-referential, where it changes both the learner and the social context (Smilde 2011: 241).

An example of learning in transition is given by cellist Fiona, who wrote in her reflective journal after the eight-week project had finished:

"I feel we have managed in moments to create a group of equals – staff, residents and musicians all as human beings together – joined by the experience of music. I think we created a place of belonging that did enable the residents to feel safe and I believe these moments of wellbeing have helped to create change, even for a few moments or perhaps long term... I feel like I have been left with something unquantifiable in terms of a human/spiritual experience. I feel like it has left a mark in the tapestry of my life and I like to think, whether it is 'remembered' or not by the residents, that it has had a similar impact on them." (Smilde et al. 2014: 24)

Fiona's reflection is not only interesting in terms of the clearly visible biographical learning, when she speaks about the "tapestry of my life". The "place of belonging" to which she refers also relates to Wenger's (1998) concept of identity ("learning as becoming") within the community of practice (Lave/Wenger 1991, Wenger 1998), which was referred to earlier on.

As also pointed out earlier on, in a community of practice, the concept of peripheral participation (Lave/Wenger 1991) is pivotal, where the learner gradually reaches a more central position, and finally achieves full membership of a community. However, Lave and Wenger (1991) warn against thinking only in terms of a linear development within the community, going from the periphery to the core. We saw that indeed this is not always the case; moreover, it turned out to be one of the most important learning points for the musicians. Sticking to their aim and desires in terms of residents' improvement initially gave the musicians a feeling of failure and low self-esteem as soon as a resident did not respond musically or got locked into the dementia. Dementia cannot improve, nor heal, and learning to accept this as it is was therefore key for the musicians: at one moment the resident can be a conductor, or a fellow musician; the next moment this can be over. Nonetheless, there is learning going on: people living with dementia can realise their biography and identity in the moment through artistic practice, as many examples in our participant observation showed (Smilde et al. 2014). Fiona reflected:

"I've been thinking a lot about how music can be inclusive without people having to actively participate. Music can simply go to people, without people having to come to it. It is a wonderful thing about music, and as a performer you can even play for someone in particular without it being known or acknowledged and yet, something of that intention can be felt by the listener." (Smilde et al. 2014: 89)

Leadership

Musicians' leadership, and in particular their shared leadership, constitutes another pivotal aspect within their learning processes. Shared leadership within the context of this particular practice requires more than the ability to read a group and having a radar for what is appropriate for a certain moment. Daniel, one of the musicians who took part in the preliminary interviews of the research project, commented on this as follows:

> "[I]t requires [...] to be very flexible to go with somebody else's ideas. [...] It's very easy to just improvise freely, and just sort of let the music go wherever, but when you have a particular agenda, [with] a person who is playing that music with a particular resident, you have to incorporate them into what you're doing. So you can't just think, 'oh well, I feel like playing it like that'. Because then that's *your* thing, you know? So it's really floating, we float around each other in that way." (Smilde et al. 2014: 27)

This reflection is revealing about what exactly makes the improvisation person-centred. In addition, Fiona also asks herself the question what sound can reflect who the residents are at a particular moment: "What sound can I try now to help either reflect who they are at this moment or what sound is going to connect? It's all about your observations about that person, rather than about what you're creating." (Smilde et al. 2014: 90)

The person-centred musical improvisation in this practice thus consists of tuning in with a resident and oneself as a musician and "sound" can therefore be considered a musical metaphor for one's own identity and one's connection with the other, as Fiona also says: "You're trying to be someone else's music for them" (Smilde et al. 2014: 79). Fiona thus tries to highlight a resident, through musically reflecting the person's identity. Music workshop leader Matthew adds in this respect:

> "I think there's [...] that sort of thing that musicians or artists can do that other people don't do or that sort of, yeah, it's another level of support, isn't it? About acknowledging who somebody is that's completely without words, completely beyond words, a sort of recognition of them [...] You know, of kind

of losing myself so much in the essence of another person." (Smilde et al. 2014: 144)

Matthew's observation can also be understood in terms of reflecting "the other". George Herbert Mead's (1934/1967) theory of the self is significant in this respect and can help understand what actually happens here. The self, Mead argues, is always a "social self". In order to gain a deeper understanding of the self, Mead distinguishes between the "I" and the "Me" as two different aspects of the self. Both have a distinct position within social interaction: the "I" is the direct utterance of the self, acting and reacting, the "Me" is the social self, the self that is aware of others and that views itself through the eyes of others. In Mead's words: "It is not initially there at birth but arises in the process of social experience and activity, that is, develops in the given individual as a result of his relations to the process as a whole, and to other individuals within that process." (Mead [1934] 1967: 168).

According to Mead, there is always, and has always been an "I". Therefore, this does not change when the cognitive competence of a person with dementia to become an "object to oneself" has diminished (Alheit/Page/Smilde 2015: 24). Even when the "Me", the social self that can see oneself through the eye of another, has disappeared, the eyes of others (here the musicians) can still be on me (the person with dementia), and the musicians can recognise and acknowledge me through their person-centred improvisation. Here they reflect musically who I really am, as the person behind my dementia. The value that the musicians give me has its basis in my biography, in my life story, in me as the person who I really am (Smilde 2016: 320).

Linda Rose, founder of the project Music for Life, observed:

"[…] if you get it right as a musician, if you match something in your music, about the person you are working with, whose identity is lost, who very often doesn't know who they are, where they are, what's going on… if that match is right, then somewhere between you and that other person, somewhere in that space where the music is happening, is that person's identity. It's in that music. And they see themselves, they feel themselves, they notice, they know that somewhere in there, is them. And that is the essence of that connection." (Smilde et al. 2014: 292)

Meaningful Music in Healthcare

With the practice on "Music and Dementia", described above, in the back of our heads, we[2] embarked from 2015 onwards upon a new, explorative research project, "Meaningful Music in Health Care" (MiMiC), now not in the care home, but in a hospital, the University Medical Center Groningen. Also in this practice, person-centred music-making and "being in the moment", where one can let go of one's anxieties and be fully present, remained at the core. This time, we did not research an existing practice, but developed a practice which we researched in an explorative way at the same time.

"MiMiC" takes place between a group of three professional musicians, patients and nurses. It consists of, as the musicians termed it, "person-centred music-making" for patients and their nurses in patient rooms for one, two or four persons. Every patient on the ward that is interested in receiving music is included in the visit. Mostly the musicians use person-centred improvisation, but also idiomatic improvisation[3], repertoire and arrangements in all sorts of styles and genres. Since the end of 2015 we executed some 20 six-mornings-in-a-row projects, all on surgical wards. We chose professional musicians who were experienced in engaging with new audiences and using improvisation in various social contexts, including health care.

In the explorative research we looked at musicians' interactions with patients and nurses, "MiMiC's" contribution to the well-being of patients and nurses, and lastly, the professional performance of musicians, by which we meant the performance of the musicians in an artistic, social and situational sense. This research was, like the one on "Music and Dementia", ethnographically informed, using participant observation, narrative episodic expert interviews with musicians and nurses, and reflective journals of musicians. Our holistic research question was: "What does music actually move in a hospital setting?" (Smilde/Heineman/De Wit/Dons/Alheit 2019). This, based on our collective data, led to a number of stories of mutual development, from the perspective of musicians, patients and nurses. These stories foreshadowed the three main themes, or core categories, that emerged from our analyses: Participation, Compassion, and Excellence. The stories, based

---

2   The research was undertaken by Rineke Smilde, Erik Heineman, Krista de Wit, Karolien Dons and Peter Alheit.
3   Idiomatic improvisation means improvisation in a certain style or genre, or e.g. based on the work of a particular composer.

on our observations, interviews and musicians' reflective journals, give a deep insight into the "MiMiC" practice and in particular into what we termed the "learning pathways" of the musicians, patients and nurses in the space of time. With the help of the scheme below we will take a look at the learning pathway of the musicians as we reconstructed them.

Fig. 1: Musicians' pathway

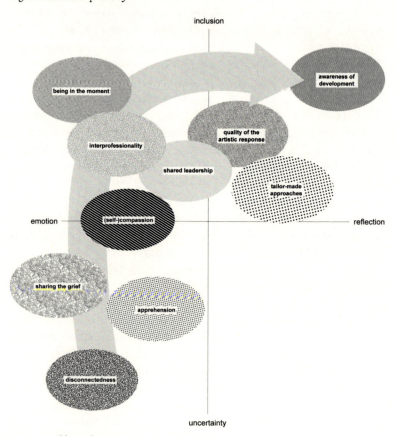

Source: Smilde et al. 2019: 77

We used our data, analysed with the grounded theory approach (Charmaz 2006), to capture the encounter between the hospital world and the live music practice in what we called a "mental field", spanned between the poles of Reflection and Emotion, and those between Uncertainty and Inclusion. Within these poles, which emerged from the data, complex social processes unfolded in time. Fig. 1 maps the biographical story of the musicians' learning pathway throughout time, brought together in what we termed "semantic clusters", which can be seen pictured in the figure.

When following the arrow in the figure, it can be observed that the musicians started from a great feeling of uncertainty, apprehension and sometimes insecurity. The social environment in the hospital was unfamiliar and challenging for them, and musicians felt hugely out of their comfort zone, their more or less natural habitat. Slowly, throughout a process of shared feeling and emotion, and not in the least through their close communication and engagement with the patients, initially also outsiders in the hospital, this journey led to a sense of inclusion. This was in particular the case when the connection with the nurses was beginning to firmly take shape, and the triangle musicians-patients-nurses became completer and more interconnected. In the end, this led to an overall reflection by the musicians on what was learnt; they could take stock of their learning, stepping back from everything that had passed, observing it, reflecting it and not only learn from it, but feel genuinely empowered (Smilde et al. 2019: 75). Below, we will take a closer look at a few examples of these semantic clusters.

Interprofessionality

The interprofessional dialogue and development between musicians and nurses was interesting to follow. Cellist Max wrote that at some point the head of surgery gave him "a unique view into the anthropology of a nursing ward" (Smilde et al. 2019: 65) and this opened his eyes. It helped get rid of feelings of uncertainty. He became determined to give things time and show the utmost modesty, respect and understanding. This can be considered transformative learning, "changing your frame of reference" in Jack Mezirow's (1990) words. It payed off, as Max wrote later on: "We have become part of the 'care framework' and that feels good. It feels as if I am part of an important part of society and that I am doing valuable work. [...] I feel that besides a musician I am even more." (Smilde et al. 2019: 66)

Being in the moment

There are a number of reflections on how "Chronos", linear clock time, and "Kairos", the moment, the now, consciousness (Lombarts 2010), can exist together, and the huge quality of the latter for everyone involved. The most striking example was that of an eighteen-year-old Iranian refugee, who was able to be completely in the moment when enjoying the music, in which he played an active role. No matter that he did not know whether he would be able to remain in the country, nor to which refugee centre he would be transferred after leaving the hospital, as the one where he was previously residing was at the time not safe enough for him, he could let go of all these anxieties during the musical session and be fully present. This made a lasting impression on the musicians, as could be read in their reflective journals.

Awareness of development

In our observations, in the interviews and in the reflective journals, we saw an increase of intuitional sensitivity in the musicians, evident in much reflection on the transferability of this practice to other social contexts, and on the question of how one might obtain this particular quality in standard classical concert situations. Cellist Max observed in his reflective journal:

> "This is not just a little different from playing for an audience in a concert hall, it is *completely* different. The relationship between musicians and audience, the function of music, and even the music changes completely. Still it remains an artistic practice [...] In [the hospital] music is not a luxury product, but something extremely important. I would love to find other contexts in which this can take shape or find ways in which a normal concert can get more urgency." (Smilde et al. 2019: 66)

We could observe recurring narratives which seemed key for artistic practices like "MiMiC", and where the three main themes, or core categories, that played a fundamental role, namely Participation, Compassion and Excellence, were clearly displayed. Throughout the musicians' journey we saw the striving to be a member of a community, in a collective identity with the nurses and patients, to "belong" (Lave/Wenger 1991, Wenger 1998) and engage profoundly with everyone involved, which is part of the participation. This required in the end compassion, for the patients in the first place, and also for the nurses. However, musicians' self-compassion also needed to be exercised, in order to let go of a perfectionism that can work against oneself as a musician, and accept and "tolerate" one's perceived shortcomings. Compassion in this context goes further than empathy (Bloom 2016), it is more active and can be defined as: "a way to develop the kindness, support and encouragement to [...] take the actions we need in order to promote the flourishing and well-being of ourselves and others" (Gilbert/Choden 2013: 138).

Excellence

As mentioned above, the third main theme, or core category, we established was excellence. After the six research-pilots had finished, Aline, one of the external advisors of the project, wrote the following beautiful observation on excellence:

> "The true artistry of the musicians from MiMiC lies in their desire to find just the right music for the right 'moment'. In the ever-changing environment of a hospital, they need to use their sensitivity, judgement and intuition to tune in to all that is happening around them and find or create the appropriate music for the person in front of them. This might be a piece of repertoire or an improvisation based on a theme or image that emerges from a conversation with a patient. Each musical encounter has the aim of connecting deeply with the patient, in whichever way feels appropriate in the moment. It is aimed to be person-centred and to 'feel personal' and therefore creates a connection with the musician and a sense of ownership and empowerment for the patient or member of staff [...] In this way a rapport was built and a sense of equality between staff and patients was created. In each encounter I have been struck by the skill of the musicians who brought their music into the hospital with great sensitivity for everyone who stayed or worked there. In what needs to be a 'clinical environment' I witnessed the cathartic power of music to help people 'feel' more human and more 'alive'. Surely, this is healing in the broadest sense and therefore an essential aspect of healthcare?" (Smilde et al. 2019: 129)

Aline talks here about musicians' artistry. We encounter that word in the work of Schön (1987), who defines it as: "the competence by which practitioners actually handle indeterminate zones of practice" (Schön 1983: 13). There are two meanings of artistry, being the "intuitive knowing", and the "reflection-in-action on the intuitive knowing". When a practitioner displays artistry, Schön says, "his intuitive knowing is richer in information than any description of it" (Schön 1983: 276, Smilde et al. 2019: 276).

It goes without saying that excellence in MiMiC extends beyond artistic excellence. Whereas artistic excellence is without any doubt an absolute prerequisite for MiMiC, in order to reach the patients and nurses, musicians cannot do without an intensely observing eye for the social situation. Therefore, what we might term "situational" and artistic excellence are married in the MiMiC practice.

The Relevance of Biographical Learning

The example of "Music and Dementia", as presented here, focused on person-centredness, which is also key in "MiMiC". The second example focused on participation, compassion and excellence, which are also critically important concepts in "Music and Dementia". In both projects as described, the biographical learning is immanent. The projects consisted of processes that unfold in time, and which changed the participants involved. These are reciprocal processes, joint learning processes. The musicians learned, their lifeworlds changed, they went through a transitional process, which is the biographical learning process. It shows for example in the following observation of cellist Max in "MiMiC":

> "Observing the 'care machine' in action gives me a lot of inspiration. No matter that there will be many obstacles for the nurses, I feel that they do their work with a lot of commitment and that they bring a quality and human aspect in their work which is admirable, and which I would like to implement myself in my work as a musician as well. To approach each human being, no matter where she or he is coming from, her or his status or age, in the same human way. Everybody can become a patient; everybody can be my audience." (Smilde et al. 2019: 129)

Biographical learning also shows in the reflection of Matthew, workshop leader of Music for Life, after the project on Music and Dementia had finished:

> "During this project I think I have learned even more deeply the importance of... valuing each person in the group; and that group consists of the musicians, the staff, the residents, the managers. Then beyond those people who

have direct contact are the receptionists, staff who bring the residents to the group and transfer them from wheelchair to armchair, relatives, cleaners... and so the list continues. And then, once the session is over and I have left the care home, something of that awareness seems to remain as I get on the tube and share that time with other strangers, as I go into a busy department store, and gradually I have to let it slip away, and adjust to being in the 'normal' world again, with its sharp edges, deadlines, and exacting demands for perfection. But I can carry what I have experienced with me and try to remember to connect with it when I can, to value this life I have for what it is." (Smilde et al. 2014: 85)

Matthew understands himself in a new way, both as a person and as a musician. His biographical learning process also reflects on the institutional level of the care home, in the awareness of the "list that continues", as the experience is more and more shared and integrated among staff, musicians and residents alike. It can lead to the perception of a "holistic learning environment", which consists of lifeworlds that include biographical learning following "[...] its own 'individual logic' that is generated by the specific, biographically layered structure of experience" (Alheit/Dausien 2007: 67).

Biographical Learning in Higher Music Education

These examples show how relevant it is to take biographical learning into account, also in the formal learning environment of higher music education. This does not necessarily need to happen through creating new curricula, but in the first place through a mindset of awareness and willingness to grant students space for their own personal and professional development (Smilde 2009).

Understanding the multifold roles of musicians in society and its values should not be in the margin, but on the contrary, be deeply rooted in higher music education. Discourses on artistic practices being either *l'art pour l'art* or social work should reversely move to the margin, and in the end could become redundant.

Higher music education is, in general, not used to considering professional training in fields where musicians engage with people in various social contexts as very important. This is remarkable, as connecting with one's audience and creating meaningful experiences has always been musicians' core business. Institutions of higher music education therefore need to be responsive and reflexive and, considering their role in contemporary society, take up responsibility to connect to society in ways that intertwine with their purpose in supporting the development of their students' artistic and personal expression (Smilde 2016). In other words, institutions need to facilitate students' ability to profoundly address the holistic key question of any musician: "Who am I as a musician, and how can I contribute to society?" This is at the core of *Musikvermittlung*; the "innovative potentials" to which this anthology aims to contribute lie exactly here, and biographical learning plays an important role in that.

This facilitation of biographical learning processes needs to come to the fore in the institutions through a clear vision, which mirrors – in open and flexible curricula and learning and teaching approaches, as well as in relevant professional partnerships, not only in the cultural sector, but also for example in health care – partnerships that are ambitious and innovative.

Last but not least, it is therefore also obvious that improvisation needs a prominent role in higher music education. We are well aware that improvisation is a fundamental means of self-expression for a musician, and we have also seen that improvisation can be crucial to the expression of "the other" in any social context, especially for those who are vulnerable and whose voices are not always heard.

Bibliography

Alheit, Peter (1994): The "biographical question" as a challenge to adult education, in: *International Review of Education* 40 (3-5), 283–298.

Alheit, Peter/Dausien, Bettina (2007): Lifelong Learning and Biography: A Competitive Dynamic Between the Macro and the Micro Levels of Education, in: West, Linden/Alheit, Peter/Andersen, Anders Siig/Merrill, Barbara (eds). *Using Biographical and Life History Approaches in the Study of Adult and Lifelong Learning: European Perspectives*, Frankfurt am Main: Peter Lang, 57–70.

Alheit, Peter/Page, Kate/Smilde, Rineke (2015): *Musik und Demenz. Das Modellprojekt ›Music for Life‹ als innovativer Ansatz der Arbeit mit Demenzkranken*, Gießen: Psychosozial Verlag.

Bennet, Dawn (ed.) (2012): *Life in the Real World: How to Make Music Graduates Employable*, Illinois: Common Ground.

Bloom, Paul (2016): *Against Empathy: The Case for Rational Compassion*, New York: HarperCollins.
Charmaz, Kathy (2006): *Constructing Grounded Theory. A Practical Guide Through Qualitative Analysis*. London: Sage.
Gilbert, Paul/Choden (2013): *Mindful Compassion*, London: Robinson.
Jarvis, Peter (2006): *Towards a Comprehensive Theory of Human Learning*, London/New York: Routledge.
Kitwood, Tom (1997): *Dementia Reconsidered: The Person Comes First*, Maidenhead Berkshire: Open University Press.
Lave, Jean/Wenger, Etienne (1991): *Situated Learning: Legitimate Peripheral Participation*, Cambridge: Cambridge University Press.
Lombarts, Kiki (2010): *Professional Performance van Artsen*, Rotterdam: Uitgevers.
Mead, George H. ([1934]1967): *Mind, Self and Society. From the Standpoint of a Social Behaviorist. Edited and with an Introduction by Charles W. Morris*. Works, Vol. 1, Chicago and London: The University of Chicago Press.
Mezirow, Jack (1990): How Critical Reflection Triggers Transformative Learning, in: Mezirow, Jack et al: *Fostering Critical Reflection in Adulthood*, San Francisco: Jossey-Bass, 1–20.
Polanyi, Michael (1966): *The Tacit Dimension*, New York: Doubleday.
Sacks, Oliver (2008): *Musicophilia, Tales of Music and the Brain*, London: Picador.
Schön, Donald (1983): *The Reflective Practitioner. How Professionals Think in Action*, Aldershot: Ashgate.
Schön, Donald (1987): *Educating the Reflective Practitioner. Toward a New Design for Teaching and Learning in the Professions*, San Francisco: Jossey-Bass.
Smilde, Rineke (2009): *Musicians as Lifelong Learners: Discovery through Biography*, Delft: Eburon.
Smilde, Rineke (2011): Musicians Reaching out to People Living with Dementia: Perspectives of Learning, in: Herzberg, Heidrun/Kammler, Eva (eds.), *Biographie und Gesellschaft; Überlegungen zu einer Theorie des modernen Selbst*, Frankfurt/New York: Campus Verlag, 229–244.
Smilde, Rineke (2016): Biography, Identity, Improvisation, Sound – intersections of personal and social identity through improvisation, in: *Arts & Humanities in Higher Education*, Vol.15. No.34, 308–324.
Smilde, Rineke (2018): Community Engagement and Lifelong Learning: musicians' artistic responses to societal change, in: Bartleet, Brydie-Leigh/Higgins, Lee (eds.), *Oxford Handbook of Community Music*, New York: Oxford University Press, 673–692.

Smilde, Rineke/Alheit, Peter (2016): On Music and Dementia: perspectives of learning, in: Evans, Rob (ed.), *Before, Beside, and After (Beyond) the Biographical Narrative*, Duisburg: Nisaba Verlag, 281–296.

Smilde, Rineke/Heineman, Erik/De Wit, Krista/Dons, Karolien/Alheit, Peter (2019): *If Music be the Food of Love, Play On – Meaningful Music in Healthcare*, Utrecht: Eburon.

Smilde, Rineke/Page, Kate/Alheit, Peter (2014): *While the Music Lasts – On Music and Dementia*, Delft: Eburon.

Wenger, Etienne (1998): *Communities of Practice, Learning, Meaning and Identity*, Cambridge, USA: Cambridge University Press.

Wenger, Etienne (2009): A social theory of learning, in: Knud Illeris (ed.), *Contemporary Theories of Learning*, London/New York: Routledge.

Biographical notes

Flautist, musicologist and music educationalist **Rineke Smilde** is professor of Lifelong Learning in Music at Hanze University in Groningen and former professor of Music Education at the University of Music & Performing Arts in Vienna. Her research group examines questions on musicians' engagement with new audiences and its meaning for their different roles, learning and leadership. Rineke's main area of research is biographical research related to musicians' lifelong and lifewide learning. She published widely on different aspects of lifelong learning in music, and lectures and gives presentations worldwide.

Hear – Taste – See: UISGE BEATHA – Waters of Life
Towards the Innovative Potential of Synaesthetic Experiences for *Musikvermittlung*

Sarah Chaker

Artists
Petra Stump-Linshalm, composer
Heinz-Peter Linshalm, contrabass clarinet
Jutta Goldgruber, painter

Programme
Petra Stump-Linshalm (2015): "UISGE BEATHA [ʊʃkʲe 'bɛha] – A Guide to Flavours for Solo Contrabass Clarinet"

1) the smooth flowing one
2) delicate spice and a whiff of smoke
3) mizuwari – mixed with water
4) nutty undertones
5) with a hint of sea salt
6) cigar box, smoky
7) angels' share
8) peat monster

Moderation
Sarah Chaker

Fig. 1: Sketch (extract) of the piece "nutty undertones" by Petra Stump-Linshalm

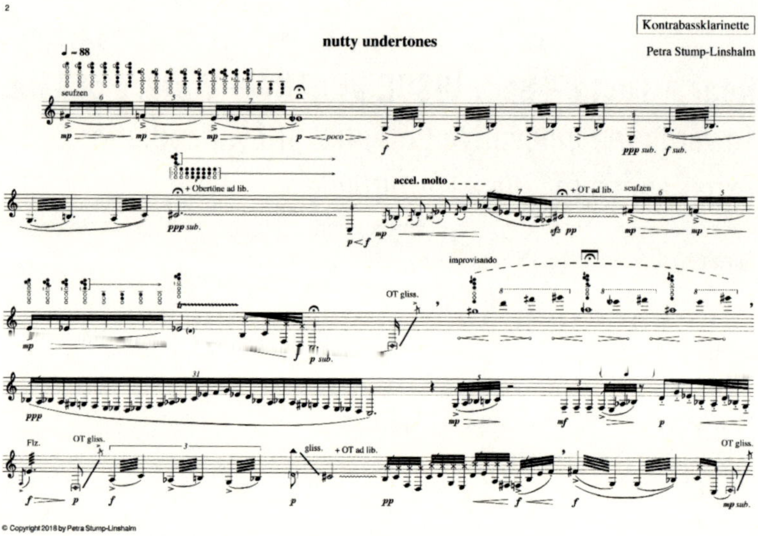

Source: with friendly permission of the composer

"UISGE BEATHA" – the Concept

Even though the "Waters of Life", set to music by Petra Stump-Linshalm, can be enjoyed purely for its sonic qualities, the special appeal of this composition – especially for *Musikvermittlung* – lies in the synaesthetic experience that the work makes possible and provokes. By serving different, seemingly appropriate types of whisky for the various pieces for contrabass clarinet solo, the senses of hearing and taste are brought into a close relationship during the performance. Even if the pieces of the composition were written in standard musical notation (see fig. 1) and are performed by the musician in a quite classical/traditional concert setting, the audience nevertheless has an active and participatory role to play, insofar as people are encouraged to relive the suggestions of the composer's sonic interpretations, brought to life by the performer's playing, and to compare them with their own gustatory sensations by tasting the different types of Scotch whisky that go with each piece. For Petra Stump-Linshalm, "the idea is that I say, 'To me, the whisky [...] sounds like this,' and then everyone can just see, do they find that too? Do they find it [the sonic correspondence] appropriate? Many people might not even think about how something might sound that tastes like this or that."[1] Jutta Goldgruber was so inspired by UISGE BEATHA that she subsequently created pen-and-ink drawings of the individual pieces – some with pen, some with brush, some with pipette – and thus helped the "Waters of Life" to find a visual equivalent in her "embodied studies" series.

Due to reasons of time and cost, only a shortened version of the actual performance concept could be presented at the lecture series, although the basic structure and sequence still corresponded to the actual concept: Jutta Goldgruber's paintings had already been positioned in various places in the hall before the event began, so that the audience had ample opportunity to view them during the event. Chronologically, the artistic performance consisted of the following elements: in a first step, Heinz-Peter Linshalm performed all the pieces of the work one after another (initially unaccompanied by whisky).

This was followed by a short break, during which the subsequent programme and the performance concept of UISGE BEATHA were briefly explained to the audience by the artists. In the course of this, two (instead of the originally planned six) varieties of whisky were handed out to the audience one after the other, and the corresponding pieces – in the case of the lecture series, we had decided in advance on "delicate spice and a whiff of smoke" as well as "nutty undertones" – were performed (once more) by Heinz-Peter Linshalm, who had also been kind enough to procure the varieties of whisky corresponding to the two pieces from his trusted whisky store before the event.[2]

---

1   Supplementing the shared podium discussion in our lecture series, the information in this article is based on a Zoom interview which Sarah Chaker conducted with Petra Stump-Linshalm, Heinz-Peter Linshalm and Jutta Goldgruber on September 6th 2021.
2   At this point we would like to offer our heartfelt thanks to the whisky store Potstill in Vienna (https://www.potstill.org) for their friendly advice and altruistic support during the lecture series event, for which the management provided us with whisky glasses for 60 people free of charge – many thanks!

The synaesthetic tastings were followed by a moderated conversation with the artists and the audience.

Genesis of the Piece: Passions and Pragmatics

UISGE BEATHA, one of the early works of the composer and clarinettist Petra Stump-Linshalm, was created in 2015, still largely free of external constraints: "It was so unintentional back then, I had no deadline, no one said how long it [the work] had to be or could be, or how many pieces it had to be. It was still such a completely free time. Then I liked this whisky description, and then this one and this one, and then at some point I thought, 'Now it's good'." (Stump-Linshalm 2021) A joint trip to Scotland by the couple Petra Stump-Linshalm and Heinz-Peter Linshalm had provided the two musicians with lasting inspiration in advance: "We were interested in whiskies at this time [around 2015], because we had been on a trip to Scotland two years earlier, and that was very interesting. We visited distilleries and learned about how whisky is made and all the different varieties. And then there are the beautiful descriptions on the whisky bottles: How does it smell? How does it taste? How does it linger? And that's very poetic." (Linshalm 2021)

In addition to the shared passion for whiskies, a more factual aspect also provided the impetus for the creation of the work. According to Heinz-Peter Linshalm, the "initial spark was something rather casual or incidental", namely the simple fact that in the field of contemporary art music, the currently available music literature for contrabass clarinet solo is very negligible[3]: "There is so little, it is a very idiosyncratic instrument, many composers find it rather difficult to use. And that was my first nudge to Petra: 'Why don't you write something especially for contrabass clarinet – for me and my contrabass clarinet!'" (Linshalm 2021)

For Petra Stump-Linshalm, *Musikvermittlung* – or the intention to create a work involving *Musikvermittlung* – did not play any role in the composition process:

> "I was really only concerned with the pieces at first. When I hear music myself, it triggers a lot of images and stories in me. [...] And it's also the same

---

3   This aspect was also mentioned by the cello quartet Die Kolophonistinnen, who are at present also faced with too little (contemporary) concert repertoire for their instrumentation (see Sarah Chaker in this anthology).

when I write [music], it's very pictorial, very emotional, much of it has a story. And with this piece I thought a lot about the sense of taste, and what it feels like in the mouth, and then I thought that others should also know that and be able to taste it. At first, I thought it was something for friends, for a fun evening, but then it grew. And then Jutta came and said she paints to my music, and I said: 'What?' [laughs] And then the project developed step by step like that." (Stump-Linshalm 2021)

In this context, it should also be mentioned that the varieties of whisky were not fixed once and for all by the composer. In principle, different whiskies can be served and drunk with the individual pieces, although they must be well suited to the taste of the individual pieces. In the preparations for a planned performance of the work, the couple therefore goes to a whisky store for precise advice: "We get something recommended to us for the respective tastes." In doing so, Heinz-Peter does not play the pieces to the salespeople in the store, but rather takes a detour via language: "We simply explain what the particular thought behind the respective piece is, how it should taste, and the salespeople then recommend something to us, and that works out well" (Stump-Linshalm 2021), whereby, according to Heinz-Peter, the advisors additionally also specifically ensure "that the sequence of whiskies is a good one" (Linshalm 2021).

Jutta Goldgruber also emphasises the effectiveness of linguistic descriptions of taste experiences in combination with sonic experiences, and how this can stimulate creative action: "I had this CD from Petra, and then listened to the pieces of UISGE BEATHA for the first time, and I found these descriptions of taste so inspiring. I didn't drink whisky [while listening to the CD] with it, but just these [literal] descriptions and the titles of the pieces in turn immediately elicited images or associations, or almost taste experiences in me." (Goldgruber 2021) So even though language cannot replace the experience of taste, it seems to trigger it at least. Language thus plays an important role in the context of this work, even if this may not be obvious at first glance (the "poetic" and thus inspiring character of whisky descriptions, which Heinz-Peter Linshalm addressed in the interview, has already been referred to above).

According to the artist, the corresponding drawings by Jutta Goldgruber for UISGE BEATHA were created individually and retrospectively, and were born "from the resonance that the respective pieces of music produced in me – in the form of moods, associations, movement [...]. The examination does not take place analytically, but is an interweaving of the music in forms, lines, inner images; a further development of motifs, a deepening, a development into something of my own." (Private mail correspondence between the author and Jutta Goldgruber) In the process of their creation, the individual paintings did not follow the sequence of the music pieces, and also differ significantly from each other in their artistic approach, as Jutta emphasises: "With some of them I came more from the descriptions and from the images, others I did at the same time and in connection with the music, and then also listened to it inwardly, and then painted. It was very different, there wasn't one approach." (Goldgruber 2021) Very openly, Jutta Goldgruber also addresses obstacles in the creative process that existed alongside feelings of success: "There were pieces that immediately flowed, and there could be two paintings to go with them. And there was one that didn't want to come into being at all. Then it was really that I thought, I still have to do this, because I want to have it [the series] complete, but it took a long time before it finally unscrambled itself for me and felt then right." (Goldgruber 2021)

Fig. 2: Ink drawing of Jutta Goldgruber corresponding to "delicate spice and a whiff of smoke" of Petra Stump-Linshalm

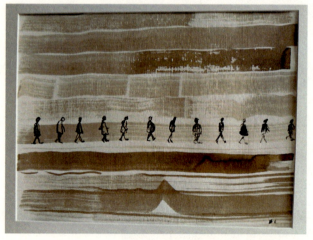

Source: Jutta Goldgruber, with friendly permission of the artist

Synaesthetic Experiences as *Musikvermittlung* (?)

According to the statements of many people present at the lecture series, the performance of UISGE BEATHA was an extraordinary and intense experience, as we can deduce from the numerous positive feedbacks that reached us during and after this performance. In their seminar papers afterwards, numerous students of mine also described this concept as a particularly successful and innovative example of *Musikvermittlung*.

This is insofar remarkable in that the work was not conceived and intended to be *Musikvermittlung*: "It was not the intention to make the music communicable to a larger audience with the help of whisky, pictures or whatever. That was not the background, or the reason why the pieces were created. Rather, it has become a *Musikvermittlung* project, despite not being intended as such" (Linshalm 2021). Even if Petra does not mind that her work has been subsequently pigeonholed as *Musikvermittlung*, she also emphasizes that it may be *Musikvermittlung* in its effect, but it was nevertheless not designed by her on the drawing board as a *Musikvermittlung* project. Whether UISGE BEATHA is interpreted as such (or not) depends on the individual perception:

> "What is *Musikvermittlung*? It is generally a broad term, or a very narrow one – depending upon how you want to see it. I do think that in the moment when you talk to the audience, when you reveal something about the music, even if it's something personal, [...] then that is already *Musikvermittlung*. That already spans a bridge, and then everyone has to decide for themselves: can I relate to that, or is it something completely different for me?" (Stump-Linshalm 2021)

In Jutta Goldgruber's view, the focus in UISGE BEATHA is rather on the transformations and effects between different sensory levels, which undoubtedly simplify the access to the work. Hence, in her opinion, it is questionable whether this effect, which results from the special performance practice of the work, can already be interpreted as *Musikvermittlung* in the narrower sense.

In general, all three artists like to perform outside traditional concert and exhibition settings. Special programmes for children, music performances at readings, in museums and in outdoors were already conceived and realised by the duo Stump-Linshalm frequently in the past, although many performances end up "in the concert hall after all" (Stump-Linshalm 2021). Currently, the composer is working on music for "Stalltänze" ["Barn Dances"] by Barbara Neu. According to Petra Stump-Linshalm, the "desire to connect with something else is [...] always there. It's just difficult to get it off the ground, and to have organisers who pay a music ensemble and maybe a dance group or something. It's almost impossible to do something like that on your own. [....] I would be a supporter of such a *Gesamtkunstwerk*, in which many things are connected with each other. There are many people out there with good ideas, but it's difficult to make it grow, to make it go somewhere." (Stump-Linshalm 2021)

In recent times, it has been observed that, in the (classical) concert life, the institutions are constantly growing, becoming larger and larger, and "they [the people in power] just organise what they want." (Stump-Linshalm 2021) For smaller projects, in contrast, the room for manoeuvre, the chance to appear and to be perceived with an idea at all, is becoming increasingly smaller a deplorable state of affairs that should be critically examined from the perspective of cultural policy, and also with regard to the possibilities of inclusion and participatory involvement.

Bibliography

Goldgruber, Jutta/Linshalm, Heinz-Peter/Stump-Linshalm, Petra (2021): Qualitative interview [via Zoom] concerning UISGE BEATHA and *Musikvermittlung*, conducted by Sarah Chaker. Vienna: 6.9.2021.

QR-code: Website for UISGE BEATHA by Duo Stump-Linshalm including audio example; [online: https://www.stump-linshalm.com/uisge-beatha].

Biographical notes

Petra Stump-Linshalm studied clarinet at the mdw – University of Music and Performing Arts Vienna, and bass clarinet at the Conservatorium van Amsterdam. As a recipient of various prizes and awards – the most recent prize awarded to her was the Publicity Prize of the SKE (an Austrian institution for composers) in 2020 – she pays special attention not only to the classical repertoire, but also to contemporary, experimental and improvised music. She is the dedicatee of numerous world premieres and has collaborated with esteemed composers such as Pierluigi Billone, Beat Furrer, Karlheinz Stockhausen and others. Her first portrait CD with her own compositions was released in 2018 by orlando records. Since 2012, Petra Stump-Linshalm has been Senior Lecturer for Chamber Music at the Joseph Haydn Institute for Chamber Music, Early Music and New Music at the mdw. More information: https ://www.stump-linshalm.com/.

Heinz-Peter Linshalm studied clarinet at the mdw – University of Music and Performing Arts Vienna, and bass clarinet at Bern University of the Arts HBK. As a musicians, he focuses not only on the classical repertoire, but above all on the contemporary repertoire. He is the dedicatee of numerous world premieres and has collaborated with esteemed composers such as Pierluigi Billone, Beat Furrer, Karlheinz Stockhausen and others. With the CD "born to be off-road", released in 2005 by ein_klang records, the duo Stump-Linshalm took stock of their successful collaboration with contemporary composers. Since 2011, Heinz-Peter Linshalm has been teaching at Leonard Bernstein institute at the mdw. More information: https://www.stump-linshalm.com/.

Jutta Goldgruber is a rhythmician, performer and painter and has been Senior Lecturer at the Department of Music & Movement/Rhythmic at the mdw – University of Music and Performing Arts Vienna. She uses music / movement / language to improvise, design and create, experiments with painting in the transformation of music, movement and body awareness, and is also an illustrator for books and kamishibai.

Artful Innovation
Learning from Experiments with Audiences in Symphonic Music Practice

Peter Peters, Ties van de Werff, Ruth Benschop & Imogen Eve

In the 21st century, symphonic music institutions face major challenges that question their traditional ways of operating. Whereas symphonic music was a vital element in the European cultural landscape until the 1960s, it has since become a museum art form, as has been argued, for example, by Peter J. Burkholder (2006), and its relevance has been questioned (see, for instance, Johnson 2002). The social value of classical orchestral music has changed profoundly, and its identification with high culture is no longer uncontested. In the Netherlands, as in many other affluent Western countries, these developments are accompanied by stagnating audience numbers (e.g. Raad voor Cultuur 2014), and a decrease in government funding. Extramusical success criteria are formulated that should ensure that government investment benefits not only the established audiences. However, a neoliberal focus on quantifiable results, fuelled by policies to increase market-generated income, has not fundamentally changed symphonic music practice. The majority of symphony orchestras continue to organise concerts in concert halls for an audience that knows what to expect (Johnson 1994). The roles of the various actors in this practice – musicians, managers, music educators, audience members – are codified in a standard model of the production and consumption of canonical compositions. Most classical music concerts have the character of a ritual that is loved and valued by musicians and audiences alike.

In recent years, however, many orchestras in European countries have taken up the challenge to innovate. They have introduced new formats to engage with existing audiences and attract new audiences, such as people of differing social and cultural backgrounds (Idema 2012, Topgaard 2014, Hamel 2016). In addition to strategies to innovate concert formats, orchestras are presenting their performances online through live or recorded streaming services. European Union research programs such as Creative Europe have funded international research projects on innovation within the classical music experience. Most orchestras are now involved in a variety of practices which we can call *Musikvermittlung*, in the form of education, new concert designs and community music projects (Wimmer 2010, Hill/de Banffy-Hall 2017, Higgins/Willingham 2017, Uhde 2018).

In this chapter we will present two experiments involving innovation with a symphony orchestra, with the aim of showing what innovation and participation entail in practice. We draw on the four-year "Artful Participation" project, funded by the Dutch research foundations NWO and SIA.[1] The "Artful Participation" project seeks to innovate within the practice of symphonic classical music by asking what it means to participate in it as an audience. How can artistically meaningful innovations be introduced into traditional forms of audience participation that are dominant in the current symphonic practice? Instead of asking how the standard model can be adjusted, we aim to more fundamentally rethink the roles and competences that the various actors bring to and develop in this practice. To do so, the project orchestrated an exchange between the symphonic music practice and social-science research on participation, experimentation and innovation, drawing on concepts and methods from audience research (e.g. Pitts et.al. 2013), science and technology studies (STS) (e.g. Bijsterveld/Schulp 2004, Lezaun et al. 2016) and artistic research (Biggs/Karlsson 2010, Borgdorff 2012). As an interdisciplinary and collaborative project, researchers, orchestra musicians and staff, as well as conservatory students and audiences, worked together on it.

The project consisted of three experiments in audience participation. In the current symphonic practice, audiences are mostly involved as passive listeners, consumers or amateurs when it comes to the expertise of assessing

---

[1] The "Artful Participation" project, funded by the Dutch Research Council (NWO) and the Dutch Taskforce for Applied Research (SIA) under the project number 314-99-204, is a collaboration between Maastricht University (UM), philharmonie zuidnederland (South Netherlands Philharmonic) and Zuyd University for Applied Sciences (Zuyd), which houses the Conservatory. These organisations started a structural collaboration at the Maastricht Centre for the Innovation of Classical Music (MCICM) in 2018. From 2018 to 2021, the researchers of the "Artful Participation" project (Peter Peters, Ruth Benschop, Ties van de Werff, Imogen Eve and Veerle Spronck), together with the musicians and staff of the orchestra, designed, organised and gave three experimental concerts.

the quality of the performance. In the "Artful Participation" project, we experimented with the contrasting roles of maker, citizen and expert by actively involving audiences in co-creating, programming and assessing symphonic music. The reflection on these experiments resulted in a learning model that will help to bring innovation to classical music practice. This learning model acknowledges that innovations in practice require specific kinds of efforts by all involved. It is through making this practical work explicit that all participants are able to learn. After having outlined our theoretical and methodological approach to the experimental research in symphonic practices, we will elaborate on two experiments and draw conclusions on learning through experimenting in orchestral practice.

Theoretical Approach: Learning in a Symphonic Practice

Drawing on studies and concepts from science and technology studies, we understand classical symphonic music as a material social practice. Our analytical focus is on all the activities that are necessary to produce, perform and distribute music, as well as on the materiality of musical performance and experience. Analogously, we radically conceptualise a musical work as an entity that has to be continually performed and worked upon to exist at all. In doing so, we intend to move beyond the traditional distinction between research on the artwork itself and the practices and contexts in which it is produced and consumed. Instead, taking an STS perspective on orchestral music, we focus on the performative ontology of artworks, such as musical compositions (Pickering 1995).

Musical performance as a socio-material practice

Following the sociologist of art Howard Becker, we open a network-perspective on art: in order to exist, art has to be performed by multiple actors in changing relational networks that constitute art worlds. These consist of "all the people whose activities are necessary to the production of the characteristic works which that world, and perhaps others as well, define as art" (Becker 1982: 34). Analogously, we understand classical symphonic music as a socio-material practice. This theoretical assumption shifts the analytical focus to the actual work necessary to produce, perform and distribute music, as well as to the materiality of musical performance and experience. This resonates with the work of Christopher Small, who has turned the noun "music" into the verb "musicking": "[T]o take part, in any capacity, in a musical performance, whether by performing, by listening, by rehearsing, or practicing, by providing material for performance (what is called composition), or by dancing" (Small 1998: 9-10). It also draws on the work by Finnegan (2007) on amateur musical practices and by Hennion (e.g. 2001), who ethnographically studies how amateurs of music form attachments to music in concrete practices (Oudshoorn/Pinch 2003, see also Born/Barry 2018). These vocabularies enable us to analyse what it means to take part in a musical performance and to question and move beyond codified repertoires of action in symphonic music practice (Acord/DeNora 2008).

Our focus on musical performance as a socio-material practice opens up the space for experimenting with new norms and forms of artistically meaningful audience participation. We deliberately do not pre-define what artistically meaningful audience participation is. Instead, this is a topic of empirical experimentation. Our notion of experiment draws on a concept of innovation that does not refer to clever inventiveness or an ideology of technological newness. Rather, we see innovation as resulting from the *capability to learn* (see Benschop/Peters 2009, Godin/Vinck 2017, Hommels et al. 2007). To innovate a practice through participatory experiments, then, means to cultivate, strengthen and deepen the capability for (mutual) learning: what can musicians, staff, and researchers collaboratively learn about their own practice when involving audiences in the organisation, performance, and assessment of symphony music?

Three forms of learning in practice

We learn by doing, in practice. Using recent studies of innovation in science and technology in practice, and building on traditions within educational theory and action research that emphasise the embodied, enacted and situational dimensions of learning over purely cognitive, applied or linear approaches (see Dewey 1933, Freire 1972, Kolb 1984, Lewin 1946), we distinguish between three forms of learning. *Therapeutic learning* takes place when practitioners, probed by an external observer, become aware of the routines, skills and knowledges that normally remain implicit and tacit in their daily activities (e.g. regarding imagined audiences or implicit notions of quality or success). This form of learning can be called therapeutic because of the traditional questioning and facilitating role of the researcher as a critical friend, slowing the practice down in order to reflect on it (see Hommels et al. 2007, Benschop/Peters 2009). *Experimental learning* denotes a collaborative learning by developing and practicing new knowledges, skills and ways of working through experiments that challenge established routines, roles and ways of working. Doing things differently deliberately generates a heightened reflexivity in which normativities, attachments, risks and stakes are made explicit (see Lury/Wakeford 2012, Marres et al. 2018, Zuiderent-Jerak 2015). This can be difficult for a symphony orchestra, where routines and ways of working have a long and highly valued tradition. Finally, *reflexive learning* takes place when reflection has become an integral part of the practice or organisation of the practitioner, which allows for improved ability to cope with uncertainties and anticipate unexpected changes (see Schön 1984, Iedema et al. 2013). Eventually, we aim to instil a willingness, openness and desire among staff and musicians of the orchestra to do things differently in order to learn.

Methodological Implications: Artistic Research and Ethnography

Our theoretical approach towards learning through experimentation with a symphony orchestra has methodological implications for the role that we as researchers can and should take. We draw on expertise in the field of artistic research and methods of ethnography. The aim of artistic research is not to explain the artistic practice, to objectify it, or to legitimise it. Artistic research presupposes that artists contribute to research through artistic practice (see Biggs/Karlsson 2010, Borgdorff 2012). Artistic research is not a goal in itself, it is a means to question and to focus artistic practice (Benschop 2020). In the context of this project, this means that research into the innovation of participation in symphonic music practices will have the explicit goal of learning through collaboratively organising, performing, and assessing symphonic music concerts. In the "Artful Participation" project, a musician-researcher – trained as a classical violinist – worked closely with researchers, musicians and staff from the orchestra to design the experiments as artistically meaningful events.

Observing and intervening

Methodologically, our experiments combine ethnographical observations and active interventions by the researchers, drawing on interventionist and action research practices (Bradbury 2015, Lezaun et al. 2016, Lury/Wakeford 2012). Ethnographic methods, and qualitative research methods in general, are especially suitable for learning in practice, as they give researchers the systematic means to hone, calibrate, position and thus critically question and develop themselves as instruments. We draw inspiration from Tim Ingold's notion of "the art of inquiry" (Ingold 2013), where he argues that the fundamental task of anthropologists is not to gather data and build knowledge, but to learn from the practices in which they immerse themselves, in order to speculate about future possibilities. Developing, performing and evaluating the experimental concerts were collaborative endeavours in which we as researchers closely worked with orchestra staff and musicians with the goal of tracing and documenting the learning that took place throughout the process. All the researchers involved (the musician-researcher and the academic researchers) took on the role of participant-observers during the organisation and performance of the experimental concerts.

In the following three sections, we present two experiments in artful participation. What these experiments share is that they took works from the canon of Western art music as a starting point. Instead of tinkering with elements of the codified performance history of these works, the musician-researcher in our project designed concert events that required all participants to adapt their expectations of what a musical performance actually entails: musicians were asked to arrange music for a specific spatial setting, such as a local pub; and audience members were invited to take a more active role in organising the concert. These experiments were designed so that new and unexpected values and qualities could emerge from the situation. Our leading question in these experiments was: how to design and experiment with artistically relevant forms of audience participation in the symphonic music practice, and learn from these experiments?

"Mahler am Tisch": An Imagined Audience

It is seven in the evening, a mid-November night in 2019 at Café Tribunal in the city centre of Maastricht, the Netherlands. The place is very crowded, as always on a normal day like this. People are chatting at the bar and sitting at tables to eat something. As in many old-fashioned Dutch cafés, the floor is covered with peanut shells: the owner offers free nuts with the drinks. There are early Christmas decorations on the walls. At one end of the café, people are sitting around a group of five string players and a harpist. One of the violinists stands up and raises her voice to speak. She says that the musicians will perform a piece by Gustav Mahler, the slow "Adagietto" from his "Fifth Symphony". She explains that this music is very soft and invites everyone to be silent for a moment. After some hushing, people stop talking or lower their voice. When the musicians start to play their first notes, they realise that their improvised audience is becoming silent and starting to listen. Emerging from the muffled buzz at the bar, Mahler's notes seem to create a shared feeling of attention to something that is not often heard in this café.

Playing the "Adagietto" had been the particular wish of the string players when they were asked to participate in the experiment "Mahler am Tisch". It was designed to enable people to experience Mahler's music through the folk music and the village songs and dances that inspired him. Three bands were formed by musicians from the philharmonie zuidnederland and local semi-professional and amateur players. The ensembles corresponded to different aspects of Mahler's music: a klezmer band, a brass band, and a string quartet. Collaborating with the musician-researcher in the project, each group chose the music that they would like to perform. The musicians actively participated in the process of arranging parts of the original orchestral score and of finding other folk music that resonated with Mahler's musical world. They created a set list that was entirely their own. The ensembles then performed on four subsequent nights at two local cafés in Maastricht, where they played "am Tisch" – around the table. One is a small music café, which regularly features jazz performances. The second is a typical local bar, where (art) students and other residents of Maastricht come for a drink after studies or work.

Arranging and rehearsing with uncertainties

The rehearsals of the musicians were an important part of the experiment. During the arrangement and practicing process, we encouraged the musicians to imagine and musically acknowledge their audiences during the concerts in the cafés (Litt 2012). Most musicians were familiar with the two bars. At the first rehearsal, the repertoire proposal made by the musician-researcher was discussed. One musician of the brass ensemble argued that he preferred to play folk music instead of excerpts from Mahler, because "Mahler's music won't work in a bar, the audience will find it boring, hearing just brass players" (Observations from brass rehearsal, written up by Ties van de Werff, November 18, 2019). Eventually, the ensembles did arrange excerpts from Mahler's music for their specific bands. The brass quintet, for example, used excerpts from Mahler as well as traditional Austrian folk songs. For one piece, they combined parts of Mahler's "Urlicht" from the "Second Symphony" and some traditional Austrian dances. The musicians negotiated between the artistic freedom of arranging Mahler for bar performance, their own habits and routines of playing, and the ideals of fidelity to the score and faithfulness to the composer's intent. After the brass quintet rehearsed "Urlicht" from beginning to end, one of the musicians remarked: "I don't know, I don't feel the interaction with the original composition anymore" (Observations from brass rehearsal, written up by Ties van de Werff, November 18 2019). The other musicians were more enthusiastic, as the trumpet player responded: "This sounds exactly like the kind of folk music that Mahler could have used" (Observations from brass rehearsal, written up by Ties van de Werff, November 18, 2019). During the rehearsals of all three ensembles, the musicians were quite reflective about the way they were supposed to play. They imagined the setting and acoustics of the bar, the people that would be present, and how the music should sound. The musicians often created a contrast between a way of playing that is common in the concert hall and a performance style that would suit a busy café on a Saturday evening. The musicians alternated between the perceived "loose" character of their own arrangements, and the more "substantial" excerpts of Mahler's compositions. For example, when talking about one particular Mahler excerpt, the trumpet player explained to his fellow brass musicians that "[i]t should sound refined, not sloppy [...] If people recognise it as Mahler, then we shouldn't play it too loosely" (Observations from brass rehearsal, written up by Ties van de Werff, November 18, 2019). When comparing the different arrangements, a musician remarked: "We have to play chic after those eight bars of vulgarity." Musicians used adjectives such as "refined", "articulated" and "precise" to refer to a more familiar way of playing Mahler. In contrast, other pieces were perceived as allowing for a different style of playing. When discussing the tempo of an arrangement and the perceived acoustics of the two bars, a musician remarked: "It should gather some pace, we are not an orchestra. If there is one moment that we can overplay it, it is here. Not too calculated, not too classical." Or: "It shouldn't sound too etude-like, we can make it a bit lighter" (Observations from brass rehearsal, written up by Ties van de Werff, November 18 2019). Discursive qualifications such as these functioned as a way for musicians to uphold their routine ways of rehearsing in an uncertain situation.

Realising the concerts according to the design was by no means a frictionless affair. In order to create a sociable atmosphere in the café, the (musician-)researcher involved encouraged the musicians to play the arrangements, where possible, by heart. Playing without scores would not only fit the folk-style of playing that we envisioned, but would also get rid of the music stands that could have the effect of being a visual barrier between the musicians and the people in the café. While some musicians in the klezmer band did play by heart, the orchestra musicians refused to do that. They argued that it was impossible to learn the score in the time that they were given for rehearsing, or that they would feel uncomfortable to do so. We also encouraged the musicians of the ensembles to pay attention to the visual presentation of their playing. In the string ensemble, for example, the musician-researcher asked the musicians to play outwards more: to show the pleasure and fun of playing together, as a team or a band, instead of focusing on the precise articulation of the music. She also encouraged the musicians to play in a more communicative style, for example by looking at each other, or using bow gestures to emphasise different parts of the music. Some musicians felt reluctant to follow these suggestions, others were more at ease with them. As a trumpet player told the tuba player: "You have to act a bit comical, don't put on such an artistic face" (Observations from brass rehearsal, written up by Ties van de Werff, November 18, 2019). Eventually, the musicians were taking more ownership of the concerts, making their own decisions instead of following the original ideas. During the concerts, some musicians did in fact respond to the encouragements of the musician-researcher to perform in a communicative style, with each other and with the audience.

An experiment in opening up routines

The "Mahler am Tisch" experiment was designed to create a situation in which going back to Mahler's folk music roots would allow for a convivial interaction between musicians and people in the café. Making music together, talking, laughing and enjoying the fun of playing together was the aim, not so much a performance that was perfect according to traditional classical music values. Trying to implement this vision, and imagining the audience, taught us and the musicians a lot about the implicit routines in the musicians' rehearsal and performance practices. The contrast that musicians made between (imagined) concert hall audiences and café audiences made them and us aware of different ways of playing, and the possible pre-conceptions about (imagined) audiences that these musical choices presuppose: even though the bar was not a concert hall, audiences present could have been (and some were) frequent classical concert visitors. This therapeutic learning by making the implicit explicit also made visible what such an experiment asked of everyone involved: the musicians, the researchers and the people present in the two cafés. Without conventional props, such as a concert costume and a stage, a clear distribution of artistic responsibilities, shared criteria for a good performance, and an attentive and silent audience, the musicians felt vulnerable. As intervening researchers, we had to find a balance between the initial artistic ideals of the experiment and the realities of tight concert schedules, planning and communication issues, shifting and contested artistic authority, and last-minute logistical improvisations to get everything and everyone in place at the right time. For the people in the café who responded to the invitation to become an audience – many of whom suddenly found themselves in a musical situation, as the event was only minimally advertised beforehand– it meant that they had to give up their conversations with others and offer their ears and attention to music that they had not asked for. Making the experimental concerts happen therefore required work that led to collaborative learning about what makes a musical performance both vulnerable and valuable.

The People's Salon: A Co-Responsible Audience

In the second experiment, entitled "The People's Salon", the Friends of philharmonie zuidnederland were invited to program a symphonic concert evening. Through qualitative interviews and two focus groups with fifteen Friends, personal stories and memories were collected about how a particular classical music composition had been important for them during certain moments or phases in their lives. In the focus groups, the Friends were very open and sometimes emotional when sharing their personal memories and stories. Some were mundane, as in the case of a Friend who liked to listen to symphonic music in her car because it made the noise of the engine less annoying. Others were more emotional, such as one Friend who listened to Rachmaninoff's "Second Piano Concerto" in the week his wife passed away, and now feels that she figuratively winks at him when he accidentally hears this music. The focus group meetings and the semi-open interviews with individual Friends made it clear that hearing other people's memories and stories about music provided a starting point for intense conversations about the meaning and importance of classical music in people's lives. This element of conversation led the musician-researcher to envision the concert as an intimate musical evening, such as had originated in bourgeois Paris salons around 1900. In these salons, musical performances facilitated and triggered a meeting of minds. Through their exchange of stories and memories about the meaning of classical music in one's life, the Friends thus took co-responsibility for the program, as well as for the character of the event.

Sharing artistic responsibilities

The main challenge in this experiment was to share and distribute the artistic tasks and responsibilities for organising the concert evening between the Friends involved, the researchers, and the orchestra staff, specifically the artistic programmer. Based on the interviews and the first focus group, the researchers proposed a storyline of recurring themes: childhood memories, love stories, everyday life situations (such as listening to the car radio), and consolation at moments of loss and sorrow. This provided a potential structure for the concert program. The group of Friends felt very responsible for the process, as one of them noted in an evaluative survey afterwards: "Especially after the first meeting, I really felt like a co-programmer, for a beautiful musical evening" (Van de Werff 2020). Responsibility in an artistic sense was also felt when making final decisions on the program for the evening. This was challenging for some Friends, as it meant that "you cannot take into account all of the beautiful, personal and dear memories, which means that we will have to disappoint some people" (Van de Werff 2020). Others found it challenging to accept "different views on musical tastes", or to come up with "workable ideas" (Van de Werff 2020).

During the second focus group, it turned out that the Friends had selected mainly solo and chamber music works, whereas a medium size symphony orchestra had been scheduled. Since there were not enough personal stories related to orchestral works, the artistic programmer of the orchestra and the researchers had to artistically intervene by suggesting some symphonic pieces. By doing so, we could also take the Friends along in the decision-making process that usually belongs to the artistic programmer: taking into account the instrumentation of the scores and the number of available musicians, the costs of hiring extra musicians or adapting an arrangement to fit the instrumentation. Eventually, the Friends, the researchers and the artistic programmer agreed on two symphonic compositions that were feasible in terms of the available musicians and rehearsing time, and also fitted the themes of the evening.

For practical and logistical reasons, such as a lack of time, finding a suitable venue for the concert evening was done by the researchers. We first enquired about two historical locations in the city centre of Maastricht which have the late nineteenth-century atmosphere that invokes the atmosphere of Proustian music salons, but they were not available in January 2020. That made us reflect on this decision: we were not aiming to re-enact the 19th century salon and its social context. Rather, we wanted to use the salon as a guiding metaphor, for bringing conversation and music together, around meanings of classical music in our lives. We then found an old cement factory just outside the city centre, called AINSI. It has been refurbished as a cultural venue, and offers a large foyer with many sofa seats placed among the remaining industrial equipment. Aesthetically, it provided a contemporary rawness of concrete walls and ceilings, combined with old carpets, tables and armchairs (see Figure 1). It also has a relatively standard black box theatre hall that accommodates an audience of 150. This limited the maximum number of Friends that could attend. Once all the 2,500 Friends of the orchestra had been informed about the concert, which was offered to them for free, it only took one day to reach the maximum number of reservations.

The idea was to use the different spaces in the AINSI venue to create not only a musical stage, but also an environment where audiences could converse. In the focus groups, we also discussed the stage design and the way we could include some stories in the set-up of the concert evening. The musician-researcher had proposed to stage the stories in various places and invite the audience members to walk from one to the other, as a metaphorical journey through life. This would require careful management of the movements of both the musicians and the audience during the concert, so shortly before the concert the researchers decided to perform all music in the hall and have the conversations in the foyer. The Friends and researchers together then decided to ask some Friends to present their stories live during the concert, in a talk-show manner with a host. This role was taken by the timpanist of the orchestra. We also asked the Friends, as ambassadors of classical music, to start conversations with audience members in the break and after the concert about the value of classical music in one's life. The Friends were motivated to take up this role, as some liked the idea of making classical music "more accessible", "closer to the people" and to reach "normal audiences, and not only the diehard experts" (Van de Werff 2020).

Fig. 1: *The foyer of the AINSI art space*

Source: Peter Peters

Staging a salon

The actual staging of the event in the days before the concert was done by the musician-researcher together with technical staff from the orchestra and AINSI. She had to constantly negotiate between her original design ideas and a host of smaller and bigger resistances: the position of the smaller ensembles that would perform chamber music, as well as the position of the orchestra; the size of the hall itself, as well as its acoustic limits with regard to where the musicians and the audience could be situated. Using coloured lights to change the atmosphere between pieces led some of the musicians to protest because they could not read their scores. In a last-minute attempt to prevent the staging from falling back into a conventional orchestral performance setting, she brought some of the sofas from the foyer and added small tables with flowers, which was met with some hesitance from the orchestra production crew. Eventually, the evening went smoothly: the alteration between the presented stories of the Friends on stage and performances of works such as Wolfgang Amadeus Mozart's "Rondo alla Turca", Nikolai Rimski-Korsakov's "Sheherazade" or Johann Sebastian Bach's "Third Brandenburg Concerto" gave the attending audience a sense of familiarity, as could be heard from their responses during the evening.

What actually happened on January 25th, 2020, in AINSI, was different from the initial design presented by the musician-researcher. Moving from the story board to the actual concert brought together a large group of people: Friends, orchestra musicians and staff, technical staff of the orchestra and the venue, and us as researchers. By deliberately changing important aspects of the programming and designing of the orchestral event, we learnt that seemingly trivial choices regarding the stage design or walk-through of the audience turned out to be artistically important for creating the right atmosphere, fitting the artistic programming of the evening. Materials – ranging from the concrete structures of the building and its acoustics, derelict industrial equipment and old sofas, to the program notes that offered the stories to the audience – all contributed to the artistic quality of the musical situation on the night of the concert. This insight in itself is obviously not new for all involved; the production leader of the orchestra was well aware of the artistic consequences of his choices. The experiment, however, made this visible and negotiable for researchers, audiences, musicians and staff alike.

While we aimed at sharing artistic responsibility with the Friends as co-designers, in the end we learnt that artistic responsibilities circulated among the people and materialities at the concert. Listening to personal stories not only contributed to a different listening experience, as some of the Friends voiced in a focus group after the concert, but also opened up ways to make classical music matter to people in a different way. For their part, the orchestra musicians said that they felt the dedication of the audience in the intensity of their attention. The artistic programmer and other orchestra staff members involved reflected on the possibility that this experiment could become a concert format that can open up the ways audiences are able to relate to classical music.

Conclusion: Learning through Experimenting

What lessons can we draw from these experiments? What does it mean for an orchestra to be a lab and collaborate with academic and artistic researchers? What do we as researchers learn from our work with orchestra musicians and staff?

Learning to do things differently

One important lesson we learned together is that in regular symphonic practices, audiences are always imagined throughout the entire process of programming, organising, producing, performing and assessing classical music concerts. To make all the musicians and staff involved aware of this, and make their imagined audiences explicit, is a first step when the aim is to rethink the artistic role that audiences can have in innovative concert formats. The artistic design of the concert events implied that the musicians rehearsed with the explicit question of how the audience would contribute to their performance, as we have seen in the experiment "Mahler am Tisch". This opened up musical and non-musical choices for the musicians, such as using music stands or not, or making on-the-spot changes to the music during rehearsals to make it fit the situation, and made them more aware of their style of playing and their stage presence. When such imaginings become part of the rehearsal practice, they can be questioned, challenged and imagined differently – only when such routines become visible through therapeutic learning, can there be experimental learning: learning to do things differently. Instead of "outsourcing" artistic responsibility to the audience members as unpaid amateurs, in "The People's Salon" they were invited to take co-responsibility as citizens for the practice they care about deeply by making visible how classical music can matter to different people in different ways. Sharing their stories showed how audience members literally live with classical music instead of just consuming it at concerts, as a neoliberal view would have it. Moreover, by experimenting with a different stage set-up and stage design, it became visible how artistic choices circulate between people and materials, helping to enable the musical situation to unfold. This awareness allows production crew, musicians and the staff of the orchestra to imagine possible different concert situations.

Reflexive learning: a challenge for a routinised practice

As in our experiments, any orchestral concert requires that everything comes together at exactly the right moment. Planning for this right moment in a large organisation is incredibly complex and requires routines and experience. We have learned that this production logic often interferes with the creation logic that is assumed in artistically meaningful experiments. In the organisation and production of classical music concerts, especially innovative concert formats, seemingly small things can come to matter artistically:

from the position of musical stands on stage and the way an ensemble is arranged, to the body language of musicians and the staging of the audience and its expectations. To acknowledge the interactions and tensions between the two logics requires stepping away from a hierarchical and compartmentalised view of artistic choices and artistic responsibility – which can be challenging and difficult in the daily practice of symphony orchestras.

In order for experiments to have an innovative and sustainable impact on the design and organisation of classical music concerts, it is evident that various forms of learning are needed. It takes time and effort to learn: to become explicitly aware of implicit routines (therapeutic learning), or to learn from trying to do it differently (experimental learning). Through the combination of observation and intervention, academic and artistic research, we aimed to cultivate forms of learning that differ in their degree of reflexivity and awareness, imagining alternative routines. In our experiments, we aimed to challenge ingrained notions of audiences or the musical work, in order for musicians and staff to become aware of the potential to change them. What our experiments suggest is that artistically meaningful innovation requires reflexive learning over time. Experiments such as "Mahler am Tisch" and "The People's Salon" – which both combined therapeutic learning with experimental learning – can be seen as stepping stones for reflexive learning: the ability of musicians and staff to cope with uncertain musical situations, and unexpected changes to their routines. Such reflexive learning has to be integrated into the everyday practices of both staff and musicians in order to benefit the workings of the entire orchestra. This implies making strategic choices, such as allocating time and money in ways that might challenge the core business of the orchestra. As there is a lot at stake when innovating an institution like a philharmonic orchestra, this requires a committed combination of care and courage from all involved.

Bibliography

Acord, Sophia Krzys/DeNora, Tia (2008): Culture and the arts: From art worlds to arts-in-action, in: *The Annals of the American Academy of Political and Social Science*, Vol. 619, No. 1, 223–237.

Becker, Howard. S. (1982): *Art Worlds*, Berkeley: University of California Press.

Benschop, Ruth/Peters, Peter (2009): *Samen Innoveren. naar een Europees niveau in de podiumkunsten*, Maastricht: Zuyd Hogeschool.

Benschop, Ruth (2020): A Thought Experiment on Artistic Research as High-Risk Ethnography, in: Borgdorff, Henk/Peters, Peter/Pinch, Trevor (eds.), *Dialogues Between Artistic Research and Science and Technology Studies*, London: Routledge, 46–60.

Biggs, Michael/Karlsson, Henrik (eds.) (2010): *The Routledge Companion to Research in the Arts*, London: Routledge.

Borgdorff, Henk (2012): *The Conflict of the Faculties. Perspectives on Artistic Research and Academia*, Leiden: Leiden University Press.

Born, Georgina/Barry, Andrew (2018): Music, Mediation Theories and Actor-Network Theory, in: *Contemporary Music Review*, Vol. 35, No. 5-6, 443–487.

Bradbury, Hilary (ed.) (2015): *The Sage Handbook of Action Research*, [3rd edition], Thousand Oaks, CA: Sage.

Burkholder, J. Peter (2006): The Twentieth Century and the Orchestra as Museum, in: Peyser, Joan (ed.), *The Orchestra: A Collection of 23 Essays on its Origins and Transformations*, Milwaukee, WI: Hal Leonard Corporation, 408–433.

Bijsterveld, Karin/Schulp, Marten (2004): Breaking into a World of Perfection. Innovation in Today's Classical Musical Instruments, in: *Social Studies of Science*, Vol. 34, No. 5, 649–674.

Dewey, John (1998) [1933]): *How we Think: A Restatement of the Relation of Reflective Thinking to the Educative Process*, Boston: Houghton Mifflin.

Finnegan, Ruth (2007): *The Hidden Musicians: Music-Making in an English town*, Middeltown, CT: Wesleyan University Press.

Freire, Paulo (1972): *Pedagogy of the Oppressed*, New York: Herder and Herder.

Godin, Benoit/Vinck, Dominique (eds.) (2017): *Critical Studies of Innovation: Alternative Approaches to the Pro-Innovation Bias*, Cheltenham (UK): Edward Elgar Publishing.

Hennion, Antoine (2001): Music Lovers. Taste as Performance, in: *Theory, Culture & Society*, Vol. 18, No. 5, 1–22.

Hamel, Micha (2016): *Speelruimte voor klassieke muziek in de 21ste eeuw*, Rotterdam: Codarts.

Higgins, Lee/Willingham, Lee (2017): *Engaging in Community Music. An Introduction*, New York/London: Routledge.

Hill, Burkhard/de Banfy-Hall, Alicia (eds.) (2017): *Community Music. Beiträge zur Theorie und Praxis aus internationaler und deutscher Perspektive*, Münster/New York: Waxmann.

Hommels, Anique/Peters, Peters/Bijker, Wiebe E. (2007): Techno therapy or nurtured niches? Technology studies and the evaluation of radical innovations, in: *Research policy*, 36(7), 1088–1099.

Idema, Johan (2012): *Present! Rethinking Live Classical Music*, Amsterdam: Music Center the Netherlands.

Iedema, Rick/Mesman, Jessica/Carroll, Katherine (2013): *Visualising Health Care Practice Improvement: Innovation from Within*, London: Radcliffe Publishing.

Johnson, James H. (1994): *Listening in Paris: A Cultural History*, Berkeley/Los Angeles/London: University of California Press.

Johnson, Julian (2002): *Who Needs Classical Music? Cultural Choice and Musical Value*, Oxford: Oxford University Press.

Kolb, David A. (1984): *Experiential Learning: Experience as the Source of Learning and Development* (Vol. 1), Englewood Cliffs, NJ: Prentice-Hall.

Lewin, Kurt (1946): Action Research and Minority Problems, in: *Journal of Social Issues*, 2(4), 34–46.

Lezaun, Javier/Marres, Noortje/Tironi, Manuel (2016): Experiments in Participation, in: Felt, Ulrike/Fouché, Rayvon/Miller, Clark A./Smith-Doerr, Laures (eds.), *The Handbook of Science and Technology Studies*, [4th edition], Cambridge, Massachusetts/London, England: The MIT Press, 195–221.

Litt, Eden (2012): Knock, Knock. Who's there? The Imagined Audience, in: *Journal of Broadcasting & Electronic Media*, Vol. 56, No. 3, 330–345.

Litt, Eden/Hargittai, Eszter (2016): The Imagined Audience on Social Network Sites, in: *Social Media + Society*, Vol. 2, No. 1, 1–12.

Lury, Celia/Wakeford, Nina (eds.) (2012): *Inventive Methods: The Happening of the Social*, London: Routledge.

Marres, Noortje/Guggenheim, Michael/Wilkie, Alex (2018): *Inventing the Social*, Manchester: Mattering Press.

Oudshoorn, Nelly/Pinch, Trevor (eds.) (2003): *How Users Matter. The Co-Construction of Users and Technology*, Cambridge, MA: MIT Press.

Pickering, Andrew (1995): *The Mangle of Practice: Time, Agency, and Science*, Chicago: University of Chicago Press.

Pitts, Stephanie E./Dobson, Melissa C./Gee, Kate/Spencer, Christopher P. (2013): Views of an audience: understanding the orchestral concert experience from player and listener perspectives, in: *Participations: Journal of Audience and Reception Studies*, Vol. 10, No. 2, 65–95.

Raad voor Cultuur (2014): *De Cultuurverkenning. Ontwikkelingen en trends in het culturele leven in Nederland*, Den Haag: Raad voor Cultuur.

Schön, Donald A. (1984): *The Reflective Practitioner: How Professionals Think in Action* (Vol. 5126), New York: Basic books.

Schulze, Gerhard (2005): *Die Erlebnisgesellschaft: Kultursoziologie der Gegenwart*, Frankfurt: Campus Verlag.

Small, Christopher (1998): *Musicking: The Meanings of Performing and Listening*, Middletown, CT: Wesleyan University Press.

Topgaard, Richard (2014): *How the Lion Learned to Moonwalk and Other Stories on How to Design for Classical Music Experiences*, Malmö: Malmö University.

Uhde, Folkert (2018): Konzertdesign: Form follows Function, in: Tröndle, Martin (ed.): *Das Konzert^{II}: Beiträge zum Forschungsfeld der Concert Studies*, Bielefeld: transcript, 121–149.

Van de Werff, Ties (2020): *Survey: Ervaringen bij het organiseren van de Vriendensalon*, retrieved May 19.

Wimmer, Constanze (2010): *Exchange. Die Kunst, Musik zu vermitteln. Qualitäten in der Musikvermittlung und Konzertpädagogik*, Salzburg: Stiftung Mozarteum Salzburg.

Zuiderent-Jerak, Teun (2015): *Situated intervention: Sociological Experiments in Health Care*, Cambridge & London: MIT Press.

Biographical notes

Peter Peters is professor at the Faculty of Arts and Social Sciences of Maastricht University and director of the Maastricht Centre for the Innovation of Classical Music (MCICM). The MCICM is a collaboration between philharmonie zuidnederland, Zuyd University of Applied Sciences and Maastricht University. Peter has a background in sociology and philosophy. His current research combines a lifelong passion for music with an interest in how artistic practices can be a context for doing academic and practice-oriented research. He focuses on innovating classical music practices, specifically symphonic music.

Ties van de Werff is a researcher at the Research Centre for Arts, Autonomy and the Public Sphere of Zuyd University of Applied Sciences, and was a postdoc at the MCICM. Ties has a background in science and technology studies, empirical philosophy, and social design. His research interests lie in the ethics of societal engagement practices, both in the sciences and in the arts. Specifically, Ties explores how artists, scientists, and societal intermediaries engage with different valuations of the good, when making their work valuable for others.

Ruth Benschop is reader at the Research Centre Autonomy and the Public Sphere in the Arts at of Zuyd University of Applied Sciences, Maastricht. Ruth was trained as a theoretical psychologist at Leiden University and finished her PhD (with honours) at the University of Groningen in 2001. Two old fascinations brought her to her current workplace at the Faculty of the Arts. Her interest in the rich interspace between academic and artistic practices on the one hand. On the other, her affinity with the innovative methodological and exploratory opportunities of qualitative, participatory research.

From an early career in classical music and theatre, **Imogen Eve** now works as an artistic researcher, writer and ethnographer in the performing arts. As a director-designer, Imogen blends her formative training as a musician and an actor to create immersive and interactive storytelling experiences through live music performance. In the Artful Participation project, Imogen developed research experiments in the form of music performance platforms. These aimed to innovate symphonic music through audience participation, and shaped the research trajectory of the project through artistic practice.

Just join in? Audience Participation in Classical Contemporary Music
Empirical Insights into Theory and Practice

Jutta Toelle

> "We just expect to have fun, to hear the piece and how it's meant to sound, to play a bit of tin foil and a bottle. I like the fact that you can just participate and you don't have to be a musician as such, 'cause I find it egalitarian and it's kind of quite... everyone's equal, I can participate in the same way anyone else can, I like that, it makes it accessible, it's a lovely idea." (Interview with participant, JT, London, June 15, 2016)

This is how one audience member, participating in a pre-concert workshop in London in June 2016, explained her expectations and motivation. The quote contains several important points: the participant, a woman in her sixties, expects to have fun and to play instruments, to produce sounds and contribute to the music. She counts on being a part of the performance, and she is looking forward to put away the differences between "us" and "them", i.e. audience and musicians. She mentions the word "accessible", and wants to derive meaning from the situation. Three areas of conflict are already noticeable from this short quote: A) the participant perceives a gap between music producers and music receivers, B) the participatory performance claims to be accessible and to bridge this gap, and C) the participant counts on getting some arcane knowledge from the other side: she hopes to be told "how it is meant to sound" (interview with participant, JT, London, June 15, 2016).

In this essay, I will present findings about a very special format of *Musikvermittlung*: participatory performances in the realm of contemporary classical music. Our study[1] is indebted to an interest in the audience experience in general and at participatory performances in particular. I will give an outline of the project, describe the performances which we evaluated and present our empirical research on audience reactions. The essay will conclude with a consideration of the promises and pitfalls of participatory projects.

Participatory Projects as Part of *Musikvermittlung*

For many reasons, institutions working in the realm of classical music have become more and more active in *Musikvermittlung* and have started looking into more inclusive, open-ended and alternative performance formats. Facilitated by practitioners of *Musikvermittlung*, audience members are invited and allowed to come closer, to enter formerly restricted spaces, to witness rehearsals, and participate in planning, organisation and performances to differing degrees. The classical and contemporary classical music scene, often criticised as over-ritualised and exclusive, has developed a considerable interest in participatory performances, supported by political considerations and demands to democratise culture (White 2013: 1, Brown/Novak-Leonard 2011). Participatory formats as a form of *Musikvermittlung*, such as the one evaluated here, have huge potential to address new audiences and to bind existing audiences closer by providing offers to connect with, think about, identify with or generally derive relevance or meaning from a performance (Barker 2006). Performances like these may loosen the strict framework of classical music in order to facilitate other experiences, and they may generally alter "the conventions of performance and audience relationships" (White 2013: 1).

Western classical music, as well as other art musics in India, Japan, and China, has gone through different stages of professionalisation; subsequently, roles in the performance of different kinds of music have become pre-determined. Today, Europe counts thousands of professional music ensembles and professional musicians who make their living (more or less) performing the kind of music they have been trained to play. In official and institutional settings of Western classical music there is usually no space for amateurs. This is why participatory performances within this ritualised and professionalised

---

[1] Research has been conducted together with John Sloboda, Guildhall School of Music. Some of the results have already been published as Toelle/Sloboda (2019). This essay, however, was written solely by Jutta Toelle.

framework might seem contradictory, at first sight. Also, some musicians and ensembles are skeptical, fearing "the dumbing down of the legacy of professional artistic production" (Brown/Novak-Leonard 2011: 12).

In general, participatory performances such as those featured in this essay are not entirely new, even in the apparently restrictive environment of a Western concert hall. Since the 1960s, composers as diverse as Iannis Xenakis ("Oresteia", 1966), Francois-Bernard Mâche ("Répliques, pour orchestre et public muni de 800 appeaux", 1969), Malcolm Williamson ("The Stone Wall", mini opera designed for audience participation, 1971), Luc Ferrari ("Société V: Participation or not participation", 1981), Dieter Schnebel ("Abfälle I. 1. Reactions", 1960), Cornelius Cardew ("The Great Learning", 1968–71), Luciano Berio ("Sequenza VII", 1969), Tan Dun ("Orchestral Theatre II: Re", for two orchestras, bass and audience, 1993) and others have experimented with audience participation in the form of singing, clapping or producing other sounds; works such as Frederic Rzewski's "Les moutons de Panurge" (1969) and Louis Andriessen's "Volkslied" (1971), for example, were composed for expressly inclusive and participatory performances: Rzewski's piece is scored "for any number of musicians playing melody instruments and any number of nonmusicians playing anything" (Rzewski 1969 [score]), while Andriessen's composition "Volkslied" calls for "an unlimited number and kinds of instruments in all octaves" (Andriessen 1971 [score]). Most of these participatory performance projects were rooted in political convictions, short-lived and bound to their time. Of these initiatives, no empirical data on participants' experiences were collected, and published accounts of these projects are largely biographical or anecdotal.

The term "participation" itself is difficult to pin down; it can mean a lot of different things. When describing performance situations, Alan S. Brown and Jennifer L. Novak-Leonard call the mere watching of a performance "observational participation" (Brown/Novak-Leonard 2011: 1) and then go on to classify participatory projects into five stages of involvement, ranging from more receptive – merely spectating or watching with "enhanced engagement" – to different stages of participatory involvement (stages 1, 2, and 3). Their participatory list starts with a performance with "crowdsourcing artistic content" (stage 1), where the audience is not on-stage but has at least contributed to the artistic work. Stage 2, "co-creation", is described as a project where "audience members become directly involved in the artistic experience" and "some level of artistic control is ceded to the participant/audience member". The authors name the highest stage 3 "audience-as-artist" ("where audience members take control, outcome depends on participants"). A lot of their classification, in a publication intended more for arts practitioners than for researchers, has to do with the ceding of control by the performance organisers, and we will see that this ceding (and the debates around it) plays a significant role in all participatory projects.

In the context of this essay, I use the term *participation* or *participatory performance* (following Astrid Breel) in order to express "the contribution of audience members, determined mainly by the composer (and to a lesser extent by the circumstances of the performance), to the performance of the musical score" (Breel 2015: 369). She distinguishes pieces like the ones that will be evaluated here, which are "constructed by the artist, but need the audience to execute the work fully", from projects with a participatory process "which involve the participants in the creation of the work" (Breel 2015: 369). The performances I will focus on could thus be called *outcome-oriented participatory performances*, as opposed to more process-oriented ones. I will also use the term *participants* more or less interchangeably with *audience members*, because in the performances we evaluated the difference between those who participated and those who did not was not quite clear. It was never questioned if all audience members were actively participating or not; at one performance, everybody did take part and play, at another, many people eventually stopped participating and just sat quietly with folded arms.

The Pieces and Performances

For this study, we evaluated three performances in three cities – London, Frankfurt am Main, s'Hertogenbosch – in which three different ensembles performed the same two commissioned and newly composed pieces: "In the Midst of the Sonorous Islands" by Christian Mason (Mason 2016), and "The Sonic Great Wall. A Resonant Theatre for Thirteen Musicians and Audience" by Huang Ruo (Ruo 2016).[2] Both compositions include parts for audience members who take the role of performers, play instruments, meditate, whisper, hum and sing. The active participation of the audience not only forms an intrinsic part of both compositions, but had already been formulated in a commission brief which the composers received from the music ensembles.

---

2   For more information concerning the planning and process of the commissions, performances etc., see Toelle/Sloboda (2019).

The piece by Mason, "In the Midst of the Sonorous Islands", relies on ensemble musicians and audience members. The orchestra consists of 15 players plus percussion; a group of soloists is positioned off-stage, a continuo group on-stage. The spatial set-up of the piece is immersive and relatively complicated: after every movement the off-stage soloists move a bit closer towards the stage. In the score, there are extra staves for the five audience instruments, glass bottles, baoding balls, aluminum foil, chains and harmonicas. Five pages of text explain the audience activities, mostly by specifying playing techniques and cues. Audience participants are divided into groups A (playing aluminum foil, chains and baoding balls, at least 30 players each) and B (playing glass bottles and harmonicas, 24 players each). According to the score, at least 138 audience participants are thus needed for the execution of the work. The preface to the score states that participation in Group A does not require preparation ("anyone who turns up on the night can play foil, chains or baoding balls"), while participants in Group B need to attend "a workshop of c. 2 hours technical preparation and will benefit from having previous musical training" (Mason 2016: 4) as two different techniques are needed to play each of the audience instruments used, glass bottles and harmonicas. Just before the premiere, Mason said that the music for participants, while looking very easy, was "much more complex sonically, [and results in] something I'd never dare to write" (Mason, interview with JT, London, October 22, 2016).

The piece by Ruo, "The Sonic Great Wall. A Resonant Theatre for Thirteen Musicians and Audience", is scored for four wind, three brass and five string instruments, one percussionist and audience participants. The nature of the audience participation is specified in the score, in an additional stave. The composition starts with a "relax[ed] meditation session with the audience in standing-up position"; then "the audience starts quietly humming [...] while standing still with eyes closed" (Ruo 2016: 1). Meanwhile, the orchestra plays sustained notes and very long, soft chords, with the occasional percussion instrument or didgeridoo joining in. After 54 bars "in total darkness", in bar 55 the lights slowly fade up, and the violin and double bass signal the audience "to slowly open their eyes and quietly sit down" (Ruo 2016: 13). In the performances investigated for the present study, the piece ended identically every time, with a mass meditation and slowly fading lights, but this is not specified in the printed score. The composition is supposed to represent the Great Wall of China as a "communication project, built to connect" (Ruo, interview with JT, London, October 22, 2016), by using a series of platforms. Some of the musicians are instructed to walk from one mini-stage to the other while playing, following pathways along which participants are seated on both sides. The audience participants on either side of the pathways are then instructed to whisper poems; later, one musician walks along the pathway "while improvising and interpreting words shown or said by audience", and each audience participant sitting alongside "writes down and displays a selected word from the poem on a blank sheet facing outward, while randomly reading out other people's displayed words" (Ruo 2016: 131). Musicians repeat the material, and the participants continue to display and read out words several times, until all musicians have arrived at their designated platform and the audience participants become quiet again.[3]

Both compositions are based on the idea of immersion in sounds and are complex in terms of their organisational structure and spatial set-up. Both compositions do not specify if all audience members present are allowed to – or have to – participate, and only one composer specified the training needed before the performance. This turned out to be a point of conflict: at one performance, audience members who had taken part in a workshop mingled with those who hadn't. Some members of the first group thus felt superior to those in the other group and complained about the alleged waste of time: why did they take part in the workshop and the other group just showed up and was still allowed to participate? (interview with participant, JT, London, June 15, 2016)

The performances took place in London (London Sinfonietta in St. John's Smith Square, October 22, 2016), Frankfurt (Ensemble Modern in Frankfurt LAB, October 20, 2016) and s'Hertogenbosch in the southern Netherlands (Ensemble ASKO Schönberg in the Muzerije, November 5, 2016). For our study, we used a multitude of empirical methods: we handed out questionnaires, which were identical in content in English, German and Dutch, to every audience member who was willing to take one. From the total of 638 paying attendees at the three performances, we received back and evaluated 273 questionnaires, which constitutes a very good return quote of 43%. In addition to the questionnaire survey, we collected ethnographic data via observation and informal interviews. Furthermore, we analysed the documentation process, including email correspondence, as well as printed and online material published by the participating ensembles.

---

3   For more detailed information concerning the compositions see Toelle/Sloboda (2019).

The quest for the audience experience

The quest to know more about what the audience really gets from a performance is alive in all sectors of the performing arts (Burland/Pitts 2014). However, not a lot of audience research (beyond marketing studies) has been conducted in the realm of classical music performances, and even though our study is based on performances of classical contemporary music, it is music with participatory elements. We therefore felt the need to look beyond the disciplines and based our study design on topics prevalent in audience research in the field of theatre studies: the active/passive binary, the question of empowerment and agency and the search for community.

The differentiation of everybody present during a performance into active and passive is of utmost importance and at the same time very contested. The debate connects to the different stages of participation described above, but researchers also ponder the question of how active or passive audience members are when "merely" sitting and listening (Bishop 2006, Rancière 2011, Reason 2015, Breel 2015). Questions of empowerment and agency have also arisen, "relationships in the concert hall" (Small 1998) have been questioned: who is allowed to do what by whom, and who commands this agency? It seems most important then to stress that the relationship between performers and audience members is no dichotomy, but a continuum. As Ioannis Tsiouladis and Elina Hytönen-Ng argue, the interaction between both sides "oscillates between brief moments of *live* co-existence and long periods of preparation, expectation and imagination" (Tsiouladis/Hytönen-Ng 2016: 5–7).

In addition, there are after-effects to be taken into consideration – even ten, twenty or fifty years later, we can still be part of an audience at a particular event. We thus "need to look at the unfolding of the whole 'communicative event' which does not only include the current performance but also a limitless range of parallel discourses, historical and contemporary" (Tsiouladis/Hytönen-Ng 2016: 5–7).

In 1998, Christopher Small issued an important challenge to traditional historical musicology by proposing that performances of music are about relationships (see also Schütz 1951). By introducing the concept of "musicking", as "an activity in which all those present are involved and for whose nature and quality, success or failure, everyone present bears some responsibility", he claimed that we can begin "to see a musical performance as an encounter between human beings" (Small 1998: 10). Audience members may seek "perfect communion with the composer through a performance" (Small 1998: 44), others may desire unity with the performers (Auslander 2008: 66), and of course audiences are also communities, defined by "publicness" and "co-presence", as David Hesmondhalgh has argued (Hesmondhalgh 2013: 86, see also Dearn 2017). Terry O'Sullivan suggests that audiences display three essential characteristics of community: shared consciousness, collective rituals and traditions, and a sense of moral responsibility (O'Sullivan 2009: 212). In our research, the contradictory situation of being single while together, and feeling excluded or included in this group plays a significant role. Georgina Born calls on audience researchers to avoid the reduction of the audience experience to listening and advocates that they "combine the practice and experience of reception with the need to attend to audiences as collectivities, in all their singularity" (Born 2020: 52). Hence, a researcher enters uncharted terrain when starting to talk about *the audience* versus *the audience member/members*.

Along these lines, in a participatory project such as the ones evaluated by us, some of the topics described become even more prevalent: the experience of being alone/alone in a crowd versus the group experience became more contested through the participatory elements of the performance, while the disputable division of everybody present into active and passive, into music producers and music receivers, turned out to be a compelling topic.

The basic research question eventually emerged behind our quest for the audience experience: given the already complicated and not very well researched "relationships in the concert hall" (Small 1998), how do the participatory elements of a performance influence these, in the experience of audience members? Exploring a core problem of participatory performances, we set out to explain the potential embarrassment raised by them, on the one hand, and the high hopes which organisers set on them, on the other:

> "What is it that makes participation exciting to some audiences, and horrifying to others? Or, perhaps, what makes some kinds of audience participation seem trivial and embarrassing, and others substantial, seductive and effective? In what ways are the additional activities (additional to the activity that usually adheres to the role of 'audience member', that is) of audience members meaningful?" (White 2013: 1)

This last concept, meaningfulness, eventually turned out to be the most compelling topic of this research, and maybe even the key to a successful participatory performance.

For the qualitative data, the focus of this essay, we used the answers to all open questions in the questionnaire:

- Question 5: "What was the best thing about the performance for you?"
- Question 6: "What – if anything – did you not like or find difficult about the performance?"
- Question 11: "What did you enjoy about the workshop?"
- Question 12: "Was there anything about the workshop you didn't enjoy?"

The comments section (question 23: "Please let us know about other thoughts or comments") was also incorporated, as was, in one case, the answer to question 22: "What is your feeling about attending a similar event again?"

Category Building and Central Findings

The transcribed questionnaire results and interviews, our collected empirical material, was analysed using a thematic analysis framework in accordance with criteria outlined by Terry et al. (2017). In addition, quotes were identified and collected as qualitative evidence. The analysis tried to take into account the "messiness" of coding and classification (Law 2004). Of the 15 themes which resulted from the categorisation process, four recurrent themes of participants' experiences eventually emerged. These categories are closely connected to the central theoretical topics mentioned above: a "special group experience", an "interactive musical experience" and the "experience of shifting power relationships". An additional, more evaluative category which emerged was an evaluation of the participatory situation, covering "attention issues" and "meaningfulness".

The category "special group experience" revolves around the group feeling; obviously audience members experienced themselves as a group of people who have something in common (Barker 2006: 125). Participants commented that they liked "sharing the experience", "to be standing in the midst of all the people" (f64F/q11)[4] and "the experience of community without religious or spiritual connection" (f52F/q23). That the contradictory feelings of being single

---

4   The participant code is as follows: m/f for gender, then the age, then the letter for the respective concert the respondent attended: L for London, F for Frankfurt am Main and DB for s'Hertogenbosch/ Den Bosch. For example, the code 'f40L' indicates a 40-year-old female attendee of the London concert. The participant codes are followed by the letter q and a number, implying which question the quotation was answering.

while in a group were not always supported and facilitated well by the organisers becomes obvious in one comment: "felt a bit isolated from the others, there were no ice breakers, so we were more a room of strangers than a team" (f29L/q12). However, such comments might relate to a workshop rather than a "standard concert" or musical performance; obviously, participants used different criteria than they would usually employ in the evaluation of a concert.

The category "interactive musical experience" points to the fact that many participants loved being so close to the music – much closer than in a standard concert – and that they actively contributed to the musical performance. It is important to note that one of the organisers said in a short speech before the performance of Mason's piece: "This piece can't be played without you" (field notes, JT, London Oct 21, 2016). In an abundance of musical metaphors, participants liked "the sense of being an instrument in an orchestra playing a part", "being a part of the sound world of Christian Mason's piece" and "that I was part of the resonating body".[5] They reported having witnessed things audiences usually do not get to see – like, for example, the trajectory from rehearsal to performance: "the sense of creating a unique performance together" (m65L/q5), "seeing how the music came together through rehearsal" (m23L/q11). References to the interactive musical experience indicate several dimensions and stages of the interaction between the listener and music, including practice, learning, expertise, rehearsal and performance. They all imply that the participants became aware of the musical process happening before and during the performance. Even more actively and already taking into account contested hierarchies, some commented that they liked "to perform with the Schönberg ensemble" (m48DB/q5) and "to make music together as the audience" (w35F/q5).

This feeling of contested hierarchies manifests itself expressly in the third category – "the experience of shifting hierarchies". Participants – originally only music receivers – used words from the other, the music producing side: "[the participation] made me feel like I was a musician", "[I liked the fact] that the audience can produce art with very few resources" (m53F/q11). Other comments mentioned the mingling of both sides by using inverted commas, such as "[I liked] having the orchestra amidst the 'audience'" (f23L/q5), "[I liked] the participation of the 'listeners'" (f67F/q5). What was experienced as most

---

5   "Dass ich Teil des Klangkörpers war". In German, the term "Klangkörper" stands not only for the sounding, resonating body of an instrument, but is also used for a music ensemble as a sound-producing unity.

special – above all in the workshops – was the exclusivity of the perceived closeness to professionals, the feeling that audience members had been let in on professional secrets. On the other hand, the fact that participants noted their unusual proximity to the musicians made the habitual gap even more visible ("It was nice to see the musicians eating for once" (f57F/q23)).

The downside to the shifting power relationships and the perceived closeness was that a few respondents complained about feeling unnecessary, about not being taken seriously or feeling underestimated, which lays bare the individuality of experience. This frustration may be a consequence of the perceived intimacy implying equality for all: several participants noticed that in the end, professionals still remained professionals, and amateurs remained amateurs. Also, it was noted that in the realm of classical contemporary music as was performed here, composers and organisers obviously beforehand had been unsure about the capabilities of the participants. The scope of activities for participants was thus quite narrow, too narrow for some attendees, and also closely supervised, especially at one of the performances: "I think the audience (particularly rehearsed) could have managed a bigger/more complicated part." (f40L/q23); "child-like participation in Mason." (m37DB/q6)

In the course of research, we also collected evaluative comments by participants; they evaluate the participatory situation instead of just describing the experience: participants reasoned about the impact of the participatory elements on their motivations and on attention issues, hinting at factors influential for future decisions for their life journey, as human beings, concert visitors and *musickers*. This *activation* of participants thus appears to have reminded people of their potential, and the short interactions with other audience members, with the music and with the professional musicians seemed to open up a small window of opportunity to show what could be possible (see also the utopian flavour in one participant's comment: "every time the divide between audience and orchestras is lifted, it becomes lively", interview with participant, JT, Frankfurt, October 28 2016). Participants reasoned about going back to musical activities ("I am inspired to pick up my flute again", f49L/q23; "[I liked] being part of an ensemble/orchestra again", f35L/q11) and cherished the motivational substance of the community situation ("[I liked] the opportunity to make music together with people who may have never done that in their lives", f40F/q23; "the search for the answer to the question of what unites us as human beings", f52F/q23).

Many of these comments related to attention issues; quite a number of participants reported a feeling of being torn between listening and participating. Both activities were often felt to vie with each other for the attention of each participant. Some people perceived the participation itself as distracting, and the handling of the cues as too complicated; on the other hand, many respondents stated that the participatory elements had made them even more attentive. This leads to a confirmation of what practitioners hope to see result from the introduction of participatory elements: that they suspend the barriers between audience and musicians and thus enhance the concert experience: "if you go along practicing the music, you hear 10x more things than when you're only listening" (m51F/q11); "participating made me watch & listen closely – more than I usually do", (m69L/q23); "the experience of 'participating' actively as listener changes the ears" (m73F/q23).

"Changing the ears" might be one result of this whole participatory project, but there were of course many more results: the world premiere of two pieces, good performances which organisers, musicians and audience members perceived as largely successful, and hundreds of audience members confronted and possibly made familiar with pieces of contemporary classical music.

Reflections on research experiences

Audience participation in classical music is a promising concept for many reasons – its utopian flavour, the activation of participants, and the fun of it – and it is eagerly embraced by organisers. Deducing this from our research, we give a couple of recommendations for participatory performances – and for researching them! As all unusual projects, participatory ones have to be organised very well, keeping in mind the concrete goals and establishing early and stable contact with audience members.

The goals of the whole project and its message must be clearly formulated: does the project happen in order to bind an existing audience closer to the ensemble, or in order to attract new audiences? Which audiences are targeted? This moment of the defining of goals had definitely been missed in the course of the project described above. Also, it was left unclear to what stage of participation (of those described by Brown/Novak-Leonard 2011, see above) the audience members would be allowed to ascend. In some comments, the disappointment by audience members about their mere spectatorship was clear, while other participants were surprised that they actually were trained to follow cues by the conductor and do "real" musical work. Audience members actually moved between stages one and four, but in the end, the audience generally had very little agency, besides merely fulfilling roles thought up by the composers. The slogan "audience as artist", which at one point was used to market the performances, was clearly exaggerated.

Early contact with (potential) audience is paramount; it is necessary – albeit very difficult – to establish contact with potential, future audience members, in order to find out what they are willing and able to do (or not), and to keep them at it. In our example, there were several early workshops (up to six months ahead of the premieres) of both composers with audience members, i.e. people from ensemble mailing lists etc. who had signed up. At the very first audience workshop, Mason stated that his goal was to find out "if the audience manages to react to gongs or any other cues, even when they're excited" (Christian Mason, conversation with JT; London, May 18, 2016). When it became obvious that his ideas were too complicated, he significantly reduced the complexity of audience activities. Generally, far more members of the public signed up for the workshops than actually attended them, and in all three cities it was problematic to recruit people willing to engage in participatory concerts in the role of audience performers (organisers of all ensembles; conversation with JT; London, May 18, 2016 and Frankfurt, Oct. 25, 2016). This probably relates back to Gareth White's question quoted above, about audience participation being exciting to some people and horrifying to others (White 2013: 1).

Interestingly enough, the compositions themselves, the written music, did not seem to matter a lot to the participating audiences. There were very few comments in direct relation to the music. Looking at our results, I think that as long as the music is perceived as accessible by a majority of the audience – and is neither too loud nor too taxing – it may serve as a mere vehicle for the participatory performance. Going back to the beginning, it might even seem strange that the realisation of the idea to promote participatory music started with commissions given out to composers. Would it not have been far more consistent to start a co-creative process, involving audience members and professional musicians alike? This of course would have been much more complicated, especially because the whole planning and organisational process – including the three performances observed – took place without any experienced practitioners in the field of *Musikvermittlung*. Compères were hired to guide people through the process, but the conductors, the composers and the ensemble directors were also present, confusing the situation at times. However, the ensembles tried their best to organise the complicated setups and withstand all confrontations with happy, tired, exhilarated or disappointed audience members.

Audience research in participatory projects and performances offers a rare glimpse into the audience experience. The situation is comparatively open, as people are willing to talk and express their feelings. Furthermore, in comparison to conventional concert formats, the researcher observing participatory formats gets the full bandwidth of reactions provoked by the unusual setting, from enthusiasm to disgust (Breel 2015).

Participatory projects are contested but they can be very effective. They can make people think – people on all sides and from all walks of life. Organisers, musicians and audience members alike profit from ongoing debates about activity and passivity and about roles and relationships in the concert hall (Small 1998). Participatory projects heighten the attention for details, but participatory elements also make any performance much more difficult. They question and challenge the concert ritual, but they also enliven it. As much as many seasoned concert attendees hate participatory projects, they may be a way to approach new or reluctant concert goers. Rather than "sedating" a sitting audience with more or deeper information about the music performed, which might be one goal of *Musikvermittlung*, participatory projects serve to highlight a paradox. In the classical music realm, they happen – have to happen – in a highly specialised and professional field with highly diversified roles, where there seems to be absolutely no place for them. 85% of participants who filled out our questionnaire declared themselves willing to visit a similar performance again; even though many respondents also expressed feelings like disappointment, boredom or disinterest. There seems to be a big interest in "joining in", even if the practice is not as simple as the theory.

Bibliography

Andriessen, Louis (1971), *Volkslied*, London: Boosey & Hawkes.
Auslander, Philip (2008): *Liveness: Performance in a Mediatized Culture*, Oxford, UK: Routledge.
Barker, Martin (2006): I have seen the future and it is not here yet...; or, on being ambitious for audience research, in: *The Communication Review*, 9, 123–141.

Bishop, Claire (Ed.). (2006): *Participation*. London, UK/Cambridge, MA: Whitechapel Gallery/The MIT Press.
Born, Georgina (2020): The Audience and Radical Democracy, in: *Darmstädter Beiträge zur Neuen Musik*, 25, 51–59.
Breel, Astrid (2015): Audience agency in participatory performance: a methodology for examining aesthetic experience, in: *Participations*, 12, 368–387.
Brown Alan S./Novak-Leonard, Jennifer L. (2011): *Getting In On the Act. How arts groups are creating opportunities for active participation*, San Francisco: The James Irvine Foundation.
Burland, Karen/Pitts, Stephanie (Eds.) (2014): *Coughing and Clapping: Investigating Audience Experience*, Farnham, UK: Ashgate.
Dearn, Lucy (2017): *Music, People and Place: Entering and Negotiating Listening Communities*. Manuscript PhD thesis, University of Sheffield.
Hesmondhalgh, David (2013): *Why Music Matters*, Chichester: Wiley Blackwell.
Law, John (2004): *After Method: Mess in Social Science*, London: Routledge.
Mason, Christian (2016): In the Midst of the Sonorous Islands, Mainz: Bärenreiter.
O'Sullivan, Terry (2009): "All together now: a classical music audience as a consuming community", in: *Consumption, Markets and Culture*, 12.3 (2009): 209–223.
Rancière, Jacques (2011): *The Emancipated Spectator*, London, UK: Verso.
Reason, Matthew (2015): Participations on Participation: Researching the 'active' theatre audience, in: *Participations*, 12, 271–280.
Ruo, Huang (2016): *The Sonic Great Wall. A Resonant Theatre for Thirteen Musicians and Audience*. Milan: Ricordi.
Schütz, Alfred (1951): Making Music Together – A Study in Social Relationship, in: *Social Research*, 18, 1, 76–97.
Small, Christopher (1998): *Musicking: The Meanings of Performing and Listening*, Middletown, CT: Wesleyan University Press.
Terry, Gareth/Hayfield, Nikki/Clarke, Victoria/Braun, Virginia (2017): Thematic analysis, in: *The Sage Handbook of Qualitative Research in Psychology*, [2nd edition], London: Sage, 17–37.
Toelle, Jutta/Sloboda, John A. (2019): The audience as artist? The audience's experience of participatory music, in: *Musicae Scientiae*, [online] https://journals.sagepub.com/doi/full/10.1177/1029864919844804 [20.10.2021].
Tsiouladis, Ioannis/Hytönen-Ng, Elina (2016, Eds.): *Musicians and their Audiences: Performance, Speech and Mediation*, London, UK: Routledge.

White, Gareth (2013): *Audience Participation in Theatre. Aesthetics of the Invitation*, Basingstoke: Palgrave MacMillan.

Biographical note

Jutta Toelle is a musicologist and historian whose research focus lies on musical live performances and the experiences of musicians and audiences. Her PhD thesis deals with the Italian opera industry of the late 19th century, while her habilitation project investigates the early modern narrative of "mission through music". Jutta was assistant professor of musicology at Humboldt University Berlin (2007-2012), Visiting Scholar at the University of Chicago (2012/13) and a PostDoc research fellow at the Max Planck Institute for Empirical Aesthetics in Frankfurt/Main (2013-2019). Since November 2019, she is Professor of Applied Musicology at the Gustav Mahler Privatuniversität für Musik in Klagenfurt, Austria.